André Kertész

Of Paris and New York

Springs Industries Series on the Art of Photography

André Kertész
Of Paris and New York

Sandra S. Phillips

David Travis

Weston J. Naef

The Art Institute of Chicago

The Metropolitan Museum of Art

Thames and Hudson

This book and the exhibition it accompanies were made possible by a generous grant from Springs Industries, Inc. Additional support has been received from a Special Exhibition grant from the National Endowment for the Arts, a Federal agency.

Exhibition schedule: The Art Institute of Chicago, May 10 to July 14, 1985; The Metropolitan Museum of Art, New York, December 19, 1985, to February 23, 1986.

Softcover catalogue for the exhibition first published in the USA in 1985 by The Art Institute of Chicago, Michigan Avenue at Adams Street, Chicago, Illinois 60603, and by The Metropolitan Museum of Art, Fifth Avenue at 82nd Street, New York, New York 10028.

Hardcover edition first published in the USA in 1985 by Thames and Hudson Inc., 500 Fifth Avenue, New York, New York 10110; hardcover edition first published in Great Britain in 1985 by Thames and Hudson Ltd, London.

Library of Congress Cataloging in Publication Data
Phillips, Sandra S.
    André Kertész : of Paris and New York.

    Bibliography: p.
    Includes index
    1. Kertész, André.   2. Photographers—United States—Biography.   I. Travis, David, 1948–
II. Naef, Weston J., 1942–   .   III. Title.
TR140.K4P47   1985   770'.92'4 [B]   84–72764
ISBN 0–500–54106–X (Thames and Hudson)
ISBN 0–86559–061–3 (pbk.)

Executive Director of Publications, The Art Institute of Chicago: Susan F. Rossen
Edited by Robert V. Sharp, Associate Editor
Designed by Katy Homans, New York

Typeset in Monotype Walbaum by Michael and Winifred Bixler, Skaneateles, New York
Printed by the Meriden Gravure Company, Meriden, Connecticut
Bound by Publishers Book Bindery, Long Island City, New York

Frontispiece: André Kertész, *Self-Portrait*, 1929. © 1985 Ullstein Bilderdienst, Berlin. Reproduced with permission.

Front cover: Detail of frontispiece
Back cover: André Kertész, *Self-Portrait with Friends in the Hôtel des Terraces*, 1926 (cat. no. 10); *Self-Portrait at Table*, 1927 (cat. no. 40); *Self-Portrait in the Hotel Beaux-Arts*, 1936 (cat. no. 112).

Photograph Credits
The authors and publishers wish to acknowledge the assistance of André Kertész and Susan Harder in supplying both original photographs and rare archival materials to be used as illustrations in the essays in this catalogue. Additional credits as follows: Berenice Abbott and Parasol Press, p. 95, fig. 2. The Art Institute of Chicago, p. 19, fig. 2; p. 21, fig. 6; pp. 23, 46; p. 50, fig. 44; p. 59, fig. 3; pp. 60, 62, 64; p. 65, fig. 14; p. 66, fig. 15; p. 67, figs. 16, 18; p. 68; p. 69, fig. 22; pp. 73, 74; p. 76, fig. 28; pp. 77, 78, 80, 82, 84, 86, 87. L'Association des Amis de Jacques-Henri Lartigue, p. 72, fig. 23. Bildarchive Preussischer Kulturbesitz, Berlin, p. 69, fig. 21. Ernő Goldfinger, London, p. 35, fig. 28. Fritz Gruber, p. 58. Edwynn Houk Gallery, Chicago, p. 33, fig. 23. Hattula Hug-Moholy-Nagy, p. 65, fig. 13. The Library of Congress, Washington, D.C., p. 94, fig. 4. The Metropolitan Museum of Art, New York, p. 95, fig. 3; pp. 96, 98–102, 110, 113–17. The New York Public Library, p. 38, fig. 30. Pritzker Collection, Chicago, p. 27, fig. 12; p. 59, fig. 2. The San Francisco Museum of Modern Art, p. 48, fig. 41. Michel Seuphor, p. 76, fig. 29. John C. Waddell, p. 76, fig. 30. Mr. and Mrs. Michael Wilson, p. 109. Paula Wright Studio, New York, p. 21, fig. 7.

Contents

Lenders to the Exhibition

Paul Arma, Paris

The Art Institute of Chicago

George H. Dalsheimer, Baltimore

The Detroit Institute of Arts

Brenda and Robert Edelson, Baltimore

Trustees of the Theodore Fried Trust

The J. Paul Getty Museum, Malibu

Ernő Goldfinger, London

Susan Harder Gallery, New York

Edwynn Houk Gallery, Chicago

Jedermann Collection, N.A.

André Kertész, New York

Robert Koch, Berkeley

Merloyd Lawrence, Boston

Harriette and Noel Levine, New York

The Metropolitan Museum of Art, New York

The Museum of Modern Art, New York

Condé Nast Publications, Inc., New York

The New Orleans Museum of Art

The New York Academy of Medicine

Petőfi Irodalmi Museum of Hungarian Literature, Budapest

Sandra S. Phillips, Annandale-on-Hudson, New York

Nicholas Pritzker, Chicago

Carlo Rim

Dr. Richard L. Sandor, Chicago

Raymond Slater, Altrincham, England

David Travis, Chicago

John C. Waddell, New York

Thomas Walther

Michael G. Wilson, London

Ealan J. Wingate, New York

Two Anonymous Lenders

Foreword

Now almost ninety-one years old, André Kertész has been actively taking photographs for seventy-three years, exactly one-half of the history of photography. Few painters, writers, or musicians maintain such long careers without eventually repeating their earlier successes, and even fewer seem to be able to retain the vigor of their first works. Kertész is an impressive exception. But the length of any career is not its lasting measure. And even if Kertész is now the oldest master of his art, such an honor is necessarily a temporary one. We can best demonstrate our true admiration for this man, who has seen so much of the twentieth century for us, by showing his photographs and recounting the history of his career in such a way that no matter how long they may stretch into the past, they do not grow old.

One of the benefits to us of Kertész's longevity is that scholarship in photography has now established itself as a serious part of the history of art. In 1936, when Kertész arrived in this country, Beaumont Newhall had not yet presented his landmark exhibition at The Museum of Modern Art, "Photography 1839–1937," which would later serve as the foundation for his *History of Photography*. Almost two generations later, we are able to call upon the expertise of curators of photography in Europe and the United States, professors of photographic history, and doctoral candidates in the history of photography, in addition to those friends and colleagues of the photographer himself, in order to prepare the present study. Even fifteen years ago, this would have been impossible. Our good fortune, of course, has been knowing that Kertész himself is one of the partners in this enterprise.

Another benefit of Kertész's longevity is that the patronage supporting such complicated projects has also begun to establish itself. The first major corporation in the United States to take the initiative in supporting not just isolated exhibitions but rather a series of studies by various museums

is Springs Industries, Inc. They have also been an inspiring partner, for they have already encouraged and underwritten the costs of important catalogues and exhibitions on some of the major photographers of our century: Ansel Adams, Eugène Atget, and Alfred Stieglitz. Their example, coupled with the support of the National Endowment for the Arts, has enabled our ambitions to attain a level proper for such a photographer as Kertész. The NEA, which provided the funding for the initial research on Kertész at The Art Institute of Chicago, gave another generous donation toward the completion of the project to The Metropolitan Museum of Art. Springs Industries and the NEA have been supporting partners in assuring that both the catalogue and the exhibition would be of lasting importance to the field.

The present catalogue is the result of two ideas. The first was an exhibition and critical biography of Kertész's life and career in Paris proposed four years ago by David Travis, Curator of Photography at The Art Institute of Chicago. It was to make use of the doctoral studies of Sandra S. Phillips; the photographs in the Julien Levy Collection, which the Art Institute houses; loans from private collections; and photographs still preserved by the photographer himself. The second idea was less of a specific proposal than a driving force: the conviction of Weston J. Naef, then Curator of Photography at the Metropolitan Museum, that Kertész was not only the oldest master of his medium but in addition one of the truly great artists of the twentieth century in any medium was the fire that forged a new shape to the study. In the end, "Kertész in Paris" became "André Kertész: Of Paris and New York"—a more appropriate title for a man who has always had more than one spiritual home for his art. The exhibition became a highly detailed study of Kertész's middle period, which was split between the two cities. The Paris work, rich with its classic images, found a new life in our discovery of the delicate beauty of the artist's rare post-card prints from the 1920s, while the New York years, the last unexplored frontier of the master's long career, yielded the freshest discoveries of images previously unknown. The curators and researchers, with the help of many others devoted to Kertész's work, were able to piece together one of the most fragmented and misunderstood periods of any photographer's career into the fascinating and inspiring history that it is. That the world has had to wait this long for a comprehensive exhibition and book on Kertész's most crucial period seems amazing, but we must bear in mind that Kertész has been waiting even longer to show us the full magnitude and charm of his creative imagination.

James N. Wood
Director
The Art Institute of Chicago

Philippe de Montebello
Director
The Metropolitan Museum of Art

Acknowledgments

As with any undertaking as ambitious as the exhibition and book *André Kertész: Of Paris and New York*, there are many people to be thanked for helping us make it all possible. Naturally, we would first like to thank André Kertész for sharing with us over the past four years the remarkable story of his career as a photographer. His recollections, photographs, and archives necessary for our research were generously presented to us and were always exceeded by the warmth of his hospitality at each visit. In addition to those remarks by the directors in the Foreword, we would like to thank our sponsors, Springs Industries, Inc., and the National Endowment for the Arts. They have been responsible, in large part, for the extensive nature of the research, and they have made it possible for us to publish it in its entirety, rather than in a more economical and abbreviated form. This is a tradition that in the field of the history of photography has become uniquely theirs.

The core of any exhibition such as this is the art itself. We are therefore deeply grateful to the lenders, listed on page 6, for generously sharing with us not only the works in their collection but also their knowledge about them.

Much of our research was accomplished through the unselfish contributions of fellow curators, scholars, and friends of André Kertész. We very much appreciate their time and efforts, as well as the confidence that the abundance of their knowledge offered us. Special thanks go to Dr. László Béke, Madeleine Fidell-Beaufort, Susan Harder, Noelle Hoeppe, Edwynn Houk, Dr. Norman Margolis and the Theodore Fried Trust, Roméo Martinez, Dr. August Molnar and the American-Hungarian Foundation, Kristina Passuth, Michel Seuphor, Michael Simon, and Ann and Jürgen Wilde.

The heretofore unwritten biography of André Kertész could not have been realized without the assistance of many individuals who helped us prepare the text and check the accuracy of recollections relayed during hundreds of interviews, as well as the dates of photographs and events. They also shared with us their own ideas that our accumulated information provoked. For their contributions and patience we would like to thank: Martha Acs, Dr. Béla Albertini, Casey Allen, Pierre Apraxine, Paul Arma, Igor Bakht, Timothy Baum, Anne Beőthy, Renée Beslon, Magdona Bilkey-Gorzó, Ilse Bing, Sandra Binyon, Hug Block, Dr. Walter Bode, Dr. Ferenc Botka, the late Brassaï, Gilberte Brassaï, Josef Breitenbach, Dr. Milton Brown, Nicholas Callaway, Anne Cartier-Bresson, Henri Cartier-Bresson, François Chapon, Jean-François Chevrier, Michele Chomette, Van Deren Coke, Patrick Coman, Consulate of the Hungarian People's Republic, New York, Jane Corkin, Ferenc Csaplar, Csilla Csorba, Michael Cullen, Bevan Davies, Robert Delpire, Sari Dienes, Ursula Dillenburger-Brendt, Penelope Dixon-Ryan, Frank Dobo, Diana Edkins, Carol Ehlers, Ute Eskildsen, Ex Libris, Matthias Fels, Bálint Flesch, Gisèle Freund, Agathe Gaillard, Peter Galassi, J.-C. Garreta, Pierre Gassmann, Raymond and Barbara Grosset, Fritz and Renate Gruber, Rune Hassner, Françoise Heilbrun, Peter Herman, François Hers, Robert Herschkowitz, the Hungarian Ministry for Foreign Affairs, André and Marie Thérèse Jammes, Isabelle Jammes, Rudolf Kicken, David Kiehl, Joyce Kim, Isaac Kitrosser, François Le Page, Maria Giovanna Eisner Lehfeldt, Jean-Claude Lemagny, Gerard Levy, Alexander Liberman, Stefan Lorant, Simon Lowinski, Harry Lunn, Peter MacGill, Bernard Marbot, Robert Mayer, Gabriella Mészáros, the Ministry of Culture for the Hungarian People's Republic, Maria Morris Hambourg, Philippe Néagu, Beaumont Newhall, Jeanne Von Oppenheim, Colin Osman, Suzanne Pastor, Alain Paviot, Cathy Payne, Pelucidar, Elizabeth Phillips, Robert Pincus-Witten, Eugene and Dorothy Prakapas, Harold Riley, John Rewald, Dr. Naomi Rosenblum, Edwin Rosskam, Sander Photographie,

Alain Sayag, Philippe Sers, Robert Shapazian, Kim Sichel, Katalin Sinko, K. Gordon Stone, John Szarkowski, Roger Thérond, Sherry Barbier Thevenot, David Tipple, Lucien Treillard, Mme. Paul Vaillant-Couturier, Julia Van Haaften, Samuel Wagstaff, Hugh and Sabine Weiss, Theodore Weiss, Richard Wheland, Wilfred Wiegand, Mrs. György Wix, Daniel Wolf, Virginia Zabriskie, and Mary Zilzer.

Within the two sponsoring institutions, there are many people who through their daily work support, in an invisible way, such undertakings as this. At The Metropolitan Museum of Art, we would like to thank especially Colta F. Ives, Curator, and Elizabeth Wyckoff of the Department of Prints and Photographs. Margaret Kress, formerly of the Metropolitan, tirelessly assisted us in researching the artist's early New York period and provided us with the ability to chart this previously unknown territory of Kertész's career with authority. As a consultant to the Metropolitan Museum, Christopher Gray supplied valuable information pertaining to the identification of buildings represented in photographs and their designers. At The Art Institute of Chicago, we are grateful to those members of the Department of Photography who worked on many aspects of the organization and preparation of the exhibition and its catalogue: Deborah Frumkin, Nancy Hamel, Douglas Severson, James Iska, and Peter Taub.

This catalogue was accomplished in large measure through the long, devoted, and determined work of the Art Institute's Associate Editor, Robert V. Sharp. Without his careful attention and guidance, the catalogue would not possess the shape, consistency, and accuracy it now has. Among the others in the Publications Department to be thanked for their help with this aspect of the exhibition are Susan F. Rossen, Terry Ann R. Neff, Cris Ligenza, Betty Seid, and Tom Fredrickson. We also thank the members of the Department of Museum Photography, especially Howard Kraywinkel and John Mahtesian. We are grateful to Katy Homans for her elegant and sensitive design of the book, to Michael Bixler for his painstaking work and beautiful typesetting, and to the staff of the Meriden Gravure Company for their care in handling the original photographs and in printing this volume.

Finally, we would like to thank our spouses— Matt Phillips, Leslie Travis, and Mary Naef—for their understanding, patience, and support during the many hours that kept us apart from our families while preparing this book and exhibition, as well as for the suggestions and encouragements that are naturally a part of such support.

Sandra S. Phillips
David Travis
Weston J. Naef

Preface

In 1962, at the age of sixty-eight, André Kertész retired as a professional photographer. For the previous fourteen years he had worked for various Condé Nast publications, sometimes as a fashion photographer, but chiefly as a photographer of decorative interiors for *House and Garden* magazine. Rarely was he seen as a photojournalist, the capacity in which he had been known in Europe. In that year, after his recovery from an illness, he celebrated his fiftieth anniversary as a photographer by becoming an amateur again. His curiosity was still as vigorous as it had been when he took his first photographs in his native Budapest; the youthful innocence of the eighteen-year-old novice was gone, but in its stead was the sophistication of a master's playfulness. The lyrical and optimistic side of a personality he had harbored throughout his career now replaced his professional self entirely.

During his first years in Paris, he had been stimulated by the atmosphere of modern art, as well as the picturesque character of the city. Between 1928 and 1931 he became one of the leading pioneers in photographic reportage, a new field fostered by the rise of the illustrated magazine that differentiated itself from previous photographic journalism by the introduction of the photographer's opinion concerning the subject being illustrated. But as Kertész made a name for himself, the private side of his artistic personality submerged slightly as his professional personality became established. He never ceased, however, taking his most innovative photographs more for himself than for his employers. By 1933 he had published his first book, *Enfants*, was searching for a publisher for his remarkable series of female nude distortions, and had begun to organize his past and current photographs into a book about Paris. His credit may have appeared under fewer photographs than it had five years earlier, but he was a different photographer with larger goals. His personal work, now sparser but richer and moodier

than the sparkling abundance of his first years in Paris, subtly began to communicate more complicated moods, and the melancholy solitude of an artist distanced, but not removed, from former enthusiasms became apparent to those who were able to read beyond the nominal subjects of his photographs.

After he moved to New York in 1936 to work one year for the Keystone agency, the amount of space Kertész was alotted in the illustrated magazines for the expression of that private self was considerably diminished. To complicate the matter even further, the demands of making a living not as a free-lance photographer but rather as a professional photographer under contract first to a photo agency and later to a magazine publisher limited the time he had on his own. In 1957, after more than a decade of obscurity, the vibrant photographic personality that was once the talk of the best photographic talents in Europe and which had produced the most mellifluous and tantalizing photographs of Paris, was nowhere to be seen—not on a gallery wall or a publisher's page. He told his friend Brassaï, visiting for the first time from Paris, that he was like a dead man.

Under ordinary circumstances a half-century career would have been enough to rank Kertész as one of the reigning masters of photography, but, in 1962, his real work was virtually unknown. From the late 1920s to the mid-1930s, in addition to having been reproduced regularly in widely circulated magazines, his photographs had appeared in several important exhibitions in France, Germany, and New York and were the subject of critical articles by leading French writers. But his luck in New York was not as good. After his one-man exhibition in 1937 at the PM Gallery, which he had hoped would introduce his photographic skills to New York and secure him some free-lance work, his former fame began to fade. Outside of his private satisfactions as a professional photographer, the brightest mo-

11

ments of the next twenty-five years were the publication of a book of his photographs, *Day of Paris*, in 1945 and his first one-man museum exhibition in 1946 at The Art Institute of Chicago. No other one-man exhibitions or publications followed until the early 1960s. Kertész's work was not included in the popular "Family of Man" exhibition organized by Edward Steichen for The Museum of Modern Art in 1955, nor was it included in Helmut Gernsheim's *Creative Photography: Aesthetic Trends, 1939–1960*. Even as late as 1963, his work was absent from a large and seemingly comprehensive exhibition entitled "Great Photographers of This Century" assembled at the annual Photokina trade fair in Cologne.

But rediscovery did come, if in stages. First there was a small exhibition in 1962 at Long Island University; then a year later an exhibition accompanied by a modest catalogue was held at the Bibliothèque Nationale in Paris. The latter exhibition resulted not only in the prestige of being recognized by a national institution, but the publicity generated by the newspapers helped Kertész in the recovery of a hoard of glass-plate negatives that he had left behind in Paris and which a friend had removed to a château in southern France during World War II. In the same year he received a Gold Medal at the Fourth Venice Biennale of Photography. But the most substantial resurrection of his career occurred when The Museum of Modern Art mounted a major retrospective in 1964 with an accompanying catalogue by John Szarkowski, and it is from this date that the current appreciation of his art has grown.

Attendant to the rediscovery of Kertész, Roméo Martinez, editor of the Swiss publication *Camera*, asked Brassaï to write an appreciation of his friend's photography for the April 1963 issue. The magazine reproduced thirty-one of Kertész's photographs, ranging from his Hungarian work to several of his recent images of New York. Most of the photographs, however, were of Paris. Brassaï perceptively observed that Paris had never left Kertész, even after he had settled down on the other side of the ocean. Perhaps some thirty years earlier, during the height of Kertész's career in Paris, someone, even Brassaï, might have noticed that Kertész's native Budapest had never left him; for, after Kertész's arrival in Paris, he was always a man of several cultures.

If we were to define Kertész's career by the cities in which he has lived, it would not be hard to demonstrate that at the beginning each city was seen in the light of the culture he had just left: there are New York photographs in which the photographer seems to look for Parisian situations, as there are Paris photographs that nostalgically seek an earlier Budapest. But unlike globe-trotting journalists who can apply but one sensibility to every encounter along the way, Kertész became a true citizen of each of the cities in which he lived. The progression of his life from the old world of Budapest to the modern world of Paris and ultimately to the new world of New York seems a fitting sequence for an artist of the twentieth century. But the separation of his career into the periods of his three homes, although convenient, is misleading. Kertész's middle period, when he first matched his newly acquired technical virtuosity against the demands of his considerable imagination and of making a living as a photographer, is actually divided between his years in Paris and his first years in New York.

Until now, it has been generally assumed that Kertész's early years in New York were fallow, even wasted ones. Kertész himself included few photographs from this period in his later books and exhibitions, and even now does not recall this time as his most fruitful. There is no question that his Paris years were happier and that the company of artists and editors there were more encouraging and receptive to his work. But if our evaluation of his career were to rest on the observation that in New York his genius was simply misplaced and undernourished, we would not be taking into consideration the possibility that the same years in Paris might have been just as difficult because of the war and the continual subordination of photographers to editors and art directors in the organization of the illustrated magazines. Just stating that his genius was misplaced does not help to explain how he kept it alive or why it appeared to be so healthy at the time of the tremendous flowering of his activity as a photographer at the beginning of his late period in the early 1960s. The fact that the problem has been oversimplified in the past masks the true nature of the situation, as well as Kertész's own personality.

From our researches we hope we are now able to present a better understanding of his career, not from the direction of his latest work but in its proper order: first as a dream that Kertész carried from Hungary to Paris, and later in New York as a struggle to preserve it in his person through his gentle sense of humor and in his photographs through the sanguine conviction that the emotions of delight can be more enduring than those of despair. The romantic spirit of such a philosophy contributes to another special character of his work: that something of what is unique about any genius must be sheltered from the detrimental, as well as the accommodating, influences of the environment in order that the chosen identity of the photographer's personality survive.

In surveying the career of a photographer whose personality neither mellows nor hardens, one expects to encounter a static homogeneity. Kertész's career, however, is dynamic, if only because of the uniformly high quality of his art over the long historical period it covers. He arrived in Paris at the beginning of one of photography's most creative periods: Man Ray had already established himself as a Dada and Surrealist painter who was equally occupied with photography, and, in the year of Kertész's arrival in Paris, the Bauhaus had just published the first edition of László Moholy-Nagy's influential book *Malerei Photographie Film.* The years immediately following saw the establishment of a new kind of illustrated magazine for mass circulation that encouraged the personal expressions and opinions of the photographer; the introduction of the 35mm camera; the rediscovery of Atget's work; and a general fascination with photography as a mechanized form of sight, which was termed "foto-auge" (photo eye) by the Germans. Supporting all of this renewed interest in photography as a form of artistic expression were exhibitions, reproductions in avant-garde magazines, and annual anthologies of the latest photographs.

During this period many photographers rose to immediate prominence and faded just as quickly, leaving behind a small body of innovative work upon which others built equally transient reputations. Through all of the experimentation with darkroom techniques, abstract composition, photomontage, bird's-eye and worm's-eye vantage points, and stop-action photography, Kertész's inner conviction that photographs should be natural both in vision and sentiment might have seemed a bit old-fashioned had he himself not been one of the leading innovators in such a fertile period. A careful study of his career makes it clear that he was not a follower who applied the innovations of others to his own work, for it was from his work that many others borrowed. His early

night photographs predate the rage for such pictures that followed in the 1930s; his sense of timing and ability to recognize that the coincidence of object and event is fundamental to the medium came before critical terms such as "the right moment" or "the decisive moment" had been coined; and his later compositions that, almost in perverse opposition to his sense of space, feature the optical flattening of the picture space by the juxtaposition of the subject with seemingly insignificant objects around it, yet holding together as a picture rather than a pattern, can be seen as a precursor of some of what was considered to be new at the time of his retirement. But at no time in his career did any one of these motifs so completely dominate his insistence on natural vision and sentiment or his classical sense of balance that he became identified as being the source of any of them. On the other hand his steadfast convictions about photography and the persistence of his artistic personality in his work were able to weather the successive tides of fashion and the changing demands of employers that exhausted the talents of many of his contemporaries.

It is satisfying for us to imagine that Kertész has been able to keep some of the childlike wonder of his amateur innocence alive for over seventy years, and that disappointment and rejection could not spoil it. But more than likely, this perception perpetuates a convenient myth that avoids understanding the true complexities of the artistic personality and disguises the fact that as historians we are unable to explain exactly what genius is. Although many of the photographs of Kertész's career have been available to us through the numerous exhibitions and publications that followed his rediscovery in the early 1960s, few of his works have been described by anything other than appreciative essays, which have not cleared the air of the romantic mists that seem to be their natural accompaniment. Perhaps, in the end, this is appropriate. But if we are to have a chance to understand the career of a great photographer, we must set aside the myth of genius long enough to establish what actually happened. Then we can decide.

Sandra S. Phillips
David Travis
Weston J. Naef

André Kertész

Of Paris and New York

André Kertész: The Years in Paris

Sandra S. Phillips

Paris was where the twentieth century was.
—Gertrude Stein, 1940

One early evening in September 1925, André Kertész stepped off the train from Budapest and entered Paris for the first time. He carried with him a Hungarian peasant flute, his cameras, and the money that he had carefully saved to permit himself a year or two of freedom to find his way as a photographer. He left behind his family and a young woman, Elizabeth Saly, whom he had promised to call for if things went well.

For the first night, and several that followed, Kertész stayed in a small hotel on rue Vavin, not far from the Montparnasse station. When he awoke, he leaned out of his window and took his first photographs of Paris, a city he had been longing to see for perhaps ten years (see fig. 1). The window view expressed both his rapturous curiosity about what he saw and his distance from it; this stance would become characteristic of Kertész. These photographs and the ones that quickly followed reveal a tourist's exhilaration—the joy of discovery. But Paris, although it had been the city of his dreams and those of many of his countrymen, was not for visiting: it was the place in which he was determined to establish himself as a photographer and make his name.

Kertész arrived in Paris with a press card in his pocket. Since Hungary had been defeated in World War I, and France was one of her former antagonists, the card made his departure easier. But Kertész was not actually interested in press or commercial photography. In fact, he had a rather nebulous idea of how he would use his photography, though he possessed a powerful drive to embark upon some new aesthetic in this medium. Kertész knew that he needed to spend time seriously making photographs without distractions. By the early 1930s, he would be described by no less a person than the great dealer Julien Levy as the "prolific leader in the new documentary school of photography."[1]

Kertész spent eleven years in Paris. Almost all of this time he lived in the Montparnasse area. After his stay at the hotel on rue Vavin, he resided for a few months near the Hôtel de Ville, where he had a friend, but his first true home was back in Montparnasse, at 5, rue de Vanves, where he lived from 1926 to 1928. His only other residences, 75, boulevard Montparnasse (1929–31) and 32 bis, rue du Cotentin (1931–36), were virtually around the corner from each other. Although he knew the city broadly and would frequently wander in such distant areas as Montmartre and Meudon, his home was in the 14th arrondissement, which was the locus of the great international cultural activity, the forum for meetings and exchanges in which Kertész would take part.

Paris of the 1920s and 1930s has been immortalized by many of its citizens and visitors. Records and images have come from Hemingway's *The Sun Also Rises* and his memoir, *A Moveable Feast*; Janet Flanner's *Paris Journal*; Gertrude Stein's *Autobiography of Alice B. Toklas*; and the lives and works of James Joyce, Marc Chagall, Henry Miller, Jean Cocteau, the Fitzgeralds, and many others who made these years a golden age for art, literature, music, and intellectual discourse. Kertész's place in all of this, however, has never been adequately discussed—perhaps because of his innate sense of modesty and privacy. Kertész was never at the center of this international activity, but he certainly was in contact with it. He did not really know Picasso or Braque, for instance, although he had a passing acquaintance with them. Many of the well-known figures he photographed were introduced to him through magazine commissions. This was certainly the case with his photographs of Chagall, Colette, Maurice de Vlaminck, and Marie Laurencin. Because of a diffidence about him that interviewers remarked upon as late as 1929, and because of his halting command of French, his first friends, and probably always his closest ones, were among the relatively small circle of Hungarian emigrés: Gyula Zilzer, Lajos Tihanyi, István Beöthy, Tivadar (later, Theodore) Fried, and Gyula Halász, who had taken the name Brassaï.

Kertész's initial circle provided a miniature

Catalogue no. 40
Self-Portrait at Table,
1927.

Figure 1
Kertész,
Rue Vavin, 1925.

world in which he could begin, a group of friends who would support his Hungarian identity while he expanded the range of his acquaintances and grew as an artist. The great meeting place favored by Kertész was the Café du Dôme, where Hungarians customarily gathered, along with nationalities of almost every sort. At the Hungarian table Kertész could watch his friend the painter Tihanyi play chess with the former president of Hungary, Count Mihály Károlyi, now as poor as they. Paris attracted the artistically adventurous as well as the politically exiled. And, to support themselves, many of these stateless people who were not artists turned to journalism. Kertész, too, was considered a journalist as much as an artist, and he had the same respect for his medium as an artisan has for his craft.

Modest, quiet, even a little withdrawn at first, Kertész soon established himself within the artistic community that was beginning to take photography seriously. From these relatively few years in Paris, he would produce an extraordinary body of creative work, some now familiar, some surprisingly still unknown. But Kertész's photography is deeply rooted in the traditions and aspirations of his Hungarian homeland. Both his subjects in Paris and the way he photographed them derived from his formative experiences. Since this heritage molded his ideas about the way art should look and the role it should play—ideas that permitted him to make such innovative photographs in Paris—a brief examination of his Hungarian origins is in order.

I. Kertész and Hungary, 1894–1925

A Cuman, open-eyed youth,
he endured many sad desires.
Tending a herd, he wandered
on the endless Hungarian plain.

A hundred times dusk
and mirages enmeshed his spirit.
But if flowers sprouted in his heart
the common herd trampled them.

A thousand times he dreamed
of beauty, wine, women, death.
But if flowers sprouted in his heart
the common herd trampled them.

Only one look at his filthy
milling comrades, and his herd,
and he, promptly dropping his song,
took to spitting, cursing.
　　　　　　—Endre Ady,
　　　　　"The Poet of the Puszta," 1906

Born in 1894 to a middle-class Budapest family, Kertész Andor, as he was named, was the second of three sons of Lipót (Leopold) and Ernesztin Kertész. His father, a businessman, contracted tuberculosis early in the marriage and died when André (as he would be called in France) was fourteen. He and his brothers, Imre (1890–1957) and Jenő (b. 1897), were thus left in their mother's care. Fortunately, her brother, Leopold Hoffman, took a strong paternal interest in his nephews and guided them as they grew up.

Although the Kertész-Hoffman family was Jewish in origin, there was no religious observance or consciousness among them. The boys were completely assimilated middle-class Hungarians and received a conventional public school education.

Their uncle Leopold worked in the Budapest Stock Exchange. Thus it was natural for the boys to follow business careers. The oldest, Imre, worked in a brokerage office; he lived his entire life in Budapest, where he died. Jenő was trained as an engineer; he immigrated to Argentina a year after André left for Paris. Conditions in Hungary then were not favorable to an energetic young man. Kertész, by his own admission a poor student, was enrolled in the Academy of Commerce in preparation for a white-collar career. As expected, he graduated at eighteen and followed his uncle into the stock exchange.

He was, however, something of an anomaly in his family. Although they respected the cultural revival in their country, no one before had taken so serious an interest in art. Kertész recalls that at about age six, in the family attic, he came upon satirical magazines with Jugendstil illustrations. They were a revelation to him. He realized that he was more interested in visual things than in anything else. He was also rebellious: he often skipped school to wander in the many parks around Budapest or to visit the amusement park, the Városliget, not far from where he lived, and the world-famous Ethnographical Museum near his school. This latter site was an

Figure 2
Kertész,
Szigetbecse, 1919.

Figure 3
Kertész,
Wandering Violinist,
1921.

important focus of national identity, a place where one could see some of the liveliest and most vivid art in Budapest, its strong and rich folk tradition. By the time he was a young man, he had developed a taste for vagabonding, for enjoying the pleasures outdoors on the streets.

Although Budapest has some impressive ancient monuments, it is principally a nineteenth-century city.[2] It was created in 1873 from three moderately small villages, Buda, Pest, and Obuda, the first two of which were linked by a chain suspension bridge, the Elizabeth Bridge, across the Danube River. An American reporter who visited Budapest during the Millenial Celebration of the Hungarian Kingdom (1896) was struck by the city's vitality, modernity, and extensive new building, and called it "the Yankee city of the whole world."[3] Though smaller than other European capitals, Budapest was nonetheless an exciting and stimulating place in which to grow up. Because of the nationalism that stirred all nineteenth-century Europe, there was both a proud and burgeoning national culture focused on the Magyars and the Magyar language, and a cosmopolitan culture that sought to move beyond the provincial limitations of strictly Magyar identity, that is, beyond glorifying the aristocrat and idealizing the happy Hungarian peasant. Kertész's work is related to this international movement.

Although established in the city, Kertész's family had strong ties to the countryside. When he was young, his family spent summers in Szigetbecse (see fig. 2) on the *puszta*, the flat plainland that comprises most of Hungary, and Tiszaszalka on the Tisza River. His relatives in Szigetbecse were farmers and vintners. The *puszta* is the historical heartland of Hungary, where the ancient Magyars arrived and settled in the year 1000.

Though protected by surrounding chains of mountains, the area was conquered by the Turks and then reconquered by the Hapsburg armies in the seventeenth century. Because the land was wasted through extensive conflict, the Hapsburgs repopulated it with many different nationalities: Serbs, Germans, Slavs—all of whom maintained their separate identity into the early twentieth century. Even beyond the *puszta*—and Hungary comprised a much vaster area then than it does today—clusters of different nationalities were scattered throughout, unified only by the Hapsburg bureaucracy. Szigetbecse was largely German, and its population was completely unassimilated, even though by the nineteenth century there was considerable pressure brought to bear on non-Magyars to speak Hungarian and to participate in the growing nationalism of the Magyar aristocracy.

Kertész instinctively despised such pressure. In the villages, his friends were peasant children and the Gypsies. There are no hierarchies in his country photographs: the spectacle of the blind fiddler (fig. 3), for example, is concrete and direct, and the figure has the timeless authority of Homer. Kertész found the arrogant parochialism of many Hungarians distasteful; in fact, he treasured the fascinating diversity and cultural richness of the countryside. In deference to peasant culture and the peasant arts he admired, he bought a flute and taught himself to play. At one point in his life, when he was dissatisfied with the course of his studies and his training as an accountant, he even considered becoming a kind of bee-keeper-farmer. All these experiences enhanced a respect for craft and a sensitivity to the out-of-doors, as well as a cultural identity that would serve him well as a photographer.

Kertész's friends at school, as they would be later, were artists. He studied drawing and learned to render light and shadow, though not in the formulaic way he was taught. While still a young boy, he became strongly interested in cameras, attracted by their capacity to capture moving, living things. The first he admired were simple ones used to make family pictures. He remembers being particularly attracted to a small box camera. He bought his first (an ICA 4.5 x 6 cm glass-plate camera), by himself, in 1912, the year he finished school. Thus, when he entered the Budapest Stock Exchange as a clerk, he was also making his first photographs. They demonstrate that his real education came from the stimulating activity in the city among his artist friends. *Boy Sleeping in a*

Figure 4
Kertész,
Boy Sleeping in a Café,
1912.

Café (fig. 4) is both amazingly natural and aesthetically cunning.

Kertész was inducted into the Austro-Hungarian army in 1914. Naturally, he packed his camera. His experiences during the war perhaps intensified his strong distaste for patriotic causes; certainly, they exposed dramatically the completely inegalitarian social system ruled by the monarchy for which he was presumably fighting. Most of the pictures Kertész made during the war emphasize the human aspect of the conflict: determinedly apolitical, they stress life carried on in the face of hardship. Esztergom, the ancient seat of the archbishop of Hungary, was a beautiful and elegant place to recover from the wounds he received in 1916. While living in an army hospital, Kertész photographed the daily events in the town: a girl carrying water uphill, peasants entering the town to pay their taxes, Gypsies living in tents on the main square—in short, the diverse activities of rural life.[4] Many are, rather surprisingly, almost holiday photographs.

At the close of World War I, the nationalities of the old Hapsburg dynasty divided the realm to form "successor states": Yugoslavia, Rumania, Czechoslovakia, and the present nation of Hungary, now vastly diminished, comprising mainly the *puszta* at the center. This new Hungary was also vastly poorer—a fact made poignantly clear in Kertész's photographs of beggars or of people lining up to buy horsemeat. Within weeks of the government's surrender, while the army was returning from the front and the emperor was still trying to hold on, Count Mihály Károlyi, a liberal member of one of Hungary's wealthiest and most aristocratic families, tried to establish a democratic republic. He could not overcome the enormous social and political problems he inherited, however, and within months he left the country as the communists entered Budapest under Béla Kun. This experiment was more divisive and almost as short-lived, and was in turn succeeded in 1920 by the conservative nationalist Admiral Horthy, who imposed a proto-Fascist government that would last until World War II.

When the war ended, Kertész returned to the stock exchange, but at every spare moment he continued to photograph. Gradually his photography claimed more and more of his attention, and he began to enjoy some success. In 1917, while he was still in the service, three of Kertész's photographs were published in an early picture magazine called *Erdekes Ujság* (interesting news) (see fig. 5). The next year he received a prize for his photographs from the satirical magazine *Borsszem Jankó*. He entered three photographs in a 1924 exhibition of amateur photography. Kertész was promised a silver medal if he would prepare bromoil prints rather than what he had submitted, the customary silver print. Out of respect for the integrity of his medium, he refused. Nevertheless, his success continued: only months before his departure for Paris, one of his night photographs from the war years appeared on the cover of *Erdekes Ujság*.

As important to Kertész as his discovery of photography was his introduction to a young girl at his office. Elizabeth Saly (born Erzsébet Salomon) was the daughter of a railroad businessman who had died when his children were small. Elizabeth was about ten years younger than Kertész. Although her family was financially comfortable, Elizabeth, an adventuresome young woman, worked occasionally at the stock exchange offices. Her mother operated a pension in a charming section of Budapest overlooking the chain bridge

Figure 5
Erdekes Ujság,
March 25, 1917, p. 13,
photograph at top by
Kertész.

Figure 6
Kertész,
Elizabeth and André,
1920.

Figure 7
Imre Révész-Biró,
Peasants in a Village,
c. 1930.

across the Danube. Elizabeth and Kertész slowly developed a relationship based on their common interests in art. Elizabeth studied art and dance and made unusual and accomplished embroideries. She first appeared in Kertész's photographs in 1919, when she is shown drawing in the country-side surrounded by peasant children. By the next year, she and Kertész had become close friends (see fig. 6).

Kertész had begun to feel that his career as a photographer might be hindered by Hungary's political and artistic climate. By 1919 he had mentioned to his mother that he might want to move to Paris. He remained at her request, but the idea of Paris persisted, and it also began to arouse Elizabeth's adventurous spirit.

Although Kertész's aesthetic regard for the intrinsic quality of his medium was unique, his subject matter was similar to that of the Salon photographers who organized the 1924 show. Hungarian pictorialist photography, an internationally acclaimed school, would continue to be known well outside Hungary.[5] Like Kertész, the Hungarian pictorialists also depicted peasants and their environment, the poor, and the romantic and ancient beauty of Budapest (see fig. 7). But, from the very beginning, Kertész's work, unlike

theirs, was more natural and real, what is today commonly termed documentary.

Kertész's photography relates not only to the work of other photographers but, more broadly, to the cultural concerns of his countrymen. Something of his character can be found in the poetry of Endre Ady (1877–1919), whose work was studied by every Hungarian schoolchild. In his clear, balladlike verse, Ady gave voice to the yearnings and sense of alienation felt by his countrymen—including Kertész (see p. 18).[6] His poetry was an inspiration not only to artists like Kertész but to liberal intellectuals and leaders in government like Mihály Károlyi. Hungary's difficulties at the turn of the century—its morass of social and economic problems, its frustrated nationalist yearnings, and its great cultural awakening—were epitomized in Ady's person as well as in his verse. Like Ady, Kertész and his friends, especially in the disillusionment that followed World War I, looked to the West for inspiration. Paris was seen as a nurturing, democratic environment where an artist could lead a meaningful and important life.

Kertész was inspired not only by Ady, but by other poets, such as Sándor Petőfi, Dezső Kosztolányi, József Kiss, and even by archaic verse. Like the poetry he admired, Kertész's work is both direct and lyrical: in addition to social concerns, it draws upon Hungarian archetypes and ancient forms and modulates them in a Western key. But it would be inaccurate to describe Kertész as an intellectual. In Paris, and perhaps even in New York, Kertész retained much of the poetic spirit, aspirations, and alienation of his Hungarian youth. In France he transformed and personalized photography in a way that was deeply rooted in his heritage. His observations of French life are

Figure 8
Pesti Napló,
Nov. 29, 1925,
cover photograph by
Martin Munkacsi.

Figure 8
Pesti Napló,
Nov. 29, 1925,
cover photograph by
Martin Munkacsi.

those of an outsider, a person romantically fascinated by the French capital—more an observer than a participant.

Another important aspect of Kertész's work is its evocation of what was called the "Budapest spirit," which thrived at the turn of the century. Characterized by a spirit of lighthearted fun, of satirizing everything, of extemporizing, this lively quality of Budapest culture was centered in the cafés and cabarets and could be found particularly in journalistic writing, an extraordinarily active field at the time. In fact, there was a tradition of eminent figures—intellectuals and serious writers —who worked as journalists in Hungary. Much of the very vitality of Hungarian literature at this time came from the writers' direct communication with their audience, confronting political issues and communicating aesthetic ones. For example, the American musical *Carousel*, the story of a charming and desperate character in a Budapest amusement park, was originally a literary sketch on street life, written for a Budapest newspaper by Ferenc Molnár.

The most important intellectual activity was

formed around the periodical *Nyugat* (i.e., the West, an allusion to its international and political aspirations). The editors of *Nyugat*, founded in 1908, were interested in discovering and promoting elements of indigenous Hungarian culture that could rival that of Western Europe. Besides discovering Ady, *Nyugat* also published another writer important to Kertész, and to whom his work has been compared: the realist novelist Zsigmond Móricz.[7] Móricz's close examination of Hungary's terrible social and political problems and his understanding and respect for the differences and particularities of its various cultures were an important antidote to the prevalent sentimental depictions of Hungarian country life—as important a difference as between Kertész's photographs in the country and the pictorialist images. The brilliant young pianist Béla Bartók, Hungary's best-known twentieth-century artist, also sought to create a national music.[8] With his close friend and associate Zoltán Kodály, Bartók recorded and annotated a vast number of peasant tunes, discovering in folk music a key to the Hungarian spirit and a source for his own compositions. His interest in the dissonant tonalities of ancient music led him by 1908 to create his unique modern style. While Kertész did not know Ady, Móricz, or Bartók personally, he was aware of their work and ideas.

Although very personal and contemporary— anticipating some of the innovations of Schoenberg and Stravinsky—Bartók's music was not a reinvention of musical structure. His structural conservatism was also true of Hungarian painting. The first important group of modern artists formed the Nagybánya School, under the leadership of Károly Ferenczy; they based their work on the direct experience of nature and Hungarian peasant life. Later, when the Nyolcak painters organized themselves in 1909, they countered the Nagybánya artists by responding to more contemporary European trends, specifically Expressionism, Futurism, and Cubism. Again, however, the structural integrity of form was not challenged. In Hungary, the tradition of realism in painting and literature was supported by even its most radical aestheticians, including the most prominent, György Lukács. Unlike many Russian artists after the revolution, these Hungarian painters—even the most political ones—did not experiment with nonobjective art. Lajos Kassák's Constructivist compositions and László Moholy-Nagy's abstractions were made only after the

Figure 9
Kertész,
Budapest, 1922.

the magazine suffered from the vicissitudes of the Hungarian state), this photographic work was vivid, contemporary, and unprepossessingly photographic in essence. The magazine's interests mirrored the liberal concerns and free, often satirical spirit of Budapest: there were illustrated articles about the hills around Buda, the street beggars of Pest, the boatmen on the Danube, as well as essays on peasant life in the countryside, Ady's biography, Bartók's compositions, and news of Western Europe.

Singling out one magazine is perhaps unfair: many others published a great diversity of documentary photographs. One of these was *Pesti Napló*, where Martin Munkacsi (then Márton Munkácsi) was a staff photographer (see fig. 8). Magazine journalism was an important aspect of Hungarian culture because of its traditional freedom and its anti-authoritarianism even when the regime was most despotic. In 1900 there were twenty-one daily newspapers published in Budapest alone.[9]

These magazines were Kertész's real education and inspiration. He turned away from the older, pictorialist tradition in photography—those scenes of village life and waving fields of ripened grain depicted in a delicate, romantic haze—to find in magazine photography, in its grasp of reality and its unique aesthetic, the source of his art. Kertész's own photographic sensibility enabled him to see his subjects with freshness and frankness. His respect for photographic journalism, at this time, was grounded in a belief that in the guise of realism it was modern and that social observation was aesthetically valid. He has never wavered from these ideals, never experimented for long with abstraction or manipulation, nor succumbed to a vision that would draw him away from a social—and thus, for him, personal—context. In Paris this "realist" sensibility flourished in complement to a growing one for formalism.

After the war, Kertész felt increasingly constrained by the limited horizons of Budapest. When Horthy came to power, everything subtly changed: opposed to Western ideas and anti-Semitic, the new government reinstitutionalized the old, aristocratic social system. It promoted sentimentality in art and repressed the intellectual liveliness of Budapest's culture. *Erdekes Ujság* collapsed into a shadow of its former self. Kertész continued to explore the countryside, but his views of Budapest (see fig. 9) are increasingly wrapped in haze, as though he were withdrawing.

artists left Hungary. Kertész's two good friends Lajos Tihanyi and Gyula Zilzer were affiliated with Kassák's *Ma* (i.e., today), a group of artists and writers who united in 1918 under the socially radical Kassák to redefine national self-consciousness and project a better order for the future. Paintings of the *Ma* artists were modernist, but not formally innovative. Their ideas were mostly expressed though posters and political cartoons in magazines and newspapers in the Kun era. For some artists the great traditions of Hungarian folk art provided the stylistic innovation they sought: this was true of Kertész's friends Noémi Ferenczy and Margit Kovács. A stylized folk motif decorated the cover of *Nyugat*, alluding to the Hungarian ethos that the magazine was trying to express and the modern inspiration it found in ancient Hungarian poetic forms.

The magazines that celebrated Budapest's new cultural eminence also nurtured Kertész. In addition to *Nyugat* and *Ma*, a large number of weekly magazines published lively articles on a wide variety of subjects and included some impressive literary writing, illustrations, and photography. The most stimulating was *Erdekes Ujság*, the magazine that published Kertész's war photographs. This unusual, small-format publication was directed at the educated lay reader. It contained examples of the best avant-garde writing—by Ady, Móricz, Molnár, György Bölöni, and many others—and devoted considerable space to photography. Especially in the beginning (before

Figure 11
Kertész,
Pont Saint Michel, 1925.

Distant and full of longing, they invite comparison with his first photographs of Paris.

Leopold Hoffman's death in 1925 severed one of Kertész's strongest links with his country. His family came to realize that his opportunities in Budapest were limited and, with Imre, his older brother, left in charge of their mother, André was finally encouraged to go to Paris. (In similar fashion, his younger brother, Jenő, was allowed the next year to seek his fortune in South America.) Elizabeth Saly wished to accompany Kertész, but he dissuaded her because of her age and promised instead to call for her when he was established. He worked at his clerk's desk only long enough to save money for two years of freedom in which he would attempt to make something of his craft. Then, in September of 1925, he boarded the train to Paris. Nothing could have stopped him.

Figure 11
Kertész,
Pont Saint Michel, 1925.

II. The Hungarian in Paris, 1925–1927

Always, the Jardin du Luxembourg has its wooden horses to ride and its tiny ships to sail; and in the Elysian Fields guignols twinkle like fireflies. Barges and bateaux mouches *glide (and will forever glide) through the exquisite river; from which old gentlemen, armed with prodigious poles and preternatural patience, will forever extract microscopic fish. Beneath "Paree," beneath the glittering victory of "civilization," a careful eye perceives the deep, extraordinary, luminous triumph of Life Itself and of a city founded upon Life—a city called "Paname," a heart which throbs always, a spirit always which cannot die. The winged monsters of the garden of Cluny do not appear to have heard of "progress." The cathedral of Notre Dame does not budge an inch for all the idiocies of this world. Meanwhile, spring and summer everywhere openingly arrive.*

—E. E. Cummings, 1926

At the time Kertész arrived in France, he knew only a few Hungarians and had only the slightest knowledge of French. Within a few days, he moved from rue Vavin to a pension run by a Hungarian near the Hôtel de Ville, upon the recommendation of a mutual friend in Hungary. In these earliest days and weeks in the city of his dreams, Kertész began to photograph extensively. These images are rich in atmosphere, very suggestive, and deeply subjective. A continuation of the dreamlike views of Budapest, they, too, were often made in fog and rain (see fig. 10). We can

Figure 10
Kertész,
Rue de Rivoli, 1925.

follow Kertész the tourist as he walked to the Eiffel Tower, the cathedral of Notre Dame, or the Place de la Concorde in the center of the city, before venturing farther out to Sacré Coeur or taking the train to the gardens at Versailles (see cat. nos. 1–3). His photographs of these monuments resonate with the aura of French civilization.

There are also photographs that capture typical Parisian details: the modest streets and quais of the Seine are similarly possessed with a special mysteriousness (see cat. nos. 4, 5). And yet these are not just tourist photographs, because Kertész endowed them with such a sense of his own intense and melancholic personality, and because he also respected the pure momentary and documentary character of his medium. Thus, we see the Eiffel Tower lit by a bolt of lightning, or Notre Dame's façade reflected in rain puddles at night, or a tree that has just fallen into the Seine and that will be cleared away the next day (fig. 11). All these are investigations as well as expressions, and as such reflect Kertész's Hungarian, "realist" heritage. Most of Kertész's early Paris pictures are devoid of people. They are also extraordinarily sensitive to the changes of weather and other effects of nature on the city. As we shall see, Kertész has always used photography as a vehicle for his own feelings, to please only himself. As a young man alone in the streets, he would gradually open to new ideas, but always—even stubbornly—retain his sense of himself.

While still in Budapest, Kertész had learned something of Paris from the reports of others; he

soon found the center of his Paris, in the heart of Montparnasse, at the Café du Dôme. From his small studio at 5, rue de Vanves, he could view the Eiffel Tower high over the rooftops (see Travis, fig. 6). His well-known photograph of his new friends at the nearby café (cat. no. 7) is a celebration of his recent discoveries. This famous café was a truly international gathering place and has been described vividly by many of its old habitués.[10] Even Hemingway said that if you got into a taxi on the right bank the driver would automatically take you straight to the Rotonde or the Dôme.[11] For Kertész, the Dôme became *the* place to meet old friends and make new ones, to find Hungarians with whom he could speak, and to enter, casually but deliberately, the larger world around him.

From this early photograph, we know that Kertész was at last part of this active, challenging arena. In the center of the picture, animated by the blurred figures in the background and to the left, is his circle of friends. Kertész has sighted this little table, the Hungarians' table, from a

distance, and will shortly join his friends. Someone has just left, the drink is still on the table, the chair pulled back to the bottom frame of the photograph. Two new friends are about to leave: the Russian artist Marie Wassilieff and the young Hungarian architect Ernő Goldfinger. At the center, still seated, is the Hungarian painter Lajos Tihanyi, a deaf mute, but from his intense and animated expression, the most active figure in the photograph.

At the Dôme, Kertész regularly met his friends, especially Hungarian artists and journalists. Most of them were living rather precariously, yet enjoying the adventure of Paris. For this first year Kertész did not worry about finances. He lived off his savings and a few sales of photographs he negotiated at the Dôme. Only rarely did he receive a commission for a portrait. He made these early photographs for himself and frequently gave them away to admirers.

Nonetheless, portraiture—whether commissioned or not—was a way to gain entrance into the new environment. Within a few months

Figure 13
Kertész,
Rooftops and Chimneys,
c. 1927.

Kertész made many portraits, most of Hungarian friends: Lajos Tihanyi, József Csáky, István Beőthy, Marcel Vertès, Gyula Zilzer, all artists; and soon also the writers György Bölöni and Sándor Kemeri, his wife; other journalists; the musician Paul Arma (then Imre Weisshaus); and Brassaï, who was then making his living as a journalist. For Kertész these were all new friends, except Zilzer (see fig. 12), who had known Jenő Kertész in school.

The artists whose work Kertész most admired were Tihanyi and Csáky (see cat. nos. 11, 12). Csáky had come to Paris earlier than the others, spoke the best French, and had even fought in the French army in World War I. He was one of the best-known Hungarian artists living in Paris, and Kertész so liked his decorative Cubist sculpture that Csáky presented him with two pieces, which he still owns. Tihanyi was also a known artist, a contemporary of Kertész, although their friendship was limited by Tihanyi's affliction. Tihanyi had been associated with Hungary's modern movements, from Nagybánya and the Group of Eight to *Ma*, and had maintained friendships with the *Nyugat* writers (including Ady) in Hungary and after. In Paris, Tihanyi's style evolved from Cubist-Expressionism to elegant abstraction. He exhibited in the same gallery as Kertész, and the two friends exchanged work. Tihanyi was sympathetic to Kertész's photography and showed him around Paris, taking him to places he thought would appeal to the photographer (see cat. no. 8). Both Tihanyi and Kertész, for instance, were attracted to the configurations of Parisian rooftops and chimneys (see fig. 13).[12]

Kertész's contact with other Hungarian artists he knew and photographed in Paris reinforced his appreciation of folk art. Noémi Ferenczy incorporated both the peasant worker in the countryside as subject and the traditional peasant folk style in her tapestries. Margit Kovács used folk ceramics as a basis for her modern approach to this craft. Folk subjects also appear in the paintings of Zilzer and Fried. Kertész was friendly with other artisans, too: Eva Révai, for instance, and her mother, the photographer Ilka Révai (see fig. 14); Géza Blattner, a puppeteer, who earned his living restoring old folk objects; and the painter Kolozs-Vári, whom he photographed in back of an old, baroquely decorated fair booth in Blattner's back-yard (fig. 15). Through his friends, Kertész was in touch with modernist art, especially Hungarian

Constructivism and the emphasis on folk and popular arts that seemed connected with an ancient, ritualistic past.

Besides their art and camaraderie, Kertész's Hungarian friends also preserved for him in Paris the playful "Budapest spirit." This quality illuminates the photograph known as *Satiric Dancer* (cat. no. 25). Magda Förstner, on Beőthy's couch, pokes fun at the artist's nearby sculpture. Kertész found revelatory importance in a moment that would be trivial to anyone else. Such observations—the relationship of shadows to individuals (see cat. no. 74), a dog leaning over a balcony like a person, mannequins in kerchiefs and underwear congregated in a shop-window like people (see cat. no. 78), the smoke curling from Tihanyi's mouth —are delicate and often ironic jokes, always seemingly insignificant momentary details. The curiously tactile smoke in the portrait of Tihanyi (fig. 16) also alludes to the painter's silence and his abstract art.

The Hungarians were drawn together through common language, general penury, social idealism, and a shared sense of the provinciality of their native country. Some, who had a command of other languages and were well educated, could make their living in journalism. Journalism also offered modest financial rewards to the artists. Marcel Vertès drew fashion and book illustration, and Imre Kelen, caricature. Few became successful commercially. Like his friends, Kertész became an artistic success, but financial rewards were often shaky. The abstract artists suffered more than the others: the French considered abstraction foreign and declined to buy much of it.

Most of the friends Kertész photographed were in the same general situation he was. Significantly, there are few portraits of older or younger people, and there are none of rival photographers. When Kertész arrived in Paris, his professional colleagues there were only Berenice Abbott, Germaine Krull, and Man Ray. Man Ray, who was only a little older but more established, was frequently surrounded by his American friends. Although Kertész and Man Ray knew each other, the latter's aloofness prevented a close relationship. Kertész met Abbott through the director of their gallery, and Krull through her work at *Vu* magazine. Brassaï at this time was still an artist and journalist. When Kertész arrived, there were really no other photographers in Paris—except pictorialists of the Salon who did not interest him.

Almost everyone who has described this period

Figure 12
Kertész,
Gyula Zilzer and Friend,
1926.

Figure 15
Kertész,
Kolozs-Vári and Friend,
1929.

Figure 14
Kertész,
Eva and Ilka Révai,
1927.

Figure 16
Kertész,
Lajos Tihanyi, 1926.

Figure 17
Kertész,
*Jean Lurçat in his
Studio*, 1927.

haus artists, Paul Dermée, Tristan Tzara, as well as Tihanyi, Zilzer, and Ida Thal.

Another important early friend of Kertész's was Jean Lurçat (see fig. 17), a painter and tapestry designer, whom he met at the Dôme his first year in Paris. He was the brother of André Lurçat, an architect whose clear geometric forms were related to both the International Style and vernacular building. Other friends were the artisans Artigas, Hilda Daus, and Wally Wieselthier; the sculptors Anne-Marie Merkel (see cat. nos. 13, 14) and Ossip Zadkine (see cat. nos. 34, 35); the Norwegian painter Gundvor Berg (see cat. no. 16), who was interested in folk art; and the artist Vincent Korda, brother of Alexander Korda, the movie producer. Nonartist friends, mostly journalists, included Jean Jaffe, correspondent for *Der Tag* (see cat. no. 15). But most of Kertész's good friends were young, aspiring artists. He was attracted by their adventuresome personalities and beautiful faces as much as by their work. He had a reverence for their idealism—their separate and lively culture—although he himself had no real theoretical interests or approach to art.

Kertész's widening circle of friends did not distract him from exploring the city itself. Where the portraits are restful, the street pictures are full of vitality. They have a terrific energy, as though Kertész had been released to wander, to do as he pleased. Although the street photographs now depict people and are not quite so moody and subjective as those taken soon after his arrival, they are still intensely personal. Kertész began to see Paris as a working city, and he discovered the reality—noticed by E. E. Cummings as well—that lay beneath the tourist's view.[13] The subjects are modified by a felicity of formal composition; they are more deliberately framed. His earlier directness became more distant or oblique, but his approach was still the response of a visitor, an onlooker, not a participant. A case in point is the photograph called *The Stairs of Montmartre* (cat. no. 18), made a few months after his arrival.

Although Montmartre was well known as an artists' quarter, Montparnasse had become the rival center for experimental art of the 1920s.[14] But Kertész was also drawn to Montmartre because its quaint cobbled streets and hilly terrain are not unlike Buda, the ancient and more picturesque section of his native city. Descending the steps of Montmartre, Kertész captured fleeting images: the *clochard* (street bum) on the steps, the woman in the street, and the shadow falling across his path,

in French history has remarked on Paris's internationalism, centered specifically in Montparnasse; these foreigners created almost a separate culture within the city. Most had little contact with the French. Man Ray found the 14th arrondissement refreshing, a change from his circle of French Surrealists, and so he moved there. Thus, when Kertész began to expand outside his Hungarian circle, his new friends were of many different nationalities and, usually, living around Montparnasse.

Brassaï stayed at the Hôtel des Terraces, an inexpensive lodging where other Hungarians also lived: Tihanyi, Zilzer, and Frank Dobo, among others. Kertész visited them frequently, using his camera to convert the ancient wallpaper and armoire mirrors into brilliantly casual compositions (see cat. no. 15). Another resident was Michel Seuphor, a Belgian who had many Hungarian friends at this moment in his life. Seuphor had only recently moved from his native Antwerp to Paris, but he was in touch with Hungarian artists because of his interest in Constructivism and abstract geometric art. In Belgium he had published an avant-garde art review, *Het Overzicht*, in which he expounded his belief in the superiority of abstraction. He was marvelously well informed and knew many writers as well as artists in Paris before he moved there in 1925. Among his acquaintances were Piet Mondrian, Theo van Doesberg, Fernand Léger, the Delaunays, Amédée Ozenfant, the Bau-

all insistently impermanent, even trivial (see cat. no. 18; Travis, fig. 2). The camera was a natural appurtenance of vision. The view down into the steps is the normal perspective of an observer, and even though it was cropped to achieve abstraction (his lens was not sharp enough to realize what he saw), this is essentially a record of his personal experience.

The social awareness that Kertész developed in Hungary accounts in great part for his choices of subject, as well as for his acceptance of the raw, "inartistic" photograph of the amateur or documentor. The "common man" was a persistent concern in Hungarian culture. We sense Kertész's identification with the *clochard*, the poor but self-sufficient man set apart from the ordinary citizen. Kertész captured these solitary figures again and again (see fig. 18); he befriended some of them, asked to see where they spent the winter months, and photographed their home, the "Hotel of Hope." Gypsies and clowns are natural, unconventional, almost folk characters, excluded from the proper adult world, and Kertész treated them with mystery and admiration. Children and their things have also been frequent subjects for his camera and, in Kertész's view, bear some similarities with the *clochards*. In a related way he also admired the parks where country impinges on the city and the effects of weather and nature can be seen. In some of his photographs, these effects acquire a certain poignant symbolism, as when the leaves littering the park steps at Sceaux almost obscure them. These special places are open to the tourist, who is excluded from the real events of the city (see cat. no. 44). Parks, marketplaces, the Seine itself—all conjoin nature and civilization, man and his environment.

Kertész's early views of Paris present the workingman's city as well as the bum's. With an intuitive sense for their culture, he went to their bars, photographed their dancing customs and their folk art—such as a decorated laundry sign—and documented their street fairs and flea markets (see cat. nos. 29, 30). His realism and documentary style complemented his love of investigation. He haunted Les Halles, the open market, the heart of working Paris (see cat. nos. 47, 55). He went to the working-class sections, the canals, the Seine outside Paris, factory areas, tumble-down neighborhoods (see cat. nos. 31, 32, 56). When he photographed the boulevards, he was more interested in the gentle *midinettes* who worked there, and documented their living quarters with the curiosity of a sensitive sociologist (see fig. 19).[15]

But there is no real politicizing or propagandizing in Kertész's work, either in Hungary or Paris. Social differences and injustices are noticed but become personalized. A case in point is *Quai d'Orsay* (cat. no. 27), a scene of confrontation between two workers and an older aristocrat.[16] The photographer has personalized this situation of "common men" in a countrylike setting juxtaposed against an old dandified aristocrat; the impact is emotional, not didactic, and is filled with poignant disorientation. When he places a man of the streets against large posters describing wealth, security, or material happiness, his intent is not only to point out the social irony, but his own uneasiness (see cat. no. 28). The crippled or maimed, especially war veterans, are also seen in this personal context.

Even a developing formalism did not disguise

the basically personal meaning of Kertész's subjects. In the spring of 1927, when Kertész bent over a parapet to observe a man sleeping on the quai below, his interest in the torque between the vantage point and ground plane did not abstract the scene in as extreme a way as do, for instance, László Moholy-Nagy's views from above. In Kertész's work (cat. no. 48), the gesture of looking down seems natural. With that of Moholy, the distance is more severe, the objectivity more complete, the visual punning of figure and form more obvious and analytical. In Kertész's photograph there is a direct but discreet relationship established between the man on the street and the photographer observing him; more than mere sympathy, it is a sense of community, but removed at the same time. Kertész also delighted in the slight irregularities that humanize the geometry of the photograph, such as the man's hat, which is a little too rumpled to be circular. He found a gentle humor in the other *clochard* walking between the two trees, a momentary counterpart to the man sleeping under them.

Around 1929 Kertész was asked to assemble some of these very tourist views for a book on the life of Endre Ady. György Bölöni, now a newspaperman, and his wife had been close friends of the poet. Bölöni selected and commissioned photographs to illustrate the interests and habits of Ady during his years in Paris. In many cases they mirror Kertész's own preferences: pictures of a tramp walking near the Luxembourg Gardens, or a delicate still life composed of Ady's papers and a Bible in a cheap hotel room. Many are views of Paris parks, a frequent subject in Ady's poetry. There are photographs of cafés where he refreshed himself and made as much contact with Parisians as was possible with his imperfect French (see cat. nos. 67–72). These images describe Ady's city of dreams; like dreams, they are intuitive and meditative, withdrawn from real contact. Kertész received many compliments on this book from Hungarians: he had drawn Paris from their point of view.

In a self-portrait made early in 1927 (see cat. no. 40), Kertész portrayed his modesty and self-sufficiency. Seated casually and quietly, he is surrounded by objects of his affection: a vase of flowers and a book on the table, other books and some Hungarian craftwork on the bookcase nearby. The tablecloth was embroidered by his mother, in a folk design. Hovering inspirationally over the whole scene, like a benevolent specter, is a small but entirely recognizable view of the Eiffel Tower, mysteriously beautiful in the fog (cat. no. 1). This photograph, made for his mother and for Elizabeth and sent to both, demonstrates Kertész's secure sense of himself.

III. Kertész's First Artistic Successes, 1927–1929

Beauty is everywhere, in the arrangement of saucepans on the white walls of your kitchen, perhaps more than in your eighteenth-century salon or in official museums.
—Fernand Léger, 1924

Kertész had arrived in Paris knowing virtually no one and with no gainful employment. Within a year-and-a-half he had a circle of good friends, was selling his photographs to illustrated magazines in France and Germany, and was building a very creditable reputation as an important artistic figure in photography. By 1927 not only was he aware of the artistic movements and events in the city, but he was also actively contributing to them.

Among the diverse group of people at the Hôtel des Terraces was Michel Seuphor, who though younger than Kertész possessed a sophisticated understanding of contemporary art. Their mutual friend Gyula Zilzer brought Seuphor to Kertész's hotel room a few months after his arrival. Seuphor vividly remembers meeting a modest and quiet young man who could speak no French and played a song on his peasant flute for his visitor. Since they were both new to Paris, they agreed to explore it together (see cat. nos. 17, 33). And although Kertész was then, as always, essentially a private man who wanted to keep his distance, he must have found Seuphor's enlightened company stimulating.

In early 1926 Piet Mondrian invited Kertész to visit his studio for the first time. At that moment the painter's true dimensions were appreciated by very few people. Seuphor, however, was an intimate friend. Although Kertész knew Mondrian from the Dôme, he was unfamiliar with his paintings before he entered the studio. Clearly, he approached his subject with reverence, interested in documenting the artist's habits, the way his spirit affected where and how he lived. In *Mondrian's Studio* (cat. no. 23), the artist's slightly rumpled bed in the middle of the photograph appears almost like an altar. A special light from the window reveals how naturally, even wonderfully, Mondrian's art merged with his surroundings and elevated them. Kertész cherished the simplicity of these rooms. Everything in his photograph reflects the harmony and spiritual essence the artist sought.

And yet, in the group of photographs Kertész made that day, he discovered telling deviations from Mondrian's precise geometry. Mondrian noticed that the photographer studied his mustache, and Kertész discovered that it was trimmed to make his face appear more regular and geometric. This aspiration to order and the slight and human divergences from it appealed to Kertész, who still has vivid memories of this visit. He went to Mondrian's living space to document it; he made still lifes that are beautiful in themselves and also inform us of the person living there. The objects in *Mondrian's Glasses and Pipe* (cat. no. 21) are simple geometric forms; the glasses are common, manufactured articles, yet we are shown their refined sculptural qualities, which Mondrian must have admired. These objects were used daily: their austere clarity, their beautiful geometry were a part of Mondrian's experience. Kertész took a few personal possessions, objects of extreme simplicity, and composed a picture that speaks of the artist's being. The artfulness of life—expanding art to incorporate seeing, as Léger demanded—clearly challenged Kertész.[17]

These aspirations are most telling in *Chez Mondrian* (cat. no. 22). Here again, Kertész found natural geometries in the door frame, table, mat, and stair railings, but these insistent angularities serve to accentuate the curve of the bannister and the hat hanging on the peg, elements absent from Mondrian's art. The diffused light that quietly enters the room seems almost a mystical force, revealing one object antithetical to the artist's painting. As Seuphor has described it:

> So strongly did [Mondrian] feel the lack of a woman in his daily life that he always kept a flower—an artificial flower suggesting a feminine presence—in the round vase standing on the hall table of his studio at the Rue du Départ. . . .
>
> I never saw the slightest trace of a living flower in Mondrian's studio. But, in a round vase on a hall table close to the door, there was always the single artificial tulip. . . . An artificial leaf which went with it was painted white by Mondrian to banish entirely any recollection of the green he found so intolerable.[18]

Mondrian had only recently stopped painting pictures of single flowers, which he relied upon for a modest income. Kertész understood the meaning Mondrian attached to his flower. Within the spare order of this image is a profound understanding of the person who lives and works there. Kertész's sensitive appreciation of light, the delicacy of his tonalities, and the directness and simplicity of these compositions were new to his work. *Chez Mondrian* also investigates the relationship of outdoors to indoors that Kertész would explore in a variety of ways. As a tourist, he had used the motif of the window to express his own psychological distance. Here, however, the opening into the stairwell plays a more formal role.

Occurring less than a year after his arrival, this contact with the most important figure in abstract painting in Paris set Kertész on a new course. We suddenly find a great number of enthusiastic experiments. His work became more formalist, more sensitive to planar tensions and geometric structure. Aware in a general way (even before he left Hungary) of the Constructivist ideas proposed in Kassák's magazine *Ma*—aware also of the *Buch neuer Künstler* Kassák had made with Moholy— and now exposed to the new architecture as well as the new art, Kertész began to show an appreciation and inspired appropriation of these ideas. But his personality was never dominated by the ideas of others, for his eye has always been primarily responsive to the human aspect of what he sees. He has always maintained that he photographs only what he feels.[19] His own Constructivism was achieved almost without mechanical objects, almost exclusively by reference to the hand-built, the man-made.

Cello Study (cat. no. 19), for instance, cut down from a close-up to form an extreme abstraction, even in its now purified state resonates with the human spirit, the touch of the bow, and the warm glow of the wooden instrument. Its companion piece, *Quartet* (cat. no. 24), was also severely cropped from a large, full-length photograph. The violinist Feri Róth, who had just assembled a new quartet, asked Kertész to make some photographs that could be used for publicity. Róth got what he desired, while Kertész the artist drew from one of these photographs the abstract composition he envisioned. True to his sense of his medium, as with *The Stairs of Montmartre*, he never interfered with its process except through cropping. Many of his photographs from this time are radically cut down, and often he

Catalogue no. 43
Avenue Junot, 1927,
from *Photographische
Rundschau und
Mitteilungen* 66,
no. 5 (1929), p. 99.

Figure 20
Kertész,
Telephone Wires, 1927.

reinvestigated these croppings like a musician experimenting with a new interpretation of his own composition. Such is the case with his variations on the portrait of Paul Arma. Kertész began with a portrait of this young Hungarian musician in a fairly standard format (cat. no. 59). Then, attracted by the delicate hands of the pianist, he made four variations on the hands, glasses, and shadows (see cat. nos. 60–62). There is in all of these, however fanciful or mysterious they may be, a sense of respect for the object: the hands are always Arma's, never merely a design. Cutting down from a larger image was Kertész's way of purifying and abstracting the subject without interfering with the integrity of the photographic medium.

Kertész photographed another artist's dwelling in 1927: Tristan Tzara's new home, designed by Adolf Loos. Again, he knew both men from the Dôme, although only casually. They invited him along when they went to visit the site in Montmartre. On this occasion Kertész photographed Tzara at the window (cat. no. 42) and then examined avenue Junot below (cat. no. 43). He admired the beautiful geometries of this architecturally important building, of Loos's sensitive adaptation of vernacular studio architecture in the Montmartre district. But what Kertész depicted, characteristically, was the personality that domi-

nated this empty building. Likewise, *Avenue Junot* is not a rigid geometric composition—the gentle sweep of the road is gracefully irregular. There is a tactile appreciation of the paving stones, the somewhat careless and dusty but delicate arrangements of tools, materials, and workers. In an age when glass and steel were often seen symbolically and were used enthusiastically by architects and artists and admired by photographers, this street seems almost hand-fashioned.

Kertész's new formalism is evident in two new subjects: the detail that is both an abstraction and a kind of document, and the found still life. For example, one can sense a change from his early depiction of chairs and their shadows (cat. no. 17) to one made the following year, in 1927 (cat. no. 49). The earlier photograph imparts a sense of place—the walk is romantic, in the nature of a tourist's enchanted view of the Luxembourg Gardens. The chairs and their shadows have a sense of mystery—the shadow shapes dance elegantly and confusingly, integrating the chairs and the path, the fence and the scattered leaves. In the later version, the mysteriousness is still present, but it does not dominate the mood. The chairs still have an appropriate Parisian air, epitomizing something about the city, but there is now a clearer geometry and a spatial flattening that together make this composition somehow purer than that of its predecessor. The view is not so clearly an onlooker's, the objects photographed are more integrated into the surrounding space, and the earlier romantic sentiment has been transformed. Now Kertész was looking for details in city views, as is evident in *Telephone Wires* (fig. 20), taken not far from rue de Vanves. Here, the space has been flattened, the forms hardened, and the composition ostensibly related to the abstractions of his friends. Other views of the river, boulevards, and parks also made at this time incorporate steel railings and chains into geometric patterns, while remaining delicate, essentially personal interpretations of Paris.

The idea of the found still life, of decoding the personal meaning in objects, was one Kertész developed in many photographs he made of artists' studios in 1926 and 1927. Most of these are views of corners or tabletops where art and real things merge. Kertész sometimes juxtaposed a still art object with something momentarily arrested, as in his image of a sculpture and newspaper transformed by the sudden appearance of a cat (cat. no. 41). Another early still life was made

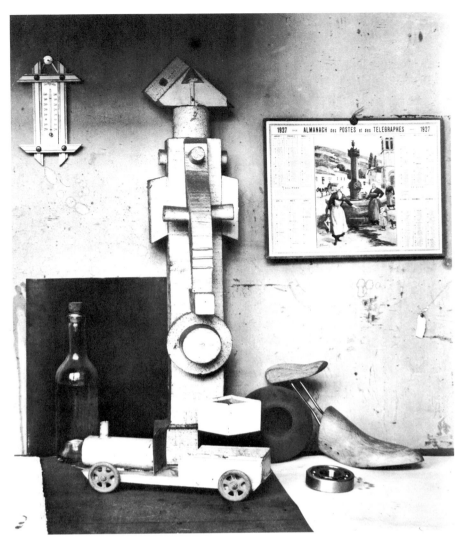

Figure 21
Kertész,
*Corner of Léger's
Studio*, 1927.

Figure 22
Kertész,
Madame Károlyi, 1927.

Figure 23
Kertész,
Jean Slivinsky, 1927.

in the studio of Fernand Léger, whom Kertész
admired both for his paintings and for his efforts
to widen the scope of modern art. In Léger's
studio the photographer discovered a wine bottle,
a shoe stretcher, a child's toy, a mechanical object,
and a piece of sculpture, all perceived so that
common objects and art are unified by the quality
of seeing (see fig. 21). Almost as if in accordance
with Léger's own dictum (see p. 30), these photographs demonstrate that Kertész had quickly
moved beyond a romantic view of the city and its
artists to find beauty in everyday things, in
unexpected or unnoticed places.

By 1927, then, Kertész was a confident young
man, now speaking some French and broadening
his horizons. His portraiture of this period reveals
a new sense of compositional formalism; the subjects are now more diversified, no longer strictly
Hungarian. In some of them, Kertész investigated
the doubling and flattening effect of mirrors. He
explored the dialogue between two different kinds
of space, the play between two different realities,
as in the portraits of Mme. Károlyi (see fig. 22),
the actor W. Aguet, and even Edward Titus
(cat. no. 57). The playing-off of flat and sculptural
elements was pursued not only in these mirrored
images, but in several views into windows
(see cat. no. 53).

Kertész had by now produced enough innovative work to merit an exhibition. A former Polish
lieder singer named Jean Slivinsky came forward
(see fig. 23). He offered Kertész an exhibition in
his gallery, Au Sacre du Printemps, on rue du
Cherche-Midi in Montparnasse. Slivinsky showed
the work of many foreign artists and of some of
Kertész's friends: Tihanyi had been given an exhibition in 1926, and Beőthy showed his sculpture
there the year after Kertész. Marie Wassilieff and

Figure 24
Kertész,
*Jean Slivinsky,
Herwarth Walden, and
Friends at Au Sacre du
Printemps*, 1927.

Figure 25
Kertész,
After the Soirée, 1927.
Ida Thal is in the center
of this group; Adolf
Loos, Piet Mondrian,
and Michel Seuphor
are at right.

Kiki—the artist's model turned popular singer and painter—were also given shows. Slivinsky exhibited Berenice Abbott's photographs in 1926, and it was he who arranged a visit between the two photographers.

Slivinsky was also involved with Michel Seuphor and his close friend the poet Paul Dermée. These two had interested the gallery director in staging a series of soirées celebrating the combined pleasures of poetry, music, and contemporary art. The first soirée coincided with the opening in March 1927 of a show of paintings by Ida Thal, a Hungarian abstract artist and friend of Seuphor, and of the photographs of André Kertész.

Kertész recorded the exhibition in a photograph of Slivinsky and Herwarth Walden, the proprietor of the gallery Der Sturm in Berlin, surrounded by friends (fig. 24). Above their heads are twelve photographs, or about a third of Kertész's show. Most are recognizable: *The Studio Cat* (cat. no. 41), a still life of objects by Hilda Daus, two unknown still lifes, the Pont Marie, *Mondrian's Glasses and Pipe*, a *fête foraine*, a Paris street with a *pissoir*, *Wall of Posters* (cat. no. 28), *Notre Dame at Night*, *Chez Mondrian*, and probably a photograph of Les Halles (perhaps cat. no. 47). There were also some portraits, *Telephone Wires*, and a view of Léger's studio. The selection reveals Kertész's attraction to crafted things, his discoveries of the city, and his responsiveness to modernist ideas like Constructivism. Ida Thal's geometric abstractions, which were hung a little higher on the walls of the gallery, only stressed Kertész's contact with the vivid world around him, and his personal transformation of it.

Slivinsky sent out three notices: one announced Ida Thal's exhibition with a brief appreciation by Seuphor; another reproduced a Kertész photograph (cat. no. 14) on one side and a poem by Paul Dermée on the other describing the character of Kertész's work. Dermée's piece, of great charm and delicacy, praises the photographer as being endowed with a vision almost like that of a child, uncommonly direct and thus revelatory (see remarks on cat. no. 52). The third card was an invitation to a soirée for works of the "new spirit" ("*oeuvres d'esprit nouveau*"), actually the opening for the show. That evening was an exciting event, a lively assortment of music and poetry, some contemporary, some old. One participant read Goethe and Villon, another the Hungarian poets Kassák and Attila József, all in the original languages.

Figure 26
*Documents internationaux
de l'esprit nouveau*, 1927,
cover.

Kertész remembers that the small rooms were fairly bulging to capacity with an enthusiastic crowd. Tzara, Loos, and Mondrian were among those who attended. After this grand evening and dinner, Kertész assembled a small crowd in front of an artists' supply store for a photograph (fig. 25).

The title Dermée and Seuphor chose for their evening events, celebrations of the "new spirit," was historically significant. Guillaume Apollinaire had originally coined the term to signify the continuing and expanding avant-garde spirit. Dermée was interested in "abstract" poetry as well as the more traditional, and he was then experimenting with "Bruitist" music and mechanically produced sounds. In 1920 Dermée, Ozenfant, and Le Corbusier had founded the magazine *L'Esprit nouveau*. Dermée was concerned with what he called the "lyric beauty of objects."[20] It soon became clear, however, that the other editors were more interested in examining the aesthetic beauty of vernacular objects such as locomotives and airplanes. In 1925, when *L'Esprit nouveau* ceased publication, Dermée and Seuphor tried to revive it on their own terms. The result was the single issue of a magazine they named *Documents internationaux de l'esprit nouveau* and published in 1927 (fig. 26).

The magazine produced by Dermée and Seuphor reflected the diverse currents of their respective interests, briefly and somewhat incongruously united. The editors wanted to avoid doctrine; their aim was to show the variety of modernism in the West. Amid this diversity, and alongside single photographs by others, Kertész was the principal photographer (although not all of his images were credited). The range of art represented in this issue was wide, but the selection favored the International Style in architecture and abstract or Constructivist art. Writings of Saint Paul and Plato were interspersed with poetry of Hans Arp and Filippo Tommaso Marinetti, as well as the Hungarian József. Léger, Mondrian, and Kurt Schwitters were also represented.

On the back of a post-card print of *Chez Mondrian* that he sent to his brother Jenő in Buenos Aires, Kertész wrote, "L'Esprit nouveau is coming out in mid-January. A new artistic magazine, this picture will be published there." Unfortunately, this expectation never materialized: the first issue, which appeared in April, was also the last. Nonetheless, these events represented a highlight in Kertész's career in Paris. A reviewer

for the *Chicago Tribune* praised the "primitive" clarity of his work, as had Dermée:

His directness in portraiture is almost disarming. With two or three exceptions the portraits are as unaffected as a snapshot. . . . Through this simplicity they show, like the still-lifes, landscapes and genres, the artistic possibilities of photography which depends purely on the most fundamental resources.[21]

He had found his place, he was productive, he retained his individual expression, and his work was admired and promoted by a small but important and internationally connected group of avant-garde artists and poets.

The next few years continued Kertész's happy involvement in photography as an artistic adventure. He made major discoveries with his new Leica camera, which he bought in 1928. The advances of this conveniently portable instrument made it easier for him to investigate arrested action, to capture several things happening in the frame at once. He no longer needed to wait for a figure to enter the scene to complete a composition. These changes are evident in more spontaneous and subtler juxtapositions—of outside and inside, of humorous coincidences, and of emotionally charged encounters. *Meudon* (cat. no. 58) is an especially haunting image: a train passes overhead on a viaduct under restoration in a run-down neighborhood, while a solitary man comes toward us. In many cases Kertész's examinations of simultaneous action involve children, whose vibrant, random activity was suitable to this new insight. His habit of vagabonding drew him to depict as well the noisy, working activity of the city (see cat. nos. 70, 75).

By 1928 Kertész was publishing work in picture magazines in France and elsewhere, and he was clearly established as an eminent personality in photography. In this year some of Kertész's colleagues decided to organize an exhibition to publicize the new photography in France. The site chosen for the exhibition—called the "1er Salon Indépendant de la Photographie"—was the Comédie within the Théâtre des Champs-Elysées. The theater had already hosted many avant-garde events—Dada manifestations, the Swedish ballet, and a raucous Surrealist demonstration. The show was hung around the large staircase of the Comédie, hence its nickname, the "Salon de l'Escalier."

The recognition that photography was receiving

in France—that is, as a new medium worthy of its own avant-garde salon—was probably inspired by German activity. The "Salon de l'Escalier," however, clearly pointed out the differences between photography in Germany and in France. It showed the work of young experimentalists (Abbott, Kertész, Krull, Man Ray, and Paul Outerbridge) and the fashion photography by George Hoyningen-Huené and d'Ora, and it contained a historical section devoted to Nadar and Atget. Distinctions between magazine photography and the medium's aesthetic potential were not so tightly drawn as in Germany. Photography in France—almost exclusively the work of foreigners—did not have the consistency of the work done in Germany: the works were more individualistic, less identified with a conceptual program. Photographers active in France did not have as strong an emotional commitment to the machine aesthetic, to the camera as an objective and truthful instrument of vision, as did their counterparts in Germany. French photography was often more personal and mysterious, though at the same time, paradoxically, much of it could be called "documentary." In this respect, Kertész's work was typical of photography in France.

One might well wonder why French writers, editors, and gallery owners became interested in photography at this time. In fact, its acceptance was part of a general return to order. The avant-garde movements that had begun before World War I had been transformed into the School of Paris. Older artists, including Picasso and Matisse, the Futurists, and even the Cubists, gravitated to a new realism, as did the adherents of the new artistic style, Surrealism, officially born in 1924.

Concurrently, there was a fascination with primitive and folk arts, related to an interest in vernacular arts, in popular culture. For example, prominent Paris dealers Wilhelm Uhde and Jeanne Bucher exhibited naive painting in the 1920s, and artists such as André Lhote and Ossip Zadkine collected naive objects. Magazines such as *Jazz* and *L'Art vivant* examined "living art"—as well as "fine art." If Le Corbusier was interested in the aesthetic of airplane hangars and American grain elevators, then Kertész was partly admired for his respect for the culture of the city, and for broadening the definition of aesthetic experience.

In this important exhibition, Kertész showed several of the same photographs as in the Sacre du Printemps show, but there were important differences. One was the greater number of portraits,

mainly of friends, although some were commissioned. Other photographs chosen for the exhibition, the *Cello Study*, chairs in the Luxembourg Gardens, *The Stairs of Montmartre*, *Chez Mondrian*, and *Hands and Books* (cat. no. 54), all demonstrate Kertész's compositional sophistication, his cunning investigation of vantage and geometry, and his elegant sense of form. The photographs are also informed with his respect for the "mystery of the object," as one reviewer noted of his work, evoked through particularly gentle tonalities and a certain directness of approach.[22]

The most important single photograph by Kertész in the exhibition was *Fork* (cat. no. 65), made that year. Other photographers, such as Paul Outerbridge, showed photographs of ordinary objects in an aesthetic context. Like Kertész's *Fork*, Outerbridge's *Ide Collar* defines its subject sculpturally. But Outerbridge gave his composition an appealing flair that made it appropriate as an advertisement. Kertész's *Fork*, on the other hand, is endowed with a personal quality: delicate, abstracted, yet communicating its essential function. The fork was photographed the day after a pleasant dinner with Kertész's friends. It is resting on a plate, as though seen at the end of a meal—it is not shown in brilliant artificial light, nor made a utopian symbol by graphic abstraction. *Fork* was made with Kertész's 9 x 12 cm glass-plate camera, which allowed for careful adjustment of the composition. With its insistent, close-up view, it also anticipates images taken around the same time with the Leica (see cat. nos. 63, 64). All Kertész's subjects have a certain concreteness and personality, yet a strangeness despite their familiarity, as Pierre Bost observed.[23] For Bost, *Fork* was a real work of art, a true indication of photography's aesthetic potential.

One of the major critical figures to emerge from the "Salon de l'Escalier" was the poet and novelist Pierre Mac Orlan, who was sympathetic to photography and appreciative of Kertész's spirit. The two men had met before the 1928 exhibition. Kertész visited Mac Orlan outside Paris, where, embittered by his earlier poverty in Montmartre, he was living in semi-isolation. Kertész photographed him several times (see cat. no. 51); Mac Orlan is usually seen playing his accordion, for which he composed popular and often strange, folk-surrealist songs.

Mac Orlan chose the working class and the lower levels of society as subjects for his somewhat grotesque, parablelike stories and poems. He was

Figure 27
L'Art vivant 5
(Mar. 1, 1929),
pp. 208–09, photo-
graphs by Kertész.

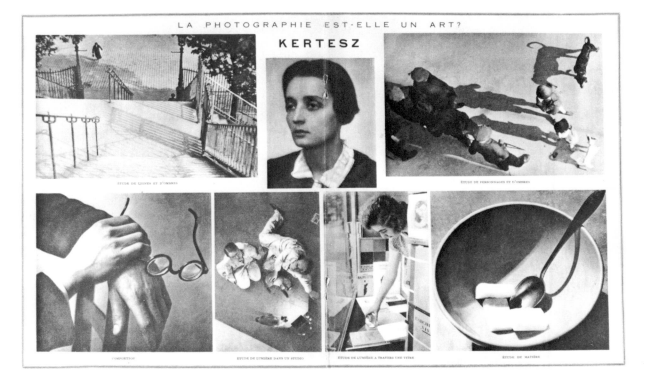

also interested in outsiders: pirates, vagabonds,
and underworld characters. Like Kertész, he was
fond of mists and nighttime shadows, urban landscapes that mirror the strangeness and fate of his
characters. No one in Paris, it would seem, could
have served Kertész so well, with such apposite
interests, as did Pierre Mac Orlan. In 1928 he
wrote an amazingly prescient article on photography in which he announced that "the true
illustrators are the photographers."[24] He saw
clearly the difference between a formalist attitude
to photography and a documentary approach that
stimulated the literary imagination. Mac Orlan
was interested in the way photographs can disturb
and dislocate, in their power to suggest the fright-
ening or mysterious. For him, as for the Surrealists, the non- or anti-artistic photograph—
the anonymous document—was the most pro-
vocative to the imagination, because it was more
purely and absolutely subconscious. Kertész's
deserted parks at night, his empty chairs, had
for Mac Orlan a deliciously vivid and pregnant
disquiet. For him, Kertész was a "poet-photog-
rapher." When Mac Orlan was later asked to
write an introduction to Kertész's book *Paris*
(1934), he said that the work spoke so eloquently
itself that he could write only what the images
dictated:

*A view of one of Paris's bridges provokes a
sense of strange larval, nocturnal life; a deserted
square is peopled by shadows; an empty street
lets us see the funeral cortège that will arrive
someday.... A simple click of the shutter will
reveal to the unbelieving an aspect so secret of
things, that they will not recognize the park
chairs they often sit in, which at other times are
taken over by children.*[25]

Another literary figure prominent at the time
was Francis Carco. His subject matter was close to
Mac Orlan's and his novels of Paris low-life have
a spirit similar to that of Kertész's photographs.
Both Carco and Mac Orlan wrote books on the
School of Paris artists (Pascin, Utrillo, Vlaminck,
and the Hungarian Marcel Vertès), whose street
views, still lifes, and figures show more concern
for a poignant and sometimes decadent realism
than for structural invention. Occasionally, Kertész's photographs illustrated Carco's and Mac
Orlan's homages to the "leprous walls" and
gritty pavements of Paris.[26]

But Kertész's close comrade in these years was
Eugène Dabit, whom he met about 1928 through
a friend and fellow art student of Elizabeth's, Vera
Braun. Because of his tragic early death, Dabit is
not as well known today as either Mac Orlan or
Carco. He was the author of *Hôtel du Nord* (1929),

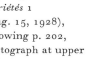

Catalogue no. 78
Storefront and
*Montparnasse, rue de
Vanves*, c. 1929, from
Bifur 1 (May 1929),
opposite p. 72.

an important, compassionate book about the lives of residents in a poor hotel in the canal district of Paris. Dabit wrote with great perception of Kertész's *Paris*.[27] His directness, realism, and clean and simple language Kertész still finds meaningful. Both men responded to the very poor, describing their lives with lyric simplicity and honesty, and extracting heroism and tragedy from their dim and grimy locale. And although he has never had a real social consciousness, Kertész was also vaguely sympathetic to his friend's leftist idealism.

The year 1929 was one of change for Kertész. He made innovations in his own photographs and his work was published in art and literary magazines and appeared extensively in the pictorial press. The adventurous art magazine *L'Art vivant*, edited by the art critic Florent Fels, published an important critical assessment of his photography by Jean Gallotti, and beautifully reproduced seven photographs.[28] True to its name, the magazine concerned itself with contemporary art in its many manifestations. It covered traditional forms of painting and sculpture, but it also included essays on the aesthetics of poster advertisement, on the street fairs, and on Gypsies camped in the outskirts of Paris. Very attracted to photography, Fels initiated a series, written mainly by Gallotti, called "La Photographie est-elle un art?" Kertész was the third photographer, after Atget and Albin-Guillot, to be interviewed (see fig. 27). The reticent Kertész, pressed for some statement about his profession, finally told his interviewer that

"photography must be realist," and that "photography is one thing, painting another, and they are not the same thing." Gallotti observed the extremely personal nature of Kertész's realist photographs, and stated that his sense of composition and lighting were as individual as a signature.

As a recognized leader in new French photography, Kertész was invited to participate in the first major international photography exhibition of this time, the 1929 "International Ausstellung von Film und Foto" in Stuttgart. Although he never visited Germany while he lived in Paris, Kertész knew something about German photography through his friends and from publications. The "Film und Foto" show was the first of a series of exhibitions designed to publicize the potentials of the medium. It was organized by the Deutscher Werkbund, an association of industrialists, architects, craftsmen, and arts educators, who wanted to promote high quality in useful objects and designed environments. László Moholy-Nagy assisted in the organization and selection of the exhibition.

The works Kertész sent to the show are congruent with Moholy's interest in seeing new objects in different ways: they emphasize vantage points from above and below, and the close-up. Some photographs, like that of *Telephone Wires* or a view of a Paris gutter, depict modern urban growth. Other studies of commonplace things, such as that of *Mondrian's Glasses and Pipe*, or *Fork*, clarify Kertész's vast difference from his German contemporaries. His photographs were motivated by feelings, not by ideals.

Kertész may not have been familiar with Moholy's work in 1929, but he did know the photographs of Albert Renger-Patzsch. His friend Anne-Marie Merkel brought back from her native Germany a copy of Renger-Patzsch's newly published book *Die Welt ist Schön* (1928). Kertész admired these photographs and felt a certain kinship with them, although he also thought them rather cold. The German book relates flowers, animals, and people of different cultures. Works by Renger-Patzsch do not have the same sense of particularity that those by Kertész do. Like many of the comparative illustrations in Moholy's books, Renger-Patzsch's images were intended, through comparison, to achieve a sense of ideal abstraction. Kertész's photographs, on the other hand, always emphasize the personal worth and specific meaningfulness of objects.

Figure 31
*Münchner Illustrierte
Presse,*
no. 40 (Oct. 6, 1929),
p. 1319, photographs by
Kertész.

Like many German and French photographers, Kertész was now finding his work reproduced in small literary reviews. *Der Querschnitt*, the oldest and most distinguished of these, published not only the elegant work of Moholy and the sensitive images of Kertész,[29] but also strange, funny, and common anonymous photographs. This little publication had been started by the art dealer Alfred Flectheim, but it was later bought by the large Ullstein publishing firm, which increased its circulation. From its first year, *Der Querschnitt* juxtaposed photographs comparatively, for instance, a close-up by Renger-Patzsch of a flower on one page and the head of a tiger on the other; but this was done for amusement, not out of any aesthetic theory.

Kertész's photography also appeared in a popular version of *Der Querschnitt*, another Ullstein publication named *Uhu*. This magazine published light fiction, chatty essays, and numerous photographs. Some of Kertész's photographs in *Uhu* were used to evoke the strange underworld of Paris at night (see fig. 28). *Uhu* also published a perceptive essay on the new photography, and included Kertész in the company of Moholy, Munkacsi, Renger-Patzsch, and Erich Salomon (see fig. 29).[30]

The Belgian magazine *Variétés*, which began

in 1928, also published photographs extensively, but treated them rather like artifacts, similar to the found objects that so interested the Surrealists. *Variétés* magnified and playfully extended this use of photographs, so that pages and pages of all kinds of images elaborated a theme that mirrored the literary content. All aspects of life interested the editors of *Variétés*, who directed much of their attention to popular culture, even fashion. Kertész's portrait of Mac Orlan illustrated an article on accordions, demonstrating that artists and poets took this instrument seriously (fig. 30). Another issue illustrated the culture of vagabonds and *clochards*, still another that of folk artists such as Kertész's friend André Bauchant.[31]

Another literary magazine that published works by Kertész was Ribemont-Dessaignes's *Bifur*. Its editors were interested in literary reportage as an aesthetic form. *Bifur* reproduced Kertész's photographs in the company of other documentary-style photographers, especially Atget, Krull, and Eli Lotar, along with anonymous photographs and even some surreal experiments by Maurice Tabard. Heavily printed in an almost grimy color and placed within some hard-hitting political discussion, Kertész's work has a sense of almost suffocating despair. A street corner at night plastered with movie posters advertising *Le Baiser qui tue* appears alongside a storefront with naked mannequins bemusedly looking around (see cat. no. 78). As so often happens in French photography of this period, the comparison was made not out of utopian idealism, but to express disorientation and alienation emanating from common phenomena. Objects of popular culture become blank substitutes for human expressions. The magazine was responsive to Surrealism, but it also reproduced a series Kertész made on the hearty naive painter André Bauchant.

By 1929 Kertész had become a successful photojournalist. The assignments he completed sometimes supplied him with photographs that he would send to exhibitions or publish later in a more specifically aesthetic context. Several of them (cat. nos. 76, 82, 86) were bought by Julien Levy, whom he met about this time. A view of the Eiffel Tower from above (cat. no. 82) was made for an essay on the monument's fortieth anniversary. The portrait of Clayton "Peg Leg" Bates (cat. no. 86) was part of a piece of reportage (see fig. 31) on an American jazz dancer, one of many who came to Europe following Josephine Baker. Despite the fact that he had an artificial limb, Bates was a successful and inventive dancer, and Kertész photographed him executing great leaps. But this close look at the artificial limb, admiring its simple and strong construction and the perfect placement and shine of the shoe, has a sense of tragedy beyond the fascinating and inventive composition. The photograph of a young archer (cat. no. 76) was part of a photoessay on an archery contest. This image would later appear in Kertész's first book, *Enfants* (1933). A portrait of

Alexander Calder, another of Kertész's companions from the Dôme, was also made in 1929 (cat. no. 77). Though he was a happy and likable man, this photograph shows Calder, surrounded by his *Circus*, in a withdrawn, even somber, mood. While Kertész had long been fascinated by shadows and other elements explored in these photographs, they nonetheless exhibit a somewhat tragic air and an ambiguity that are new to his work.

IV. Kertész and Magazine Photography of the 1920s and 1930s

I am an amateur and I intend to be one all my life. For me, photography should capture the true personality of things. . . . Remember the reporters and the amateurs—both of them want only to make a souvenir or a document: that is pure photography.

—André Kertész, 1930

Because of the richness and variety of popular magazines in Hungary, it is not surprising that many Hungarians—Kertész among them—readily became involved in popular journalism in both Germany and France. The new, postwar mass-publication market had suddenly made these fields invitingly lucrative. Whether they left home for political reasons or, as he had, for professional ones, most of Kertész's compatriots showed their inventiveness in adapting to many kinds of journalism—caricature, for instance, and fashion illustration. The cinema was a rival field, an art form with interrelated aesthetic parts, and it was also heavily endowed with Hungarians. Kertész himself was briefly attracted to filmmaking at this time, though nothing came of it.[32]

While the Hungarian precedent was certainly important, Germany was really the birthplace of the photographically illustrated magazine addressed to a large, generally middle-class audience. Ullstein's *Berliner Illustrirte Zeitung* was the most established, but other cities like Munich and Frankfurt also had important magazines. The great bulk of each issue was devoted to a serialized popular novel, but the most interesting sections were found at the front and back, where photography was lavishly used, interspersed with text, drawings, and collage so that each element interacted playfully and evocatively with the others. These German magazines sought to portray life, not to reproduce art. They featured "human interest" stories—lighthearted, entertaining

sketches, rather than really informational essays. Politics were only touched upon, if included at all. Their goal was rather to demonstrate the basic similarities between people from exotic countries and those nearer home whose circumstances were unknown or frequently overlooked. Therefore, Kertész's photographs were a natural, even inspired addition to this German fare; his interest in the "common man" and the folklore of peoples was a valuable extension for the German magazines.

Kertész first published several single images in German magazines: *Café du Dôme* appeared in 1926 in *Das Illustrierte Blatt*, and *Satiric Dancer* was used as an illustration in *Die Dame* the following year.[33] Thus, his work appeared in the mass pictorial magazines at the same time that it was being published in such literary journals as *Der Querschnitt* and *Variétés*. But although Kertész continued to publish single photographs throughout his stay in Paris, he also played an important part in the development of the photoessay in Germany and France.

Kertész remembers that the German editors from the Ullstein firm complained that he was not sending them enough material. While single photographs were welcome, they preferred him to engage in reportage. "If we give you a subject," he recalls them telling him, "will you make a series of photographs?" The idea appealed to Kertész, and in fact the arrangement left him with considerable imaginative freedom. In the early period of pictorial magazines, the relationships between staff and free-lance photographers were very casual. Usually an editor would suggest a timely subject and commission a writer. The editor would then show the essay to a photographer, and if the photographer thought he could illustrate the article, he took on the assignment. Sometimes the photographer suggested particular ideas to the editor or writer, but always his task

LA FORÊT PARISIENNE

Figure 32
Vu, no. 23
(Aug. 22, 1928),
pp. 530–31, photo-
graphs by Kertész.

was to demonstrate how things looked and to complement the essay.

Kertész's closest relationship with a European magazine, however, developed not in Germany but in France. A gregarious Alsatian named Lucien Vogel stepped into Kertész's exhibition at the Sacre du Printemps gallery in 1927 and, impressed by the work on the walls, he invited the younger man to participate in a magazine he was planning, a pictorial weekly called *Vu*. This magazine and, later, *Art et Médecine* were to become the mainstays of Kertész's career in Paris. In addition to a steady income, they provided him with the opportunity to make photographs congruent with his own interests. In the pages of *Vu* and *Art et Médecine*, he was able to explore many of the themes from his noncommercial work, and to continue his commitment to the photograph as a document.

Vu was the most attractive and adventurous pictorial magazine of its time and clearly bore the mark of its originator, a man Kertész greatly respected. Vogel had had extensive experience in magazine publication before *Vu*: he started his career editing *Art et Décoration* and then, with his wife, Cosette de Brunhoff, created and managed first *Gazette du Bon Ton* and then *Jardin des Modes*. Both of these were essentially fashion magazines, the former luxuriously printed and colored by hand-stencilling. *Bon Ton* also included illustrations by important contemporary artists

such as Marie Laurencin, and essays by writers like Jean Cocteau. By the time he met Kertész, Vogel was feeling the limitations of these publications, and he wanted to create a magazine more reflective of his liberal political ideas. His solution was a visually stimulating journal, confronting a wide range of current events, and based generally on German models.

For *Vu*, Vogel at first followed the German formula for a cheaply produced picture magazine whose chief selling point was a serialized popular novel. Vogel's version, however, was better printed, more unified and elegantly designed, and in general had more flair and style. Where there was minimal communication between Germany's artistic innovators at the Bauhaus and the country's magazines, Vogel, quite consciously, sought the best designers. Cassandre designed the logo, and Alexander Liberman, brought in to replace another Russian, Irène Lidova, as art director, made the layout more graphically adventurous and appealing. *Vu* also published essays by some of the best writers of the period, such as Colette, Mac Orlan, and Philippe Soupault.

But the real beauty of *Vu* was its photography. Again, Vogel sought the best. He was himself a talented amateur photographer, and the magazine frequently carried some of his own work. Vogel published most of France's innovative photographers—Brassaï, Kertész, Krull, Man Ray, Tabard. *Vu* was the most important place to see contemporary photography regularly: the art galleries and museums that were beginning to exhibit photographs could not approach the sheer volume of first-rate photographic images that appeared every week in this magazine.

Kertész's photographs first appeared in the fifth issue of *Vu* (April 18, 1928), and, significantly, this work was used decoratively—not as reportage. More extensively than the Germans, Vogel featured photographs for their aesthetic pleasure, to set the proper tone of an essay or novel. Thus, *Quartet*, a harmonious, meditative picture, introduced a section of a serialized novel that had nothing intrinsically to do with the illustration. In 1930 Kertész suggested to the editors that he photograph Miss France by close-ups of her mouth, lips, and ear; these images were assembled into a lighthearted collage.[34] Vogel also frequently published a nonnarrative and usually entirely photographic centerfold. Kertész's work was regularly used in this decorative capacity. One of his earliest essays was the "Forests of Paris," evocative photo-

Figure 33
Vu, no. 36
(Nov. 21, 1928), p. 788,
photographs by Kertész.

Figure 34
*Münchner Illustrierte
    Presse*,
no. 19 (May 12, 1929),
p. 637, photographs by
Kertész.

graphs of the woodlands in the Bois de Boulogne and other parks, with lines of poetry by Baudelaire, Valéry, and Victor Hugo serving as captions (see fig. 32).[35]

When Vogel used Kertész for reportage, as he often did, his interests melded with Kertész's own. Occasionally the photographer proposed subjects that appealed to him, and Vogel enthusiastically let him experiment. For "Au Souffle du verrier" (the glassblower's breath), Vogel, who had suggested the topic, arranged for Kertész to visit the old Daum glassworks in Paris. As fascinated by the craft itself as by the human dimension—the poor craftsman and his child apprentice—Kertész carefully followed the old man's work from beginning to finished product and produced a true piece of early photoreportage (see fig. 33).[36]

In the magazine's first years, Kertész produced many essays: one of his favorites was on Chartres cathedral, celebrating the last time its bell was rung manually. His lighthearted, poetic use of documentary photographs was naturally extended as Kertész examined French culture. According to his editors, Kertész was called upon whenever they wanted a specific kind of reportage: gentle, amusing pictures of Paris or of French country life; or images of events and occurrences that

were nearby but not usually seen, like the views of life in a Trappist monastery that Kertész was the first photographer to penetrate, made at Vogel's behest (see Travis, fig. 5).[37] Although Kertész's work of this kind was distinctive, it was related to that of his contemporaries, Krull, Isaac Kitrosser, Hug Block, and others.

For the German magazines, Kertész usually acted as a reporter of cultural events. This was particularly true of *Die Dame*, a women's magazine similar to *Vogue*, produced by the Ullstein firm. For them, he produced a series on children watching a puppet show, another on a German banquet in Paris, still another of an opening for a showing of Marcel Vertès's paintings, or, for the cover, a portrait of the popular guitarist Alina da Silvia.[38] For Ullstein's prestigious *Berliner Illustrirte Zeitung* he photographed the customs of Germans in Paris.[39] Occasionally, Kertész worked with Brassaï on such topics as popular dances and the use of technology (e.g., hidden microphones) in church.[40] Most of Kertész's German articles were occasional pieces, usually arranged through some intermediary, most often a friend at the Dôme. But he did have direct contact with one German magazine: through Bölöni, Kertész had met the Hungarian Stefan Lorant, the most vital

PAYSAGES BARRÉSIENS

Figure 35
Vu, no. 28
(Sept. 26, 1928),
pp. 630–31, photographs by Kertész.

Catalogue no. 92
From the Louvre,
c. 1931, from *Art et
Médecine*, Oct. 1931,
p. 21; photograph at
left by Man Ray.

editor for the *Münchner Illustrierte Presse*. Lorant's uncle had been editor of *Erdekes Ujság*. Familiar with the popular Hungarian magazine, Lorant helped to transform his German periodical into something more vivid than the older, slightly stodgy *Berliner Illustrirte Zeitung*. The *Münchner Illustrierte Presse* had a reputation for paying well, and Lorant understood Kertész's special gifts and interests. For instance, he asked Kertész in 1929 to travel to Lyon to report on a congress of international puppeteers—a subject that certainly interested the photographer. Lorant also published reportage that had already appeared, or would appear, in France. In 1930 the *Münchner Illustrierte Presse* carried Kertész's photographs of

student life in Paris, which *Vu* published two years later. Both magazines reproduced Kertész's photographs of the Eiffel Tower on its fortieth anniversary (see fig. 34).[41]

Having become familiar with Paris, Kertész began to look outside the city and discover its refreshing pastoral surroundings. Many of his truly spectacular images from the late 1920s were made of the countryside around France; his special understanding of peasant cultures enabled him to describe the French country to Frenchmen in a new way. In a period of growing nationalism, Kertész admired what he called the "international" aspect of the countryside. Although a number of these landscapes were made in his early years at *Vu* (see fig. 35), the subject became one of Kertész's specialties in the thirties.

In the 1930s Kertész's photographs of French folk culture regularly appeared in *Vu* and, even more extensively, in *Art et Médecine*. This magazine, financed by Dr. Fernand Debat, inventor of a patent medicine, was a lavishly printed monthly intended for reading in waiting rooms.[42] Since *Art et Médecine* paid well and let photographers follow their own interests, it published some of the finest photographic work of the decade (see cat. no. 92). Good photography was complemented by evocative essays from well-known writers. The editor, Anna Marsan, attached great importance to the selection of texts and appropriate photographers. Kertész was a regular and important contributor for the whole span of the magazine, from 1930 to 1936. His principal essays included ones on the Lorraine, Lyon (see cat. no. 93), the Ile de France, Brittany, Corsica, and several on the Symbolist poet Maurice Maeterlinck, whose reverence for mystery and folklore especially appealed to Kertész (see cat. no. 80).[43] He was also frequently assigned portraits of artists and celebrities—for *Vu*; its sister publication, *Lu*; and *Art et Médecine*. In this way he photographed Carco, Chagall, Colette, and Vlaminck, as well as Maeterlinck, all people whose work Kertész appreciated.

But France's political mood was changing in the early thirties, and the recurring anxieties were reflected in its illustrated magazines. A great amount of space was devoted to France itself, to a rediscovery and redefinition of French national identity. Ironically, many of the photographs were made by foreigners, a great number of them Hungarian. Kertész's photographs of the working class and peasant cultures of France were easily adapted to these new nationalistic concerns, of

Catalogue no. 93
*Quartier Saint-Jean,
Lyon,* and *The Saint-
Barthélemy Steps, Lyon,*
1932, from *Art et
Médecine,* Apr. 1932,
pp. 20–21.

Figure 36
Regards,
July 16, 1936, p. 15,
photographs by Kertész.

which he himself was probably unaware. Besides photographing the royalist Marshal Lyautey at home, the arch-conservative Charles Maurras in the offices of *L'Action française,* and landscapes memorializing the conservative man of letters of Lorraine, Maurice Barrès, he extensively documented the Colonial Exposition, a great popular event of 1931. Kertész emphasized the diverse beauties of folk architecture and the attractive native populations, while others (such as his friend Ilya Ehrenburg) criticized the organizers for displaying these same peoples and their environments like exhibits at a zoo.[44]

A gradual polarization of public opinion was evident not only in *Vu* but also in the distinguished literary periodical *Nouvelle Revue française.* As the 1930s wore on, *Vu*'s visual style reflected this increasingly charged political atmosphere, as well as a contemporary fascination with sensational events: the Stavisky affair, the violent murders of Nozières and the Papin sisters, even Edward VII's abdication. Interest in religious mysticism, occultism, and superstition showed up in some of Kertész's commissions for *Vu* (see cat. nos. 87, fig. 41). Vogel's leftist sympathies became more and more evident. The magazine's layout, now under Alexander Liberman's general direction, became more graphic, and he used photo-

graphs not as evocative instruments but, more concretely, as documents.[45] Liberman's photocollage covers were effective evocations of the issues discussed within. It was he who transformed one of Kertész's delicate early photographs of the Eiffel Tower at night into a terrifying image by superimposing a German bomber overhead (see Travis, figs. 6, 7). The work of Kertész that appeared in *Vu* in the 1930s was treated in a more documentary and concrete fashion generally, as when his photographs of simple things—a bottle of milk or a loaf of bread—were cropped and collaged with text, graphs, and other elements to create a fully integrated visual and verbal statement dramatizing the high cost of necessities. Thus the style mirrored the times, and was probably related to the expanded use of photographs as documents in the newspapers.[46]

Kertész also briefly published work in *Regards* —the Communist *Vu*—at this moment of increased political consciousness. Here again, his natural sympathy for the common man was used for purposes other than the spirit in which they were taken. Some of his older photographs of disabled veterans of World War I singing under his window were used in a political—not personal —fashion (see fig. 36). Kertész, for all his leftist sympathies, has always been essentially a bourgeois liberal. But the political climate was intensifying. In 1934 *Vu* covered the storming of the Chamber of Deputies by the French Fascists, and, on the other side, the rising of the Popular Front under Léon Blum. Robert Capa's partisan reportage of the Spanish Civil War was given extensive exposure; in fact, Vogel's sympathy for the Republican cause in Spain during 1935 and 1936 and

his impassioned coverage of the conflict caused his backers generally to withdraw. Vogel lost his magazine to a group of conservatives who bought it out in 1936, the year Kertész left France. By that time, his apolitical style was no longer in keeping with the whirlwind of events that were to engulf everyone in Western Europe.

V. Kertész's Artistic Photography in the 1930s

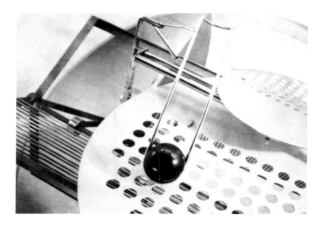

Photography has its own folklore, its primitives, academics and fauves. But its youthful vigor, its new faith, its means, rapid and sure, have permitted it to run through, in less than forty years, what painting has carefully paced for centuries. The hare has reached the finish line the same time as the tortoise.

—Carlo Rim, 1930

Figure 37
Kertész,
László Moholy-Nagy's "Light Modulator," 1930.

When Kertész moved out of the little studio in rue de Vanves and into the apartments at 75, boulevard Montparnasse, he was an accomplished photographer, a consummate photojournalist, an exhibited and published artist. In several ways the year 1930 marked a turning point. The tension and disquiet of the period and the special problems he faced as an artist and professional photographer provoked changes that formed a new dimension in his work. Although the totality of his oeuvre has a continuity unusual in photography, he now pursued simultaneously several quite different aesthetic ideas.

In 1930 Kertész was asked to contribute photographs to the "11e Salon de l'Araignée." This had been an annual show for illustrators. Thanks to the enthusiastic energy of Carlo Rim, the Araignée—only in this year—invited a wide range of artists and photographers, along with commercial artists and illustrators, to exhibit their work. The show was a fascinating jumble of sober art and irreverent artifacts, and was put together with a serious sense of play—the improvisational quality and lightheartedness that Kertész admired. Jules Pascin invited Calder to show his *Circus*, and Cassandre showed his enormously popular posters. But the photography section was especially diversified and exciting. Eight of Kertész's photographs were exhibited with works by Abbott, Atget, Krull, Parry, Sougez, and Tabard, alongside photographs from agencies, commercial photographs, and amateur snapshots. The show

was an extension of Rim's interest in the valid pleasures of everyday experiences, of widening the aesthetic parameters to include the old and the new, the more serious figures, and vernacular and folk expressions. As Carlo Rim said in the catalogue for the exhibition, photography now had its own history.[47] It had also become fashionable.

But the same year there was another show that used photography in quite a different way. The Grand Palais held a large exhibition of German design organized by the Deutscher Werkbund. This was another interdisciplinary exhibition, but different in kind from the Araignée. The French show stressed variety as well as amusement; the Germans were clearer and very sober. In the Werkbund show, the first widely seen exhibition in France of Bauhaus work, photography was integrated into design and displayed along with furniture, architectural plans, and teapots. It was clearly presented as part of a larger utopian scheme. Moholy came to Paris to help install it, and brought along his *Light Modulator*. He sought out Kertész and met him for the first time. Moholy asked Kertész to photograph his sculpture, and he obliged with a very precise, descriptive image (fig. 37). But Moholy seemed to Kertész to be a jack-of-all-trades, and his photography—admittedly only a part of his total work—too cold,

Figure 38
Kertész,
*Steps Near the Quai de
la Loire*, 1930.

Figure 39
Kertész,
Place Saint Sulpice,
1934.

too purely experimental. Kertész, as always committed to the realism of his medium, could not take Moholy's theoretical ideas seriously, just as he felt that Man Ray's experimental photography was something of a joke.

The Werkbund show was enormously popular in Paris. The two shows sharply defined the different attitudes to photography that Kertész now encountered: one, a fantastic approach, the other, formal. For Paris, the seriousness of the Werkbund show signaled a change in attitude toward the medium. Lines were gradually drawn: one could be a commercial photographer, a photojournalist, or an artist. The connecting links, which Kertész had always found stimulating, were now harder to maintain.

The inventive and improvisational qualities of the early years of photojournalism had led to increased specialization in this field as well, and Kertész's contributions reflected the change. Increasingly in the 1930s he received assignments to photograph landscapes and France's great artistic personalities. At the same time he also began to take more or less routine assignments, doing photographs of tropical fish, surgery, medical experiments, or the cosmetic implanting of eyelashes. These essays were made with taste and care, but they were not intrinsically interesting to

him. In some of his reportage there is a sense of professional distance that is new. In the last two years he spent in Paris, the number of photographs Kertész published in magazines declined dramatically, and most were, in fact, old images.

Kertész saw himself as an artistic photographer, and he concentrated his efforts on making himself known as such. Therefore, in the thirties he devoted most of his creative energy to exhibitions and publications, especially books exclusively of his work, carefully printed and presented. He supported these projects with photoreportage and the sale of earlier work. In both his professional activity and his creative photography, he reexamined old subjects, such as the steps of Montmartre (see fig. 38) and the nearby Daisy Bar (see cat. no. 91). But he also found new compositional subjects. By 1930 he had discovered two important formal ideas he would explore for the rest of his stay in Paris: one was a kind of collage composition, and the other, the Distortions. Both appeared in his reportage, as well as in his exhibitions and publications.

Kertész visited the Académie Française in 1929 with the intention of producing a marketable piece of reportage on that most private establishment. Just as he had been fascinated by the hidden lives of the Trappist monks at Soligny, so he

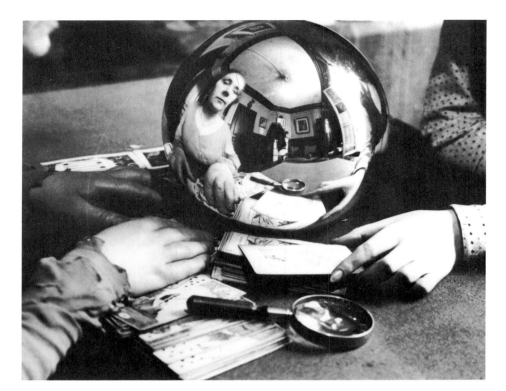

was intrigued to penetrate this equally remote and austere institution. He discovered many obscure parts of the building, and one was its old glass clock. When he climbed up to examine the clock tower, he viewed through the clock mechanism the bridge reaching over the Seine to the Louvre (see cat. no. 83). This layering of one space, flat and close, upon another, deeper view, was a new compositional idea for him. It appears also in several views he sold as illustrations for the book *La Route de Paris à la Méditerranée.*[48] He continued to explore this juxtaposition of a frontal element with a deep view into space in several important photographs (see cat. no. 101). He even severely cropped a view from above to produce such a composition (see cat. no. 110, fig. 39).

In 1929 he had begun seriously to investigate distortion. Although he had certainly been fascinated by shadows, mirrors, and reflections long before, his renewed interest was sparked by an assignment for *Vu.* His friend Carlo Rim, a caricaturist, editor, and organizer, was appointed chief editor at *Vu* in 1930. Vogel asked Kertész for a portrait to suggest Rim's evanescent personality. Kertész remembered the mirrors he had seen at Luna Park, Paris's Coney Island, and thought how appropriate it would be to depict Rim (always interested in popular subjects and in amusements and jokes) distorted in a circus mirror (see cat. nos.

88, 89). Both men enjoyed the project immensely. A few years earlier Kertész had experimented with distortions of a woman's face in a garden globe (see fig. 40). Now he sent the image to an important exhibition in Germany.[49] A distorted photograph of Edouard Loewy's bookstore was used by the owner and published at this time. In September 1930 Kertész was assigned a reportage on fortune-tellers in Paris, and this gave him the further opportunity to explore the strange, disfiguring, and mysterious shapes found in their crystal balls (see cat. no. 87, fig. 41).

Also in this year Kertész decided to revisit Hungary for the first time since he had arrived in Paris. He wanted to see his mother and older brother, Imre, and at this time he discovered that Elizabeth believed he had forgotten her. He persuaded her to come to Paris. In 1931 Elizabeth joined Kertész in his new quarters at 32 bis, rue du Cotentin, where they would live until 1936.[50]

When he and Elizabeth began their life together, Kertész must have carefully considered his position as a photographer of reputation, and taken some quite deliberate steps to advance himself. The relationship clarified his aims to concentrate on publications and continue with exhibitions. The photographs from 1931 that document Kertész with Elizabeth reflect his exuberance and his tenderness toward her. He made

Figure 42
Kertész,
Elizabeth and Gypsies,
1931.

Figure 43
Kertész,
At the Bistro, 1932.

a formal portrait of them both, and then sharply cut it down, monumentalizing her and stressing their bond (see cat. nos. 94, 95). He took another of her with him at a small bistro near rue du Cotentin. He photographed her with Gypsies, underscoring their Hungarian identity (fig. 42). He photographed a couple on the street—a man in a soldier's uniform accompanied by a young girl—because they reminded him of himself and Elizabeth when they had just met. He began to take views of the environs of rue du Cotentin, much as he had discovered his first neighborhood around rue de Vanves. Elizabeth accompanied him on his trips to the countryside and was really the only person he concentrated on during these years. Clearly, he did not feel the need to photograph his friends as he had earlier. Even when he did happen to record a friend, he made subtle allusions to Elizabeth and himself, as in the wine glasses left behind on a table (see fig. 43).

Paradoxically, at this time, other images begin to emerge, reflecting a sense of strangeness that runs parallel to surrealism. Kertész has always adamantly refused to admit any specifically Surrealist involvement or interest. It is true that he was never a member of André Breton's tight coterie of friends, but he did have certain connections with them: Kertész published work in magazines that had Surrealist affinities, such as *Bifur*, *Variétés*, and *Minotaure*; some his friends were involved in the movement; and his Distortion series relates formally to the second phase of Surrealist photography, the period of active manipulation of images.[51] In addition, Kertész shared some interests and common themes with the Surrealists: folk culture stimulated both the Surrealist poets and Kertész. He and Atget were published by the Surrealists not only for their styles but for their subjects—whether these were store mannequins, empty carousels, or marionettes and circus figures.[52] Kertész, like Atget, produced work that is at once real, tactile, primitive, and childlike. Both were seen as modern naive artists. Like Kertész, the Surrealists were also interested in such subjects as derelicts, night scenes, enigmatic objects, shadows, mists, reflections, and mirrors, all of which hint at the reality of dreams. The Surrealists had discovered the resonance of "found objects," common things or curious ones, such as a wine glass distended from a volcanic eruption. For them, something in this kind of juxtaposition revealed a higher, mysterious order of things. They treasured pictures of such curiosities. Kertész's

Figure 45
Kertész,
*Near Saint Lazare
Station*, 1933.

Figure 46
Kertész,
At the Bobino, 1932.

Figure 44
Kertész,
*Study of Plants and
Shadows*, c. 1936,
reproduced in *Minotaure*,
no. 9 (1936), p. 67.

haunting photographs of plants removed from their
original context and placed in modern, architectural settings appeared in *Minotaure* (see fig. 44).
Photography's concreteness and commonness attracted Breton. Many of the photographs printed in
his first magazine, *La Révolution Surréaliste*, were
documentary; some were anonymous, banal, and
intriguingly ambiguous. Instead of "found objects,"
they were "found photographs."

The conjunctions of objects that Kertész found
on the streets move, in the 1930s, from his earlier
irony toward a deeper mystery. Thus, where
before he photographed an old street bum examining the word "*sécurité*" on a poster, by 1928 a
sense of disquiet pervades *Meudon* (cat. no. 58).
The connection between the man on the street,
holding a carelessly wrapped package, and the
train speeding overhead, has no logical or compositional rationale. It is certainly not ironic. Rather,
it shares the strangeness and disjuncture found in
de Chirico's or Balthus's views of city streets. Such
conjunctions of people and things on the street continued throughout the decade (see fig. 45).
Another is the street scene where Cassandre's
poster figures, advertising Dubonnet, have more
rhythm and personality, despite their stylization,
than do the real people below (cat. no. 107). The

heavy atmosphere and a mysterious hollowness in
the streets are new.[53]

Kertész's continuing explorations of distorted
reflections, blurred and apparitionlike figures, and
vapors (see fig. 46) led naturally to the next major
phase of his career. His Distortions (cat. nos. 102–
09), a concentrated group of figure studies he made
in 1933, were done on commission from a slightly
off-color magazine, *Le Sourire*. The artist himself
has described the experience:

*They had used graphic arts in their magazine
but had never used photography and wanted me
to photograph women. Of course I told them I
liked the idea—I liked women too. I thought I
could do something nice using my ideas about
distorting the human figure.*

*[The editor] was excited and promised to pro-
vide everthing I would need—model, studio,
everything. The studio was arranged with two
large circus mirrors which were quite beautiful in
themselves. Originally there were two women for
contrast—the young and the old—then I settled
on one. She was a society girl in Paris, a White
Russian. The older model was a cabaret dancer.*

*I photographed the young woman over a period
of four weeks, usually twice a week. I would*

Catalogue no. 98
Infant on a Scale, and
*Two Mothers and
Infants Waiting for
the Doctor*, 1931, from
Art et Médecine,
May 1931, pp. 12–13.

*develop glass plates and make prints for myself.
When I showed them to the model, she told me
she was quite sure that it was not her in all of
the photographs. When I exhausted the possibilities of the mirror after making about 200
negatives, I stopped.*[54]

Kertész's natural discretion had prevented him
earlier from making photographs of nudes, but the
fun-house mirror from Luna Park quickly released
these compelling images. His life also changed
dramatically in 1933. He and Elizabeth were
married—a welcome and happy event—but his
mother died the same year. And at the same time
that he carefully composed these distended nudes
in a large-format camera, Hitler was threatening
not only Germany's tenuous democracy, but Kertész's comfortable livelihood. The editors intended
to publish the Distortions in Germany after they
appeared in *Le Sourire*, and he expected to make
good money. Suddenly he could no longer sell his
photographs to any of the lucrative German mass
magazines. Immigrants from Germany soon
crowded into France, adding further to an already
large foreign population. The competition for
magazine space, which had become increasingly
tight by the entrance of the younger generation
of photographers in France, now became fierce,
affecting even one so esteemed and established as
Kertész. Editors lowered pay, particularly for
foreigners. The transformation from ideal to
nightmare seen in the Distortions, like Picasso's
Guernica images, must reflect the intensely dis-
orienting circumstances of this period.

At the very moment that he was concentrating
on these grotesque, distended female nudes, he
published his first book, *Enfants* (1933). These
unaffected images—the true opposite of the
Distortions—show his enormous fascination
with the difference of children from adults and
his respect for their special world (see cat. nos.
98, 99). The author of the text, Jean Nohain, suggested that these photographs could have a cura-
tive value for the malaise of adulthood and too
much civilization. He also noted that they could
cure the affectation of "art" photography, now
almost a commonplace.[55] Kertész dedicated this
first book to his wife and mother.

The next year, 1934, Kertész completed two
more books, the Ady biography written by his
friend György Bölöni (see cat. nos. 67–70), and
Paris.[56] Again, both retreat from contemporary
events. They are also retrospective in character,
reminiscent of his early days in Paris. In his last

year in the city, Kertész assembled two final books, *Nos Amies les bêtes* and *Les Cathédrales du vin*, in which he continued his exploration of two seemingly disparate themes.[57] In the first he renewed contact with a primitive spirit, showing animals as somehow more direct and human than their human counterparts. These photographs were made on his travels to isolated regions of France: Savoie, Brittany, and Corsica. The other book is a very beautiful publication for a vat manufacturing company whose products Kertész transformed into masterful compositions. And yet, in almost every image, a strange, somehow displaced human figure seems to be in tenuous control of the firm's glassy and brilliant new architecture.

In his last years in Paris, Kertész also broadened the range of his magazine commissions. In 1933 he worked for French *Vogue* for the first time, and intermittently continued with fashion—in his own naturalistic manner—until he emigrated. During the last two years he also published views of interiors for *Art et Médecine* and the Paris Electric Company, and he photographed elegant country châteaux. He was to continue this type of enterprise after his move to New York.

Because photography was becoming increasingly interesting to the art audience but was economically infeasible to sell in galleries, books became photographers' vehicles for major aesthetic statements. There was a great abundance of photographic books, most of them carefully, luminously printed in gravure. With the increased interest in photographic art, there was a consequent rise in the number of publications on photography. In 1936 Gisèle Freund published her study of the social implications of photography. The same year, Georges Besson's modest history, *La Photographie française*, reproduced a Kertész Distortion; the popular but elegant book by Marcel Natkin, *L'Art de voir et la photographie*, discusses his other work. *Vert Galant on a Wintry Day* (cat. no. 79) was presented (complete with diagrams) for its lessons in mise-en-page.[58] The aesthetic experience in photography had shifted from appreciation of realism to something more considered, more studied. Natkin considered *Vert Galant* a perfect picture, carefully composed, although it includes an important element of animation in the scarcely visible figure.

The 1930s was an active period for photography exhibitions. Kertész showed his work regularly in Paris, and he was invited to participate in exhibitions throughout Europe and America. His work could be seen in the annual photography shows at new galleries that regularly displayed photographs, such as Galerie de la Pléiade, and extensively in Germany before the rise of Hitler. For the most part, Kertész included older photographs with work done recently on assignment. But his spirit of adventure became more practical and specialized in the exhibitions too; in England and the United States, his work was included in shows on advertising and photography.[59]

Increasingly, as photography was exhibited in an artistic context, reviewers stressed the thoughtfulness and sensitivity of certain photographs over their realism and instantaneousness.[60] Photographers were experimenting with solarization, double exposure, and other obvious manipulations. In 1934 Kertész participated in a group exhibition at Leleu's, an establishment run by a fashionable decorator who thought that the new photography might look well hung on the walls of modern interiors. Kertész showed only Distortions. It was as though he also sensed the increasing division of his medium—either it was used in reportage, where its instantaneousness was a useful indicator of authenticity, or it was treated experimentally and with deliberate expressiveness as a rival of the other arts. His Distortions were a specifically photographic way of manipulating the image as an artist would.

Around 1935 Kertész received a telephone call from Alexandre Garai of the Keystone agency. They had an office in New York run by one of his relatives, Erney Prince. Garai suggested that Kertész take a "sabbatical" and photograph in New York for about a year. At first Kertész resisted, then gradually it seemed to him a welcome opportunity to grow, to find new subjects, to stretch his ideas. He was also attracted by the possibility of making money. Tihanyi had gone briefly to the United States for the same reason, but returned unsuccessful. While Kertész was a known artistic figure in France, a successful photographer, he was not prosperous. America offered him this chance.

In 1936 the Musée des Arts Décoratifs in Paris staged a major retrospective of contemporary photography from many countries that included a large selection of work by rediscovered nineteenth-century masters as well as scientific and documentary images.[61] This was a major evaluation of photography in all its diversity. But like the critical examinations of Natkin and others, the show expressed a tiredness. It constituted a codification instead of a critical reawakening. While serious, complete, and determinedly aesthetic, the show lacked spontaneity and creative excitement. Kertész was again represented by older work. But he missed his old freedom, the exhilaration of new discoveries, the escape into new countryside. Hardening political lines and the pressures of *patrie*, which he despised, were increasingly distasteful to Kertész, who had no taste for ideology. Formalism had lost its intensity in the new seriousness of "art" photography. Garai and Erney Prince promised Kertész new possibilities in reportage in America: a return to realism, to his old habit of looking on from a distance. They also offered a welcome opportunity for material success where there had been only artistic rewards. And so in September 1936, Kertész and Elizabeth set sail for New York.

Notes

I am extremely grateful to André Kertész for his generosity in granting me a number of interviews between 1981 and 1984. Much of the information contained herein is derived from these conversations as well as from archival materials supplied to me by Mr. Kertész.

1. Julien Levy in a letter to Nora Christiansen, Feb. 2, 1932. Archives, Albright-Knox Art Gallery, Buffalo, New York.

2. For historical background on Hungary, see Paul Ignotus, *Hungary* (New York: Praeger Publications, 1972), and Andrew C. Janos, *The Politics of Backwardness in Hungary* (Princeton: Princeton University Press, 1982). For a personal view of Hungary, see Arthur Koestler's autobiographies, *Arrow in the Blue* and *The Invisible Writing* (New York: Macmillan Company, 1952, 1954). See also Robert Desnos, *Tihanyi, Peintures, 1908–1922* (Paris: Editions Ars, 1936).

3. Richard H. Davis, *A Year from a Reporter's Note-Book* (New York: Harper's, 1898), p. 71.

4. Kertész also made his first photographs of distorted figures in the swimming pool of the soldier's hospital in 1917. See his *Hungarian Memories* (Boston: New York Graphic Society and Little, Brown and Company, 1982), p. 5.

5. To cite only one example—and that in the United States in the 1930s—*Coronet* magazine published Kertész's work and that of a surprisingly large number of Hungarians still in Hungary who were working in the pictorialist tradition. Among them were Rudolf Balogh, Imre Révész-Biró, and Ernő Vadas.

6. The Hungarian title is "A hortobagy poétája." I am much indebted to Michael Simon and the poet Theodore Weiss for this translation.

7. See, for instance, Imre Tagai, "A Fotómüvészet a Lukácsi esztétika tükreben" (Photographic art in the mirror of the Lukacs aesthetic), *Fotómüvészet*, no. 4 (1980), pp. 41–42. In the 1930s Horthy's right-wing government became more tolerant, and a group of leftist photographers developed who were called "Szociofotó" (i.e., social realist photographers). One of the most interesting documents of this movement is the book *Tiborc*, with a text by Zsigmond Móricz and photographs of peasants by Kata Kálmán (Budapest, 1937). See also Imre Kinski, "Hungarian Photography—Its Purpose and Methods," trans. Frank R. Fraprie, *American Photography* 33 (Mar. 1939), pp. 232–35.

8. On Bartók's music and its relationship to the search for Hungarian culture, see Halsey Stevens, *The Life and Music of Béla Bartók* (New York: Oxford University Press, 1953). Franz Liszt considered the Gypsies to represent the essential Hungarian soul, and he therefore concentrated his attentions on their music. See Alan Wallar, *Franz Liszt: The Virtuoso Years, 1811–1847* (New York: Alfred A. Knopf, 1983). Bartók saw much of his own work as a corrective to Liszt's misperceptions.

9. On the importance of Hungarian newspapers, see Janos (note 2), p. 102.

10. Of the many books on this period, several are outstanding. See Samuel Putnam, *Paris Was Our Mistress: Memoirs of a Lost and Found Generation* (New York: Viking Press, 1947); Robert McAlmon and Kay Boyle, *Being Geniuses Together, 1920–1930* (San Francisco: North Point Press, 1984).

11. Ernest Hemingway, *The Sun Also Rises* (1926; rpt. New York: Charles Scribners Sons, 1954), p. 42.

12. Kertész has in his collection a Tihanyi drawing that is a study of chimney shapes.

13. E. E. Cummings, "Conflicting Aspects of Paris, Being an Eyewitness Report on the Two Cities in the French Metropolis," *Vanity Fair* 26 (1926), p. 82.

14. See Michel Seuphor, *Dictionary of Abstract Painting*, trans. L. Izod, J. Montagne, and F. Scarfe (New York: Tudor Publications, 1957), p. 51.

15. See Brassaï's quite similar ideas as expressed in *The Secret Paris of the 30's*, trans. Richard Miller (New York: Pantheon Books, 1976): "Rightly or wrongly, I felt at the time that this underground world represented Paris at its least cosmopolitan, at its most alive, its most authentic, that in these colorful faces of the underworld there had been preserved, from age to age, almost without alteration, the folklore of its most remote past" (n. pag.).

16. Kertész himself has described this photograph as a description of an older aristocratic "snob," "playing the gentry," approached by two "proletarians." There is a similar confrontation between two aristocratic (or simply wealthy) men riding horses in the Bois de Boulogne and two poor men out of work in his *J'aime Paris: Photographs Since the Twenties* (New York: Grossman, 1974), p. 214.

17. Fernand Léger, "L'Esthétique de la Machine—l'objet fabriqué, l'artisan et l'artiste," *Bulletin de L'Effort*

Moderne, nos. 1 and 2 (Jan., Feb., 1924); reprinted as "The Machine Aesthetic," trans. C. Green, in *Léger and Purist Paris* (London: The Tate Gallery, 1970–71), pp. 87–88. See also the exhibition catalogue from the Musée d'art moderne de la ville de Paris and the Museum of Fine Arts, Houston, *Léger and the Modern Spirit: An Avant-Garde Alternative to Non-Objective Art* (Houston, 1982).

18. Michel Seuphor, *Piet Mondrian: Life and Work* (New York: Harry N. Abrams, n.d.), pp. 86, 160.

19. See Denes Devenyi, "Kertész: Denes Devenyi Interviews the Father of 35mm Vision," *PhotoLife*, Jan. 1978, pp. 10–13, 30.

20. See Paul Dermée, "Découverte du Lyrisme," *L'Esprit nouveau*, no. 1 (1920), pp. 29–37. See also John Golding, "Guillaume Apollinaire and the Art of the Twentieth Century," *Baltimore Museum of Art News*, Summer/Fall, 1963, pp. 2–31. Dermée also published in 1924, with Ivan Goll, a single issue of a revue called *Surréalisme* (before Breton took possession of this word). I also refer the reader to a statement by Léger quoted in Maurice Reynal, *Modern French Painters*, trans. Ralph Roeder (New York: Brentano's, 1928), "Technic must become more and more exact, the execution must be perfect; the influence of the Primitives should be preserved. At all costs we must get beyond Impressionistic or Cubist-Impressionistic painting, beyond all forms of painting determined by intention. . . . Nowadays a work of art must bear comparison with any manufactured object. The artistic picture is false and out-of-date. Only the picture, which is an object, can sustain that comparison and challenge time" (p. 112).

21. "Art and Artist," *Chicago Tribune* (Paris), Mar. 13, 1927. According to Samuel Putnam (note 10), Elliott Paul and Eugene Jolas were both on the staff of the *Chicago Tribune* at this time.

22. See the review of the catalogue for Kertész's Sacre du Printemps show by Rolf Henkl, "Neue Fotografie, Austellungen/Kunstbücher/Theatreaufführungen," *Tageschronik der Kunst* 8, no. 4 (July 1927), pp. 26–30. Reproduced with this essay were the chairs in the Luxembourg gardens (cat. no. 17) and the portrait of Jean Slivinsky (fig. 23).

23. Pierre Bost reviewed the exhibition in "Spectacles et Promenades," *Revue hebdomadaire* 37, no. 24 (1928), pp. 356–59.

24. Pierre Mac Orlan, "La Photographie et la fantastique sociale," *Les Annales politiques et littéraires*, no. 2321 (Nov. 1, 1928), p. 413.

25. André Kertész, *Paris*, text by Pierre Mac Orlan (Paris: Librairie Plon, 1934), n. pag.

26. See Francis Carco, "Paname," *Art et Médecine*, Oct. 1931, pp. 42–45, and Pierre Mac Orlan, "Visages et paysages populaires de Paris," *Art et Médecine*, Oct. 1931, pp. 46–49.

27. Eugène Dabit, "Paris, par André Kertész," *La Nouvelle Revue française* 43 (March 1, 1935), pp. 474–75. Dabit's parents owned a hotel that became the model for the Hôtel du Nord. He died in Russia while on a trip with André Gide and other writers.

28. Jean Gallotti, "La Photographie est-elle un art?—Kertész," *L'Art vivant* 5 (Mar. 1, 1929), pp. 208–09, 211.

29. See *Der Querschnitt* 1 (1926), between pp. 192 and 193. Kertész was reproduced several times in this magazine, but not in a deliberately comparative manner. See, for example, vol. 8, no. 9 (Sept. 1928), between pp. 630 and 631, where the chairs in the Luxembourg Gardens (cat. no. 17; though it was unfortunately flopped) were included with three other photographs by different photographers under the heading "Neue Sachlichkeit."

30. See "Eine neue Künstler-Gilde: Der Fotograf erobert Neuland," *Uhu* 6, no. 1 (Oct. 1929), pp. 34–41. The article reproduced Kertész's *Fork* and a small portrait of him.

31. The articles on popular arts in *Variétés* are extremely numerous, but see especially the Nov. 15, 1929, issue, where Kertész's photographs on Bauchant are part of an entire issue more or less devoted to popular and naive arts.

32. Kertész had been invited to work with the filmmaker Rudolf Matthé, a cameraman who worked with Carl Dreyer on *Joan of Arc*. Kertész did not like the dependency on teamwork and the need for compromise in film, however, and he never worked with Matthé or anyone else in film.

33. See *Das Illustrierte Blatt*, no. 44 (1962), p. 984, and *Die Dame*, Oct. 1927, p. 2.

34. See Edmond Wellhoff, "Le Triomphe de la femme, Miss France vue à la loupe," *Vu*, no. 104 (Mar. 1930), p. 203.

35. See Paul Dollfus, "La Forêt Parisienne," *Vu*, no. 23 (Aug. 22, 1928), pp. 530–32.

36. See Jean Gallotti, "Au Souffle du verrier, l'industrie du verre," *Vu*, no. 36 (Nov. 21, 1928), pp. 788–90.

37. This information comes from interviews with Alexander Liberman, Stefan Lorant, Hug Block, and Isaac Kitrosser conducted in 1982. See also Philippe Soupault, "Les Vacances à Paris," *Vu*, no. 128 (Aug. 27, 1930), pp. 846–47, and Carlo Rim, "Les Petits Matins," *Vu*, no. 145 (Dec. 24, 1930), pp. 1424–25.

38. See, for example, *Die Dame* 57, no. 5 (Dec. 1929), pp. 12–13, for Kertész's photographs of children with puppets, or "Ein Deutsches Ballfest in Paris," *Die Dame* 57, no. 11 (Feb. 1930), p. 18, and the cover of Nov. 1930 issue entitled "Die Kabarettgangerin Alina da Silvia."

39. For the *Berliner Illustrirte Zeitung*, see "Was den Deutschen in Paris auffält," July 28, 1929, pp. 1363–64.

40. See Brassaï, "Die Technik in der Kirche," *Das Illustierte Blatt*, no. 12 (Mar. 27, 1930), p. 324.

41. See "40 Jahre Eiffelturm," *Münchner Illustrierte Presse* 1, no. 19 (May 12, 1929), p. 637; "Puppenspieler: Eine Revue der heutigen Meister der Marionette," *Münchner Illustrierte Presse* 1 (Jan. 5, 1930), pp. 5–6; and "Die Studentenstadt von Paris," *Münchner Illustrierte Presse* 1 (1930), pp. 198–99, 224.

42. I am indebted to Mrs. Maria Giovanna Eisner Lehfeldt for information on *Art et Médecine* and on French magazines of this period in general.

43. See the following pieces from *Art et Médecine*: Maurice Barrès, "Les Grands Horizons de Lorraine," no. 7 (Apr. 1931), pp. 14–21; Pierre Scize, "Simplicité de Lyon," Apr. 1932, pp. 11–23; Abel Bonnard, "L'Ame de l'Ile de France," July 1932, pp. 12–21; Charles Le Goffic, "Le Bretagne et les bretons," Feb. 1932, pp. 12–25; André Thérive, "Maurice Maeterlinck," Nov. 1932, pp. 10–11; F. Vallon, "Maeterlinck, Ronsard, Medan," Nov. 1932, pp. 12–19; Abel Bonnard, "La Corse," Dec. 1933, pp. 10–15; and René de la Romiguière, "Chez Maurice Maeterlinck," Nov. 1933, pp. 28–35.

44. Examples of Kertész's photographs of the Exposition Coloniale can be found in Jean Gallotti, "Les Merveilles de l'exposition coloniale," and idem, "Traité de géographie de l'exposition coloniale," *Vu*, no. 154 (Feb. 25, 1931), pp. 800–801, and no. 168 (June 3, 1931), pp. 775–84. For Ehrenburg's view of the exposition, see his *Memoirs: 1921–1941*, trans. Tatania Shebunina and Yvonne Karp (New York: World Publishing Co., 1964), pp. 181ff; for his photographs of same, see his volume *Moj Pariz* (My Paris) (Moscow, 1933). Ehrenburg and Kertész were neighbors.

45. Liberman has stated that he is principally interested in photographs for their documentary quality: "My first consciousness of modern journalistic photography was Salomon. He photographed all the great political figures as if they were unobserved, which for me was marvellous. He always succeeded in getting the impossible picture. That was what I was interested in. When you are involved in great political events you are not interested in the medium esthetically. You want a document." See my essay "The French Picture Magazine *Vu*," in the exhibition brochure *Picture Magazines Before "Life"* (Woodstock, New York: Catskill Center for Photography, 1982), p. 3.

46. See *Histoire générale de la presse française*, vol. 3, *De 1871 à 1948* (Paris: Presses universitaires de France, 1972), pp. 476–77, 479–80.

47. Carlo Rim, 11e *Salon de l'Araignée* (Paris: Galerie G. L. Manuel Frères, 1930). Kertész is listed as exhibiting about eight works. In his general introductory remarks, Rim also stated that "genius, which formerly was an article of luxury, has become a common commodity. The fine arts, casting off their old arrogance, have stepped down into the streets" (n. pag).

48. Paul Morand, *La Route de Paris a la Méditerranée* (Paris: Firmin-Didot, 1931). See especially "St. Pierre-sous-Vézelay," pl. 21.

49. The photograph was published in a review of the exhibition; see K. Wilhelm-Kästner, "Die Fotografie von Heute, zur Ausstellung 'Das Lichtbild' in Essen," *Die Wochenschau*, no. 20 (July 19, 1931), pp. 4–5.

50. For a brief period between 1928 and 1930 Kertész was married to the Hungarian Rosza Klein, who later became known as a photographer under the professional name Rogie (or Rogi) André.

51. Kertész knew Man Ray, although not very well, but one of his close friends was Brassaï, whose connections with Surrealism are well known. Rogie André photographed the Surrealists, specifically Breton and Eluard, and her photographs were used to illustrate Breton's "La Nuit de tournesol," in *Minotaure* 7 (1935), and were later included in *L'Amour fou* (Paris: Gallimard, 1937) in the company of works by Man Ray, Brassaï, Dora Maar, and Cartier-Bresson.

52. See John Fuller, "Atget and Man Ray in the Context of Surrealism," *Art Journal* 36, no. 2 (Winter 1976–77), pp. 130–38, and Maria Morris Hambourg, "Atget, Precursor of Modern Documentary Photography," unpublished manuscript, 1983.

53. See Paul Hill and Thomas Cooper, *Dialogue with Photography* (New York: Farrar, Straus and Giroux, 1979), p. 75, and Bela Ugrin, "Kertész's Photography in Full Bloom," *Houston Post*, Jan. 2, 1983, sec. G, pp. 12–13.

54. Quoted in the gallery flyer to the exhibition "André Kertész: Distortions," Pace MacGill Gallery, New York, Nov. 1983.

55. André Kertész, *Enfants*, text by Jaboune (Jean Nohain) (Paris: Librairie Plon, 1933), n. pag.

56. György Bölöni, *Az Igazi Ady* (The real Ady) (Paris: Editions Atelier, 1934), and André Kertész, *Paris*, text by Pierre Mac Orlan (Paris: Librairie Plon, 1934).

57. André Kertész, *Nos Amies les bêtes*, text by Jaboune (Jean Nohain) (Paris: Librairie Plon, 1936) and *Les Cathédrales du vin*, text by Pierre Hamp (Paris: Sainrept et Brice, 1937).

58. Marcel Natkin, *L'Art de voir et la photographie* (Paris: Editions Tiranty, 1935), p. 22; see also a photograph of shadows of people on the street, taken from Kertész's window, analyzed on pp. 34–35. Gisèle Freund, *La Photographie en France au XIX siècle, essai de sociologie et d'esthétique* (Paris: La Maison des Amis des Livre, 1936), reprinted as *Photography and Society* (Boston: David R. Godine, 1980). Georges Besson, *La Photographie française* (Paris: Les Editions Braun, 1936). Another contemporary essay on photography is Emmanuel Sougez, "La Photographie," *Le Point* 1, no. 6 (Dec. 1936), pp. 6–26.

59. For example, "An Exhibition of Foreign Photography," The Art Center, New York, 1931, and two exhibitions sponsored by the Royal Photographic Society of Great Britain, "The Modern Spirit in Photography," London, 1933, and "The Modern Spirit in Photography and Advertising," London, 1934.

60. The critic H. Alloend Bessand remarked on the care with which *Chez Mondrian* was made. See "La Photographie est-elle un art?" *Photocinegraphie*, May 1934, pp. 3–4. After discussing the aesthetic merits of *Chez Mondrian*, Alloend Bessand states, "By this brief analysis, I believe I have answered the reproach of automatism. In the hands of someone who knows how to use it, guided by the eye and spirit of an artist, the anastigmat need not be implacable in terms of detail" (p. 4).

61. "Exposition internationale de la photographie contemporaine," Musée des Arts Décoratifs, Pavilion de Marsan, 1936. Kertész was represented by *Vert Galant* and other works entitled *Savoie*, *Moutons*, and *Rue*. An exhibition of photography at The Museum of Modern Art, "Photography 1839–1937," organized by Beaumont Newhall (the text for the catalogue became the first version of his *History of Photography*) included the following Kertész images: two Distortions, *Vert Galant*, *Road Mender* (dated 1936), and *Fashion Plate* (dated 1937), which must have been made in New York.

Kertész and his Contemporaries in Germany and France

David Travis

When André Kertész arrived in Paris, photography was on the edge of a drastic change. Most photographers who had staked the claim of artist for themselves were still under the general influence of the medium's first international style, pictorialism. Although Kertész had seen pictorial photography in Budapest, he was not attracted to it. He began as an amateur who appreciated more the straightforward documentary photographs that appeared in illustrated newspapers like *Erdekes Ujság*, as well as those unexpected curiosities of camera vision that accompany a photographer at the beginning of his career.

In Paris he was momentarily isolated from the city by his language. He found Hungarian artists and writers who could speak of Budapest in his native language, and he was immediately accepted into their circle and seated at their table at the Café du Dôme. He began to learn French. He was soon meeting with leading artists of various nationalities who had made Paris their home or photographing them in their studios. His circle widened. Kertész was not, however, a man to join artistic movements or schools of thought, nor was he aspiring to be a writer, a painter, or a sculptor. He was an independent photographer who knew how to draw strength from solitude.

One may draw strength from solitude, but rarely does one change or effect a change in isolation. The world of photography during Kertész's years in Paris was pieced together by an evolving technology and the work of many talents, none of whom can be understood as separate entities. In order to bring Kertész's special genius into relief, it is essential for us to have a map of the changing topography of the photography of his time.

I. Technique

In the summer of 1925, a few months before Kertész's arrival, the VIe Congrès International de Photographie convened in Paris; in the following year, the reports and statements of their meetings were published by the Société Française de Photographie. This was photography at its most official. Those inventors and industrial research scientists who determined the technical character of photography were in attendance, not to promote the medium as an art, but rather to exchange useful information and announce discoveries. In the mid-nineteenth century, scientists and artists had shared equally in determining the technical characteristics of the medium, but as photography became an industry, fewer and fewer artists had the training to contribute to a field that had become a sophisticated technology. The published reports were devoted in large part to the fields of sensitometry, optics, and photochemistry, with articles by Josef Maria Eder, Louis-Philippe Clerc, and other specialists. In a section labeled "diverse applications," buried among articles on photography for palimpsests, photocartography, photo-

microradiography, and instructions on how to photograph the tails of comets, was an article by the French pictorial photographer and president of the Photo-Club de Paris, Commandant Constant Puyo, entitled "Report on Amateur Photography."[1]

Puyo's subject, amateur photography, which in the early days of photography had been limited to those who had the means to purchase expensive equipment and the leisure time to use it, had by the 1890s grown to such an extent that it was becoming the basis for a major industry. The quest for convenience through the introduction of the inexpensive hand-held camera, ready-to-use materials, and the service of photoprocessing mitigated the rigors of photographic practice, producing tens of thousands of customers/photographers who might otherwise have been discouraged by the necessity of learning photochemistry and optics. From that time on, one could become a photographer through curiosity rather than through a disciplined apprenticeship. Puyo had made a report on the same subject at the preceding congress in

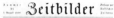

Figure 1
Zeitbilder, no. 31
(Aug. 3, 1930), cover
photograph by Felix H.
Man, *Toscanini Conducting at Bayreuth*.

1910 in Brussels. His current report stated that the fifteen years covered in his first report, 1895–1910, were unmatched in their encouragement of amateur photography because of the numerous innovations and improvements in optics, emulsion sensitivity, efficient shutters, and the new cameras that were more precise and lighter than their nineteenth-century ancestors.[2] In comparison, the period between 1910 and 1925 seemed to him to be very poor.

After 1910 a conservative outlook was characteristic of most amateur photography that had institutionalized itself in clubs and societies. The movement that had set out in the 1890s to establish photography as an art had by now lost its vitality with the resignation of most of its artistically adventurous members. In looking back on the movement of pictorial photography, one of its English founders, Dudley Johnson, wrote: "It was about this date that there began to appear some photographs that were regarded at the time as freaks, but in reality marked the embryonic germs of a new development."[3] The new development was not associated with a facility gained in a new printing technique, as Edward Steichen had once displayed in gum printing, nor simply with amateur conveniences. Rather, it was associated with personalities and ideas. In light of this, we can credit Puyo with a perceptive observation, even though it was meant to apply to pictorialists: "Today photographic equipment has arrived at a point such that progress for the amateur no longer depends on the equipment but rather on the practitioner himself."[4]

But it cannot be said that the improvement of equipment and its subsequent manufacture did not aid photographers in uncovering further clues to a more complete understanding of the character of their medium. It might even be argued that the introduction of any new convenience or improvement has the potential to alter the character of the medium. In the case of Kertész and several other photojournalists who followed, the most significant innovation of the period was the invention and trial introduction of the 35mm camera. Between 1914 and 1923 several small, hand-held cameras that used 35mm motion-picture film were produced for the amateur in Germany, France, and the United States. The format for the earliest models was of the same proportion of the aspect ratio of motion-picture cameras: 18 x 24mm, a size that proved to be too small for acceptable enlargements for professional photographers. Most

of the early 35mm cameras were more clever than serious: one camera could be used for motion-picture sequences or stills; another contained enough film for 750 exposures and was advertised as being ideal for round-the-world trips.[5]

As clever as the early 35mm cameras were, none of them caught the imagination of the public like the Leica. The Leica was the brainchild of Oskar Barnack (1879–1936), who in 1911 had come to work for Ernst Leitz in Wetzlar, Germany, as head of the research department from the Zeiss Company. By early 1914, Barnack had made two prototypes for Leitz of a camera that was designed basically to be used as a kind of light meter for cinematographers.[6] The shutter speed was compatible with that of the motion-picture camera and only the lens aperture could be changed. By developing the film from this instrument, the cinematographer could judge his exposures accurately. As an amateur photographer and enthusiastic hiker, Barnack realized early on many of the possibilities of a miniature camera of professional quality. The "Ur-Leica," as the prototype was later called, was destined to become more than a light meter.

Even in his early design, Barnack incorporated a lengthwise format (the largest format that the camera-film arrangement would allow: 24 x 36 mm), which framed a beautifully proportioned 2:3 rectangle.[7] Following World War I, which interrupted his research, Barnack's idea was rejuvenated, and between 1923 and 1924 thirty-one of the cameras were made to determine whether it would succeed in the market. Although the test responses were not enthusiastic, mostly because the motion-picture film was designed not for enlargements onto photographic paper, but rather for the projection of moving images that did not require fine grain or perfect sharpness, the company, now led by Ernst Leitz II, decided to take the risk. The camera was christened the Leica from the words LEItz CAmera, and in early 1925, the Leica I, with an f3.5 lens, a focal plane shutter with speeds between 1/5 and 1/500 of a second, and a "double" (24 x 36 mm) format, first appeared at a trade fair in Leipzig.[8]

A year earlier, another innovation in camera design, the Ermanox, had been placed on the market. Although the Ermanox was a glass-plate camera, this inconvenience was compensated by its extraordinary lens. The lens had a maximum opening of f2 (later an f1.8 was available), which permitted photographers to record certain spontaneous

Figure 2
Kertész,
*The Steps of
Montmartre*, 1926.

Figure 3
Henri Cartier-Bresson,
Hyeres, France, 1930.

indoor scenes without the aid of artificial light. This convenience led to what was called "candid photography," which became the basic working procedure of the great photojournalists of the next several decades. Such innovations, resulting from the motion-picture industry, appropriately sharpened the photographer's awareness of motion and the possibility of taking photographs in situations without flash powder. Even before the introduction of the Ermanox and the Leica, however, photographers had pushed the limits of their medium in order to depict dimly lit scenes or motion with available light only. Kertész's first successes in this regard were as an amateur in Budapest. The work of his German contemporaries Erich Salomon and Felix H. Man (see fig. 1) in the late 1920s is in the same spirit of obtaining seemingly impossible photographs from improved equipment but from relatively slow emulsions.

The camera commonly used by reporters in the late 1920s was one that used 9 x 12 cm glass plates, which had to be inserted for each exposure. Although Kertész used this popular camera, his preference was always for the smallest and lightest models. One of his favorite cameras, a Goertz Tenax with a Dagor f6.3 lens, a popular, collapsible-bellows pocket camera, used 4.5 x 6 cm glass plates. Because these plates, which were carried separately in metal sleeves, had to be loaded into the camera one at a time, Kertész disciplined himself to anticipate the action of a scene in order to capture it in a single exposure. One of the classic motifs he invented in this regard was to find a vantage point of a rigidly structured composition a few moments before the picture he wanted would be completed by a moving figure. This procedure of setting a "photographic trap" was adopted by several photographers, most notably Henri Cartier-Bresson (see figs. 2, 3).

After his Tenax camera was stolen from him in the Luxembourg Gardens during his second year in Paris, Kertész replaced it with a 6 x 9 cm French reporter's camera made in imitation of a better German model. But in 1928 Kertész found his ideal camera, the Leica. He felt as if it had been manufactured just for him: it was well made, light, responsive, and did not require separate loading for each exposure. In order to improve its versatility further, he had his friend Isaac Kitrosser, who owned the first camera store in Paris to sell Leicas, fit it with a Busch f2 lens that was used on motion-picture cameras. The first test with the new combination, to photograph

Josephine Baker in an evening performance on stage at the Moulin Rouge, failed. The fitting was readjusted until it worked satisfactorily for candid indoor photographs.[9] The film for the Leica had the advantage of being easily and cheaply obtained from cinematographers, but the disadvantage that it was not as sensitive to light as photographers required. Despite these few initial shortcomings, the Leica was unsurpassed for capturing the ephemeral dramatics of the street. Kertész's famous 1928 view of a man with a package crossing a street in Meudon simul- taneously with a locomotive crossing a bridge in the background was made possible because he did not have to reload the Leica after he had made a previous exposure without the train (cat. no. 58). The anticipatory sense that he had developed by using glass-plate cameras and the sequential nature of the Leica exposures, as well as its eye-level view finder, allowed him to capture the second picture with ease.[10] With the aid of the Leica, the lost pictures photographers saw in front of them after the shutter had closed were within their grasp.

II. The Illustrated Press

Although Puyo did not mention it as an innovation, the emergence of a new illustrated press in Germany had taken its first steps in the period before 1925. At the height of its success in the late 1920s and early 1930s, it affected publishers and photographers all over the world, especially in France, England, and the United States. As early as 1923, the *Berliner Illustrirte Zeitung* had published remarkable single photographs by the Hungarian photographer Martin Munkacsi, but it was not until 1928 that Salomon's astounding, candid, natural-light photographs of diplomats and political figures appeared for the first time. As this kind of photography was not, strictly speaking, a technique that could be applied to the procedures or added to the equipment of the amateur, Puyo would have been unusually prescient to have remarked upon it. Besides, as a leading pictorialist, Puyo would have found little of interest in what was a professional field for a new kind of photographer. What was just coming into being was the photojournalist who *did* have a personality, a point of view, and an appreciation of the special character of photography that distinguished this medium from all others.

One of the ascending personalities in photojournalism at the time was Munkacsi. Born in 1896 to a large family, Munkacsi in 1912 left his small village for Budapest, where sometime later he began writing for the newspaper *Az Est*. By 1921 he was contributing sports photographs as well. His career as a news photographer began almost overnight. When returning home one day, he photographed two men in a quarrel. One of the men was later killed, and Munkacsi's photograph was sensational evidence in a successful self-defense plea. In 1927, at the age of thirty-one, he left for Berlin, which more than Paris was the route by which Hungarian artists and photographers found their way out of Budapest, and accepted a three-year contract with the publisher Ullstein.[11] From then on, Munkacsi's name was known in Europe by his numerous credit lines under the incredible stop-action photographs that became his trademark (see fig. 4). Kertész, who by the time of Munkacsi's Ullstein work had already begun his career in Paris, did not share the same enthusiasm for the unnatural situations that resulted from the climax-moment photographs, even though he too was fascinated with arresting motion. The amateur background from which Kertész developed his skills as a photographer did allow for climax-moment photographs as a technical tour de force or as a humorous touch, but such photographs for Kertész, although stimulating, were amusing exceptions. His consistent and abiding interest was a kind of snapshot naturalism. On the other hand, Munkacsi's background as a sports photographer allowed him to function outside of the constraints of naturalistic representation.

In his history of modern photojournalism, Tim N. Gidal, a photographer of the 1930s, has given a good description of this period: "The Leica and the Ermanox were both born reporter cameras. All that was missing were born photoreporters. Almost without exception, these first appeared on the scene in 1928 and 1929. . . . The editors-in-chief of the magazines recognized his [i.e., the photoreporter's] importance for photojournalism and they quickly welcomed him with open arms, incorporating him into the format of the modern illustrated magazine."[12] Kertész received a special mention in Gidal's history.

The year 1929 began with a photojournalistic sensation. In the first issue of the Berliner Illustri-

Figure 4
Martin Munkacsi,
Spanish Dancers, 1932.

Figure 5
*Berliner Illustrirte
Zeitung*,
no. 1 (June 1, 1929),
pp. 35–37, photographs
by Kertész.

rte, *three pages were devoted to "The House of
Silence," a series of pictures on the Mother-
house of the Trappist order, Notre-Dame de la
Grande Trappe, in Soligny. It was unusual to
devote three pages to a single theme, but in this
case it was thoroughly justified. The unposed
photographs by the Paris photographer André
Kertész showed scenes, never before made public,
of the daily lives of the Trappists in their secluded
monastery of silence. . . . The reportage did more
than present a visual image of the subject. It
transported the viewer into the atmosphere of the
monastery, conveying vividly not only the environment, but also the monks' feelings and way
of life.*[13]

This landmark assignment (see fig. 5) was not
originally given to Kertész by the *Berliner Illustrirte Zeitung* but by Lucien Vogel, publisher of the
Paris weekly illustrated magazine *Vu*. At the time,
the extension of an article illustrated with photographs over three pages was new for the *Berliner
Illustrirte Zeitung* but not for *Vu*, which had initiated such a layout a year before. The outstanding
feature of Kertész's assignment was not the length
of the article, but rather the special quality of the
photographs and the way in which they could
communicate not just as single images but as a set.
The photographs had found their way to Berlin
through a German correspondent or editorial
assistant Kertész knew at the Dôme. Kertész's

understanding had been that they would be reproduced as single photographs, which more or less
had been the habit of the *Berliner Illustrirte Zeitung*. The *Vu* story, "Sous la règle de St. Benoît,"
using most of the same photographs, was not
printed until the next year.[14]

The idea of the picture story evolved at this time
through the work of photographers such as Kertész
and sympathetic editors such as Vogel or Stefan
Lorant, a Hungarian who had moved from Budapest to Vienna and who became first a still photographer for a motion-picture company and then a
cinematographer. Lorant gave up working as a
cameraman in Berlin when he began to write.
In 1928 he was promoted to Berlin editor of the
Münchner Illustrierte Presse and later editor-in-
chief for a short period. He exemplified the new
editorial direction of visual story-telling by empha-
sizing the "essay" character of photoreportage and
by permitting his photographers to make editorial
comments and decisions as they photographed.

In Paris, after 1928, it was *Vu* and not the older,
conservative *L'Illustration* that set a new pace in
photoreportage. Vogel and the writer Carlo Rim,
who became his editor-in-chief in 1930, instinctively knew it was the photographer as a personality who was able to create a story of human
interest or a stunning image of beauty from a
medium that was often criticized for its mechanical
indifference. Other editors applied these developments to their own publications or refined their

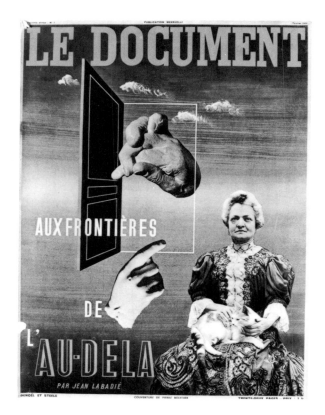

Figure 8
Voilà 2, no. 61
(May 21, 1932), pp. 8–9,
photographs by Kertész,
Germaine Krull, and
others.

Figure 7
Vu, no. 371
(Apr. 24, 1935),
cover design by
Alexander Liberman,
employing photograph
by Kertész.

Figure 10
Regards, no. 175
(May 20, 1937), pp. 6–7,
photographs by
Henri Cartier-Bresson.

Figure 9
Le Document 2, no. 7
(Feb. 1936),
cover design by
Pierre Boucher.

Figure 6
Kertész,
Eiffel Tower, 1926.

techniques to fit their own purposes and tastes. *Voilà*, for instance, founded in 1931 and published by Florent Fels, integrated photographs and sequences by Kertész, Germaine Krull, and Kitrosser with the anonymous news photographs from international agencies like Keystone, Associated Press, Universal, or Wide World into a collagelike layout of popular appeal. This format, however, placed less emphasis on the personality of the photographer than on the style of the art director, whose rise in the 1930s eventually began to overshadow the work of independent photographers like Kertész. Kertész's photographs were used in photomontages by Alexander Liberman (under the credit "Alexandre") for *Vu* (see figs. 6, 7) or pieced together with the work of other photographers or agencies into two-page spread designs in *Voilà* (see fig. 8). In this form they were not things in themselves, but rather were useful parts of a whole that did not belong to the photographer. The photographic essay had given way to a fascination for layout design that more properly belonged to the medium of the printed page than to the eye of the photographer. Even photographers became designers, as in the case of Pierre Boucher, who made montage covers for the magazine *Le Document* (founded in 1934) (see fig. 9). The Communist magazine *Regards* (founded in 1934) gave the work of the politically sensitive photographers like Robert Capa, Chim (David Seymour), or Henri Cartier-Bresson (Henri Cartier) prominent place and credit, but without the clever visual flair and imagination of *Vu* or *Voilà* (see fig. 10).

III. The New Vision

In his 1925 article, Puyo cautioned against a technical invasion of the territory of natural vision by the "implacable vision" of the photographic lens. He noted how some lens designs deviated more and more from the vision of the eye. His objection was not to progress in optical technology but to the threat of the subordination of human perception to the camera's lens: "Our images are not made to be measured, but rather to be contemplated by our eyes. It is the eye that, in the end, decides their quality."[15] Kertész, who was not a pictorialist but who nonetheless insisted on a naturalistic camera image, would have agreed.

An opposing view was expressed in the same year by the Hungarian artist László Moholy-Nagy (1895–1946), who found new advantages for the artist in the optical character of the medium of photography. In *Malerei Fotographie Film* he stated: "I seek to comprehend the problems of present-day optical form. . . . In the expanded consideration of the visual image, modern lenses are not bound to the narrow limits of our eyes. . . . The photographic camera can improve and complement our optical instrument, the eye."[16] In 1925 Moholy appears to have been enthusiastically flushed with demonstrating the development of his own general aesthetic theories with the camera.[17] But this was not his first encounter with photography. In 1922 he and his wife, Lucia Moholy, had discovered the technique of cameraless photography called the photogram, which Moholy proceeded to employ as another mechanical method of constructing abstract geometric painting or drawing.[18] A year later he began to make photocollages that used already existing photographs cut out of their normal photographic context and combined with his own drawing. Lucia began to study photography in order that their collaborative efforts along these lines could proceed with greater facility. Despite the later reputation of the Bauhaus for fostering the teaching and practice of innovative photography, it was not until 1926, after the school was established in new quarters in Dessau, that there was an acceptable darkroom arrangement in which Moholy and Lucia could work. Perhaps it was Moholy's theoretical mind and this lack of facilities that caused them to work more with ideas of photography than with its equipment.

Moholy's enthusiasm for knowing the full character of the photographic medium firsthand received an important impetus in 1925 in Paris

Figure 11
László Moholy-Nagy,
Belle-Ile-en-Mer, 1925.

when Theo van Doesburg, the Dutch abstract painter whom he had known from his first days in Berlin, induced him, the painter Sigfried Giedion, and their wives to spend part of the summer in Brittany on Belle-Ile-en-Mer. Up to this time, Moholy had taken very few "camera" photographs. The unusual angles of the resulting photographs, with their pronounced diagonal lines, coincided with van Doesburg's ideas of the use of diagonal lines in the dynamics of abstract composition (see fig. 11). The unconventional vantage point of these photographs and the ones that followed in the next decade hint at the fact that Moholy had discovered a tool that, as the title of his book suggests, was somewhere between painting and film.

The mobility of Moholy's photographic vision has been likened to the sensations produced by the avant-garde Russian filmmakers.[19] The viewer is assaulted by a world in flux that flashes new relationships through the effects of images previously unrelated (i.e., montage) and previously unobserved (special vantage point). The importance of the special vantage point that mobility provided and the consequent relationship of objects in front of the camera received a strong emphasis in Moholy's photographs, as well as in those by the Russian photographer Alexander Rodchenko. The undiluted strength of this approach to photography can be caught in the words of the Russian filmmaker Dziga Vertov:

> *I am eye, I am a mechanical eye.*
> *I, a machine, am showing you a world, the likes of which only I can see.*
> *I free myself from today and forever from human immobility, I am in constant movement, I approach and draw away from objects, I crawl under them, I move alongside the mouth of a running horse, I cut into a crowd at full speed, I run in front of running soldiers, I turn my back, I rise with an airplane, I fall and soar together with falling and rising bodies.*
> *This is I, apparatus, maneuvering in the chaos of movements, recording one movement after another in the most complex combinations. . . . My road is toward the creation of a fresh perception of the world. Thus I decipher in a new way the world unknown to you.*[20]

One of the characteristics or laws of the photographic medium that Moholy began to help to clarify is photography's relation to coincidence. In his collages, as in the collages of the Dadaists, images taken at different times could be combined

into one picture, a kind of constructed coincidence of events and objects. In this period, camera photographs that showed a conscious attempt to organize an artistic concept of coincidence in a single exposure were extremely rare. This fact alone begs the question, what makes a photographer great? Would those, like Christian Schad, Kurt Schwitters, John Heartfield, Hannah Höch, etc., who worked in photocollage and photomontage have made great photographers or would they have been frustrated with the limitations of mastering its complicated techniques? The collage or montage that combined single still photographs into a whole was similar to the "montage" of cinematographers, whose medium could not exist as a single picture, but had to be experienced through time. However, Moholy's camera photographs, as well as those of the Dadaist Raoul Hausmann, were based not on simultaneity, the coincidence of events, but rather on juxtaposition, the coincidence of objects, and its resulting design. Conceptually, the approach employed in his camera photographs was closer to his painting, which emphasized the relationship of shapes, than to his photomontage, which tried to present a notion of simultaneity.

Even in 1925, before Moholy's camera photography had matured from its initial experimental stages, the differences and similarities with Kertész's work can be accurately compared. Both were fascinated with the ability of the camera to move with the observer. The photographer could be part of the flux of change and observe it from his special vantage point. One of Kertész's first photographs of Paris (cat. no. 6), for example, was taken out of the window of a gallery where his friend Gyula Zilzer was exhibiting work.[21] A lonely policeman, almost a symbol for the solitary Kertész in a new environment, is engulfed in a stream of traffic. The photograph appears as if it were printed from a single, well-chosen moment of newsreel footage. It was rare—although isolated examples exist— that Moholy photographed situations of flux as in this Kertész view. Instead, he gave the viewer the sense that *he* as a photographer was mobile. His sense of the mobility of position was more acute than Kertész's, as he was not looking at the subject but rather for those laws or characteristics of the medium that may be forced out into the open through what appeared at the time to be optical exaggerations.

Moholy's photographs of the Eiffel Tower are similar to those taken by an amateur during its

Figure 12
Anonymous photograph
of the Eiffel Tower,
1888.

Figure 13
László Moholy-Nagy,
Eiffel Tower, 1925.

Figure 14
Germaine Krull,
Eiffel Tower, 1928.

construction or those taken by Germaine Krull; they are all photographs caught up in the design of the ironwork or with the idea of moving inside a structure.[22] Without the aid of a title or caption the viewer could not know that the subject was the Eiffel Tower (see figs. 12–14). Kertész's first views, taken from Paris rooftops, show the Eiffel Tower too, not as an iron web of engineering surrounding the photographer, but rather as a tower magically hovering above the city it symbolizes (cat. no. 1). The associations that the Eiffel Tower, Notre Dame, or the streets of Paris might have for the viewer were antithetical to Moholy's purpose in seeking an illustration of photography as the modulator of light or as a method of optically composing lines and shapes. Kertész, on the other hand, dealt with such associations at the same time as he experimented with the graphic organization of the image in its relationship to the light that makes it visible. Moholy wanted to know the medium; Kertész wanted to know the subject as well.

It was perhaps Kertész's lack of a theoretical discipline and identity that allowed him to function as a photographer on several levels at once. His atmospheric and picturesque approach to Paris, which is evident in his first photographs of the city, was not abandoned when his attention was drawn to the clean, exacting rigidities of Dutch abstract art that he knew through his introduction to Mondrian and his circle. Rather it was invigorated and continued as a separate theme of his photog-

raphy. Nor did his immediate assimilation of the work of the abstractionists preclude the fundamental search for the character of photography through his tentative, but pioneering, development of an expression of simultaneous events. In addition, he was also able to maintain a position as one of the leading photojournalists.

The difference between Kertész and Moholy might be clarified a bit further if the latter is viewed as an artist with a scientist's methodology: one who searches systematically toward a goal of definition. Moholy was a teacher of great talent, as well as an artist who was able to produce works of art that could also serve as pedagogical examples of his ideas. It would be handy if Kertész could be sketched as his opposite, but such is not quite the case. He was not a teacher, nor did he author any credos or manifestos about art or photography. Even though they differed radically, if not quite diametrically, about the value of the subject, they did share the trait that what is done in photography must be done in the vocabulary of the medium and in the spirit of the time. Kertész's work reveals this feature as an instinct, rather than as a commitment to a revolutionary theory, as is evident in Moholy's photographs. In this regard, Kertész is the poet who dwells in the creations of the associating imagination, and Moholy the grammarian who clarifies one situation and complicates the next with his illuminating definitions.

IV. German Photography

One might wonder why Kertész did not leave Budapest for Germany as Moholy and Brassaï had done before him or as Munkacsi would do a few years afterwards, or why as a photographer he did not end up at the Bauhaus. To understand this, one must keep in mind the fact that in 1925, when he moved to Paris, he was thirty-one years of age and had been a photographer, if not by profession, by serious desire, almost since his first photograph in 1912. Kertész felt he had had his beginning and training from thirteen years of amateur photography. Some of Kertész's deeply seated attitudes would have been out of place at the Bauhaus, where most of the students were looking for an unconventional beginning. He had a respect for tradition and heritage and did not seek to deny in his photographs the culture-bound associations that subject matter might bring up from the viewer's memory or feelings. With that background and with his interest in photojournalism, Kertész was temperamentally unsuited to the Bauhaus either as a student or as a teacher. Perhaps the most compelling reason Kertész did not go first to Berlin was he had always had a very difficult time learning the compulsory German taught in Hungarian schools. In addition, Paris had been Endre Ady's refuge of the generation

past, and, although several had come by way of Berlin, there were already modern Hungarian artists settled in Montparnasse.

Moholy's theoretical and revolutionary temperament fit better with the developments in abstract art that had originated in Russia and Holland. He and many of the photographers who were connected with the Bauhaus as students or teachers, such as Walter Peterhans, Herbert Bayer, T. Lux Feininger, Wols, or the American Florence Henri, can be characterized by a tendency to analyze, to find through experiment the laws they felt to be special to photography. Their photographs from these experiments were characteristically organized with an appreciation for the abstract composition. Not every one who studied at the Bauhaus, however, can be placed exactly into this broad, convenient category.

Umbo (Otto Umbehr, 1902–1980), for example, whose work Kertész later came to admire, studied at the Bauhaus before Moholy's arrival. Umbo's interests at the time were not photography but acting, pottery, and woodcarving. In 1923 he moved to Berlin, where he was a house painter, a clown, and a production assistant to the filmmaker Kurt Bernhardt, and later, a camera assistant to Walter Ruttmann. Through Ruttmann, Umbo

Figure 16
Karl Blossfeldt,
Larkspur, plate 45
from *Urformen der
Kunst* (1929).

Figure 17
Kertész,
Rose, c. 1930.

Figure 18
Albert Renger-Patzsch,
*Sempervivum
percarneum*, plate 5
from *Die Welt ist Schön*
(1928).

met Simon Guttmann, who founded the first collective of photojournalists, "Dephot." Felix H. Man (then Hans Baumann) served as the director of press photography, and it was through this agency that Robert Capa (then André Friedmann) and Andreas Feininger began their professional careers. Umbo and Kertész both had a facility for introducing wit into their photographs; Umbo's was theatrical and Kertész's resided on the naturalistic side of the surreal (see cat. no. 8, fig. 15). This sense of wit separated them from the other photojournalists, as well as from those, like Moholy, who had refined photography's new appeal through a search for its fundamental aesthetic. Yet, despite exceptional figures like Umbo, the tendency towards analysis—that is, the reduction of the medium or the subject to a piece-by-piece inspection—was a strong characteristic of German photography, which can be seen especially in the work of several major German photographers whose careers were established either long before or independent of the founding of the Bauhaus.

Karl Blossfeldt (1865–1932), who by 1925 had been photographing for over a quarter of a century, was unknown to photographers, having spent most of his photographic career as a university professor. He had gone to Berlin in 1884 from a small town in the Harz mountains to study sculpture, and he had the good fortune to be chosen to accompany one of his professors to Italy, Greece, and North Africa to collect samples of plant and natural forms. The drawings, plaster casts, and pressed samples were to be used in a source book

for demonstrating the relation of natural shapes to those used by artists and architects. Before going to Berlin as a student, Blossfeldt had had an interest in photography, and during his Mediterranean travels he took some photographs, which were later published by the professor for whom he had worked.[23] By 1901 he was making excursions from Berlin to photograph plants for his own teaching and lecturing. Once his procedure for making detailed, close-up studies was established, it remained unchanged for the rest of his career. Until 1926, when some of his photographs were published in the popular magazine *Uhu*, his work was known only to a very small circle of professors and students in Berlin. His first book, *Urformen der Kunst*, was not published until 1928, when he was sixty-three years old, and was a popular success. His analysis of plant forms, which had begun at the turn of the century, finally found an audience.[24]

Although Kertész's photography was never as systematic as Blossfeldt's, he and many other photographers produced photographs that underscored the same fascination between the graphic appearance of nature and design (see figs. 16–18). Because Blossfeldt's photographs had remained unknown for so long, the sudden interest in the parallels of the form of nature and artistic design in the 1920s cannot be credited to his work. It is the other way around: because of this general interest by artists and editors, such work by photographers like Blossfeldt was uncovered and publicized. Other photographers of the older generation, who had remained

unknown for most of their careers or whose work was unfamiliar to those interested in modern art, would also be discovered at this time.

August Sander (1876–1964) was also a systematic photographer, but less scientific in his approach than Blossfeldt. He learned his craft in a traditional way, by being a journeyman and an assistant. His first successes at the turn of the century were in "artistic" portrait photography. For these portraits Sander slaved over the retouching and manipulation of the print. The *edeldruck*, or finely crafted print, won him awards at various photographic competitions and exhibitions, giving him the inner satisfaction that he had finally achieved the status of artist-photographer in the pictorial tradition of his successful contemporaries Rudolf Dührkoop, Nicola Perscheid, and Hugo Erfurth. During hard times after World War I, Sander began to travel into the countryside around Cologne with his equipment, and he established a business making portraits of the peasants, a subject he had begun as early as 1913. His portrait studies were later extended to include laborers, tradesmen, businessmen, officials, soldiers, students, professionals, and aristocrats—almost a complete sociological spectrum of the Weimar Republic. Sander's collection of portraits, which he

called "People of the 20th Century," was known to a group of progressive painters in Cologne, who were enthusiastic about his work.[25] But it was Alfred Döblin, the author of the great novel of Berlin society, *Berlin Alexanderplatz*, who first pointed out the analytic character of Sander's work in his 1928 introduction to the photographer's one and only book, *Anlitz der Zeit*.

You have in front of you a kind of cultural history, better, a sociology of the last 30 years. How to write sociology without writing, but presenting photographs instead. . . . Only through the study of comparative anatomy can we come to an understanding of nature and the history of the internal organs. In the same way this photographer has practiced comparative photography and therefore found a scientific point of view beyond the conventional photographer.[26]

The German photography that was objective, systematic, and analytic came from photographers who used the medium as a *tool* of study in science, aesthetics, or sociology. Kertész might, with some profit, be compared to any one of these photographers, even to those like Henri who adopted German attitudes, but only if the comparison is

Figure 21
Friedrich Seidenstücker,
Puddle Jumping, 1925.

though the illustrated photographic annuals that became popular in the 1930s (see fig. 21). Like Kertész, he was not a photojournalist who stood shoulder to shoulder in the press lines at major political and publicity events. His interest was not in news but in the conditions of everyday life.

During his career in Paris, Kertész did not know Seidenstücker's work, as it was not well published in France. Later he would only have been able to see it occasionally in photographic annuals. He did, however, know the work of one German photographer well. Some time shortly after its 1928 publication, Kertész received a copy of *Die Welt ist Schön*.[27] He was immediately attracted to it, as it displayed a sympathy for an attitude he shared towards the discovery of the beautiful in the natural or man-made, although his photographs were different. The book was the work of a thirty-one-year-old photographer named Albert Renger-Patzsch (1897–1966). As a boy, he had become interested in photography through his father, who was an amateur. By the age of fourteen he was already well acquainted with multiple gum printing.[28] After World War I he studied chemistry, but by 1925 he had set himself up as a photographer. He had taken close-up photographs of flowers for a series called "The World of Plants," which was published at that time. His first book, *Das Chorgestuhl von Cappenberg*, published in 1925, was one of several he would do on the subject of churches.[29] It was *Die Welt ist Schön*, however, that drew attention to his work.

Renger-Patzsch originally wanted to call the book *Die Dinge* (i.e., objects or things), but the publisher, with some inspired marketing wisdom, changed the title. The photographer's title emphasized the matter of factness of the approach and his fascination with the physical world. The publisher's title emphasized a basic attitude toward the things photographed in the simple and direct terms that a large public could understand. The cover illustration—a structure for power lines drawn to be the same height as a plant, under which are inscribed the photographer's initials—introduced the idea of the equality that objects can achieve from the photographer's point of view (see fig. 22). The book was laid out to show the compatibility of nature's design and pattern to that of everyday objects, architecture, and industrial products. First there were flowers and leaves, then animals, faces, manufactured objects, architecture, machines, and industrial scenes, then a mixture of some of the previous subjects among two photo-

made one photograph at a time, for he sought to find a tessitura that was uniquely his in the new and expanding range of the photographic voice of his day (see figs. 19, 20). His method was not objective, systematic, or analytic, but he learned from those whose methods were. He was able to retain his own personality in his photographs, rather than substituting for it one suggested by the medium.

The two photographers in Germany with whom we might best compare Kertész's attitude, rather than certain of his individual photographs, were photographers of his own generation who had also begun as amateurs just before World War I. During his college years as an engineering student in Berlin, Friedrich Seidenstücker (1882–1966) was constantly to be found in the sculpture studios of a nearby art school drawing and modeling animals. He took advantage of his early interest in photography to make photographs in the zoo. After the war he enrolled in art school and pursued his study of animals and human figures in motion. As his sculpture was not a commercial success, he turned more and more to photography as a source of income. In 1930 he gave up sculpture and signed a contract with Ullstein. His name as a photographer became known through his picture credits in the illustrated press, through a book on animals, and graphs of the vaulting of a church and a crucified Christ, and finally a picture of praying hands; the arrangement suggested that there is a divine order to the design found both in nature and in that which man has created.

Renger-Patzsch's photographs fit well into a movement in German painting that had been called Die Neue Sachlichkeit (the new objectivity), after a 1925 exhibition organized by G. F. Hartlaub, director of the Mannheim Kunsthalle ("Malerei der Neuen Sachlichkeit"). They also would have found a welcoming reception among American photographers already working along the same lines, such as Alfred Stieglitz, Paul Strand, Charles Sheeler, or Edward Weston and the group of California photographers who later (1932) would call themselves the *f64* group because of their preference for sharp photographs. The new realism, especially in Germany, emphasized the "implacable vision" of the photographic medium and established what was nominally a new sense of objectivity; in German, French, and English, the term "objective" appropriately carries the second meaning of the lens of a camera or optical instrument.

The new photography represented by Renger-Patzsch was not embraced by everyone. The critic Walter Benjamin found little to admire by 1931 in the approach: "The 'creative' principle in photography is its surrender to fashion. Its motto: the world is beautiful. In it is unmasked photography, which raises every tin can into the realm of Art but can not grasp any of the human connections that it enters into, and which, even in its most dreamy subject, is more a function of its merchandisability than of its discovery."[30] By the term "merchandisability," Benjamin may have meant not only that the new photography was easily recognized and accepted, but also that one of the chief applications of its style was in advertising illustration.

The photographs by Renger-Patzsch were reproduced in the three major books that promoted a "new photography": Moholy's 1927 edition of *Malerei Fotographie Film*, Franz Roh's *Foto-Auge* of 1929, and Werner Gräff's *Es kommt der neue Fotograf!* also of 1929, all of which showed the work of a variety of photographers, who ranged between the experimental approach of Moholy and the optical purity of Renger-Patzsch, or asked the viewer to consider a new assessment of the medium from photographs made for industrial, medical, scientific, or journalistic illustrations.[31]

Although Kertész's photographs were not known to the authors of these books at the time of their publication, and therefore were not included, they came into contact with the work of these "new" German photographers in 1929. His work was included in two touring exhibitions of contemporary photography: "Fotographie der Gegenwart" (photography of the present) at the Museum Folkwang in Essen and "Der International Ausstellung von Film und Foto" (the international exhibition of film and photography) in Stuttgart. Through these touring exhibitions Kertész's photographs were seen in galleries in Berlin, Hanover, Dresden, Magdeburg, Vienna, Agram, and Zurich, just at the time he was gaining a wider recognition in the illustrated press in Germany and France. The most influential of the two was "Film und Foto," which had been organized by Gustav Stotz for the Deutscher Werkbund, an organization whose "primary interest was in bridging the gap between inventor, producer, and consumer."[32]

The "Film und Foto" exhibition began with a large room laid out by Moholy that compared two aspects of photography: the documentary comprehension of the world and the study of motion in one group and the conscious composition of light and shadow in another. Although Moholy did not hang Kertész's work in this introductory room, he did include photographs by Ergy Landau, a Hungarian photographer whom he had known in Budapest, but who, like Kertész, was now living in Paris. Other photographers from Paris in "Film und Foto" were Eugène Atget (who had died in 1927), Florence Henri, the fashion photographer George Hoyningen-Huené, the photojournalist Germaine Krull, Eli Lotar, and Man Ray. Most of the remaining photographers were German or Russian, but a few were British or Czech. Photographs by Berenice Abbott, Charles Sheeler, Edward Steichen, Paul Outerbridge, Imogen Cunningham, Brett Weston, and Edward Weston represented the United States. The catalogue included two short essays about American and Russian photography and three about film.

The basic aim of the exhibition was to introduce the conception of photography that had been developing in the work of the "new photographers." The organizers did not attempt to describe the full spectrum of photography as had some of the previous German photographic trade exhibitions, nor to survey the world for all the types of work being created. The exhibition did have its limits and its prejudices. Although Krull's street scenes were hung, the work of Seidenstücker, Sander, Salomon, Man, and Munkacsi was not, either because it was not known to the organizers or because it was considered to be professional photojournalism or social documentary photography. Industrial photographs, which had always had a separate section in exhibitions organized in connection with trade fairs, were also not included.

The fact that Moholy did not instigate the exhibition, but was invited to participate by an organization founded in 1907, and the fact that the exhibition included the work of photographers from other countries in good number illustrate that the "new photography" was not another stylistic "ism" that looked to one or two artists as leaders or spokesmen. Much of the work was compatible with the attitude that had been developing as a general reaction against pictorial photography in Germany, Russia, Paris, New York, or California.

The "Film und Foto" exhibition was not the first time Kertész's photographs had been exhibited outside of Paris. For example, his work had been seen in the Third International Salon of Photography in Zaragosa in 1927. A large 1928 exhibition in Prague and a similar exhibition in the same year in Rotterdam included his photographs, along with the work of amateurs and pictorialists. The most important exhibition of his work outside of Paris in this early period was held in Brussels at the gallery L'Epoque in the fall of 1928. There he was in the company only of French, Dutch, and German photographers who might be considered practitioners of the "new photography." The catalogue carried an important statement about photography by the French writer Pierre Mac Orlan, which is discussed below.

V. The Unknown French Photographers: Atget and Lartigue

Curiously, Eugène Atget was the only photographer born of a French family in the selection representing France made by the organizers of "Film und Foto." The final selection was made by Gustav Stotz through consultation with Christian Zervos, a writer who had become acquainted in Paris with Atget's work through Abbott and had written about his work, as well as that of Kertész, in the Brussels exhibition.[33] Because Atget was dead, the selection was tantamount to saying that the only photographers in Paris who expressed any modern sensibilities in their medium were not French. Perhaps it was easy for a German eye to discard the professional photographic illustrations of Laure Albin-Guillot and Emmanuel Sougez, as well as the surrealistic statements of Jacques-André Boiffard, the first photographs of Roger Parry, and those made by Maurice Tabard on his return from the United States. Or perhaps they were just unknown. To be fair to the organizers, it should be stated that the primary aim of the selection was to show the "new photography" as it existed in different locations and not to define any national characteristics of French, German, or American photography. Understandably, it was not easy to separate nonpictorial French photography from the photography done by foreign photographers in France, for not only did photography itself have to prove its artistic worth and to gain public visibility, but the work of two of the great geniuses of French photography, Jacques-Henri Lartigue and Eugène Atget, was unknown to art critics and historians and virtually unknown even to photographers.

Jacques-Henri Lartigue was Kertész's exact contemporary, having been born in Courbevoie, near Paris, in 1894. Unlike Kertész, however, Lartigue was born to a wealthy family who pampered him because he was the younger of two boys and of delicate health. His father, the founder of the newspaper *Le Soir* and later a banker, had many passions that centered on his family. In addition to taking long vacations with them, he made detailed dollhouses, involved the family in the craze for automobiles as early as 1900, and took up photography. Fortunately for Lartigue, his father was an excellent amateur photographer. In 1901, at the age of seven, Lartigue himself began taking photographs. He learned quickly and was soon taking hundreds of photographs each year, the best of which he kept in a scrapbook. The scrapbooks, which begin with his father's photographs of the family before Lartigue was born, form a history of a photographer's progress in learning the technical and artistic aspects of the medium unencumbered by the prejudices and restrictions of styles or the latest theories.[34] Consequently, one can find individual photographs in his albums of the kind that would have been labeled "new photography" almost twenty years later in Germany. For example, there is a 1908 view looking straight down from his playroom (fig. 23) that prefigures Moholy's work of 1925 and any number of stop-action scenes that equal

Figure 23
Jacques-Henri Lartigue,
*Making Bouquets for the
Flower Festival*, 1908.

largest and most sensitive study of its subject ever accomplished by a single photographer. It was, like many beginnings, Kertész's work in Paris included, a way to earn a living.

Fortunately, Atget had a long career. In 1920 he sold 2,600 of his glass-plate negatives to the Service Photographique des Monuments Historiques. By then he had acquired what he felt was a substantial collection of cultural and historic value, and he offered the collection to the government with confidence in its importance:

For more than twenty years I have been working alone and of my own initiative in all the old streets of Old Paris to make a collection of 18 x 24 cm photographic negatives: artistic documents of beautiful urban architecture from the 16th to the 19th centuries. . . . Today this enormous artistic and documentary collection is finished; I can say that I possess all of Old Paris. Getting on in years, that is to say approaching seventy, and having neither heir nor successor to follow me, I am uneasy and tormented about the future of this beautiful collection of negatives which might fall into hands unaware of its value and ultimately disappear—to no one's benefit.[35]

It was a handsome business transaction for Atget, but one prompted by the unselfish motive of wanting to preserve something of the past. His aims appear to be nearly opposite those of Moholy, who felt that the past stifled the modern artist. They were aims that through sacrifice and concentration could be accomplished by one person, like Sander's portraits, Walter Hege's humanizing illustrations for a series of books on German churches, or Josef Sudek's sensitive views of Prague and the Czech countryside. Perhaps an equally sensitive collection on Hungarian culture in photographs might also have become the aim of Kertész, had he stayed on native soil for his whole life and not been attracted, like Lartigue, to the immediate present that played before his eyes.

Like Blossfeldt and Sander, Atget holds that unusual position of having established a documentary style of photography that he maintained over a long period without radical shifts of style or attitude, and that towards the very end of his life was discovered by his fellow photographers. All three worked in near isolation keeping a ritual flame of pure photography burning through the beautiful entanglements of painting and photography during the pictorial period. All three avoided

Munkacsi's. But in their time they were passing, private snapshots pasted in a scrapbook.

Lartigue's photographs were not known to anyone outside of his family circle and therefore exerted no influence on the course of photography in his own time. The pictures reveal the possibilities of the equipment and techniques, stretched by the photographer's ingenuity and the demands of his subjects, such as racing cars, early aviation, sporting events, and spontaneous street scenes. Their special quality communicates a sense of the innocent observer and displays a great facility in the execution of the snapshot, which are two of the ingredients of Kertész's early work in Budapest and Paris and of all amateur photography.

The second genius of photography in France at this time was not an amateur, but a professional with the private, monumental goal of recording the greatness of the urban and architectural artifacts of French culture. Jean-Eugène-Auguste Atget (1857–1927) was born in a small town near Bordeaux to a working-class family. He lost his father at the age of five and his mother soon after. He was raised by his maternal grandparents and after school went off to sea. By the age of twenty-one he had moved to Paris. Until the mid- to late 1880s, he was in the army and attempted to make a career of acting. He began to photograph soon after, and he eventually developed a business in which he supplied artists with photographs. Like Sander, Atget probably did not envision at the beginning that he would become a collector of photographic views, nor that his work would become the

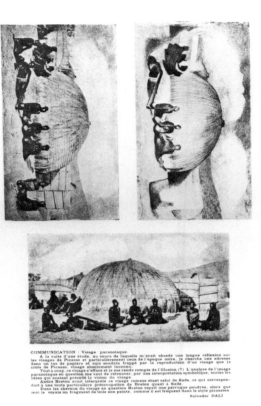

bending to the changing winds of aesthetic fashion. This is explained easily in the case of Blossfeldt by the fact that photography of plants was achieved through systematic methods and an appreciation for scientific observation. Sander, too, built his career through an accumulation of images of a

single subject. In Atget's case, it is not so straightforward. One might simply posit that he was not a social or aesthetic revolutionary and when at the age of thirty-five he first hung out his sign "Documents pour Artistes," his initial aspirations were as conservative as they were modest.

VI. The Surrealists

In 1925 Atget's work was discovered by the Surrealists through the American photographer Man Ray, who lived at number 31, rue Campagne-Première just down the street from Atget at number 17. To understand the interest the Surrealists found in the work of a conservative documentary photographer or why a movement conceived by a poet became fascinated with the photograph at all, one must understand the connection its founder, André Breton, made between the poetic imagination and the visual object. Sometime in 1919, just before going to sleep, Breton encountered

a curious sort of sentence which came to me bearing—in sober truth—not a trace of any relation whatever to any incidents I may at that time have been involved in; an insistent sentence . . . it

ran approximately like this: "A man is cut in half by the window." What made it plainer was the fact that it was accompanied by a feeble visual representation of a man in the process of walking, but cloven, at half his height, by a window perpendicular to the axis of his body. . . . I understood that I was dealing with an image of great rarity. Instantly the idea came to me to use it as material for poetic construction.[36]

The bizarre image of a man cut in half by a window could symbolize a photographer as easily as a Surrealist poet: a man who though grounded in reality views a transformed world and merges partly with it. Surrealism for Breton was a perceptual attitude primarily for poets, allowing a reader (or a viewer) to begin with the image of

Figure 26
Vu, no. 10
(May 23, 1928),
cover photograph by
Man Ray,
Vincente Escudero.

Figure 27
Vu, no. 56
(Apr. 10, 1929),
cover photograph by
Maurice Tabard,
Little Esther.

physical reality, supplied automatically (in our case the camera's view), and then to transfer it into one psychically rich in associations and symbolism. For the Surrealists, the more firmly the beginning of this process was attached to a reality ripe with existing conventional associations, the more contrast was achieved. The greater the contrast, the more marvelous and consequently more surreal the result could be (see figs. 24, 25).

Breton, however, did not, as it might appear, give Surrealism to visual artists. In his statements about reality, he reclaimed it for the poet: "Let us not forget that in this epoch it is reality itself that is in question. . . . The very narrow concept of *imitation* which art has been given as its aim is at the bottom of the serious misunderstanding that we see continuing right up to the present . . . so that our eyes, our precious eyes, have to reflect that which, while not existing, is yet as intense as that which does exist. . . ."[37] Although the nonexistent cannot be photographed, it can be indicated by the auxiliary meanings of photographs that do exist by isolating them from their original context, a technique first realized in Dada photocollages, photomontages, and photograms.

The photographer who fit perfectly with the ideas of Surrealism came to Paris, like Kertész, at the age of thirty-one. He was an American

who had known the work of Cézanne, Brancusi, Picasso, and Rodin in New York from visits to Alfred Stieglitz's gallery "291." His first actual contacts with European avant-garde artists were in New York with Marcel Duchamp and Francis Picabia. Man Ray (1890–1976) was born in Philadelphia and moved to New York at the age of seven. He studied architectural drawing and engineering, but decided to devote himself to painting. He met Duchamp in 1915 and, six years later, in his company, he found himself on his first day in Paris at a table in a Montmartre café being introduced not to painters but to writers then of the Dada movement: Breton, Louis Aragon, Paul Eluard, and Philippe Soupault. Man Ray could hardly speak French and so could not participate in their discussion, but the introduction was made, and they accepted him, although he was a foreigner, into their circle. It was a little later that he learned of the Montparnasse section of Paris, which was much more international than the city he had discovered so far. Even though the Dadaists considered it too bohemian and too arty, Man Ray found it comforting to hear English, German, Hungarian, and the French of his own level being spoken. He moved in and made acquaintances through the cafés on the boulevard Montparnasse, as Kertész was to do a few years later.

There was no way to support himself through painting, so Man Ray turned, as he had for a short period in New York, to photography. At first he took portraits, especially of the artists and writers he knew. A short time later, through an introduction to Paul Poiret by Madame Picabia, he embarked on a career as a fashion photographer. His photographic talent and inventiveness overcame his lack of training and equipment. In fact, it led him in 1922 to discover by accident or good fortune first the photogram and later the technique of solarization. His less radical work appeared on covers of *Vu* (see fig. 26) or occasionally as illustrations in other magazines. At the time of Kertész's arrival in 1925, he was the only avant-garde photographer residing in Paris.

Beyond his own photography, Man Ray is important to the photography of the period in that his studio served as an encouragement, as well as a modest financial first step, to the careers of several others. The first was Berenice Abbott (b. 1898), who went to Europe in 1921, first to Paris and then to Berlin to study sculpture. From 1923 to 1925 she served as Man Ray's assistant and learned portrait photography, which she practiced until she returned to New York in 1929. Her first exhibition was held in 1926 at the gallery Au Sacre du Printemps, the same gallery in which Kertész would have his first exhibition one year later. Jacques-André Boiffard (1902–1947), a medical student who wrote for the first issue of *La Revolution Surréaliste* in 1924, illustrated Breton's *Nadja* in 1928, and, after leaving Man Ray's studio in 1929, worked with the photographer Eli Lotar for a few years. In 1935 Boiffard returned to his medical studies and later became a radiologist. Bill Brandt (1904–1983), who arrived in Paris in 1929 and returned in 1932 to England, where his real fame as a photographer began, was another to benefit from Man Ray's instruction and encouragement.

The last of Man Ray's assistants/students was also his favorite. Lee Miller (1908–1977) had been a model for Steichen and Arnold Genthe in New York before she settled in Paris in 1929.

She modeled not only for Man Ray, but for Hoyningen-Huené and Horst in fashion photographs and appeared in Cocteau's film *Blood of a Poet*. During her work with Man Ray, she discovered the technique of solarization when she accidentally turned the darkroom lights on during the development of a negative. Man Ray instantly recognized the positive side of the mistake and perfected it into a serviceable and stylish photographic technique.

Although not connected with Man Ray's studio or with official members of the Surrealists, several other photographers in Paris worked in a manner that shows their influence. The first, Maurice Tabard (1897–1984), was a Frenchman who had spent his boyhood in France but moved to the United States at the age of seventeen and later became a professional portrait photographer. In 1928 he returned to France and settled in Paris. He was immediately drawn to Man Ray's photography. His own work expanded in range to include handsome advertising photography of automobiles and other products; experiments in photomontage, double exposure, and solarization; and street scenes and reportage assignments (see fig. 27). He established the first advertising studios for the type foundry Deberney-Peignot and helped to revolutionize the appearance of advertising photography in France. In 1932 he discovered solarization on his own and a year later wrote an article about the subject for *Arts et métiers graphiques*. The second, Roger Parry (1905–1977), was also a Frenchman. He had studied at the Ecole des Beaux-Arts in Paris and was working as a draftsman in 1928 when he met Tabard and became interested in photography. Tabard took him on as an assistant for a brief period. In 1930 his photographs, some of which were made with the aid of Tabard, served as the illustrations for a book of poems by Léon-Paul Fargue entitled *Banalités*. He, like Tabard, worked for several of the illustrated magazines of Paris, participated in exhibitions of photography in the 1930s, and was represented in several photographic annuals.

VII. The Photographers of Paris

Not everyone in Paris who made a name in photography or dabbled in its practice came to it through an interest in art or an affinity with Surrealism. Photography in the 1920s was not a subject taught in art schools, which might lure students with nothing better to do, nor a medium held in high respect, which might entice those seeking fame and prestige. Many attracted to the medium were fascinated with its curious ability to manipulate and record reality. Poets and jour-

Figure 28
Germaine Krull
Pont Neuf, c. 1928.

Figure 29
Michel Seuphor,
Pont Neuf, c. 1928.

Figure 30
Bill Brandt,
*Clochards along the
Seine*, c. 1931/32.

nalists such as Harry Crosby, Ilya Ehrenburg, and
Brassaï, and German students and scholars (after
1933) such as Ilse Bing and Gisèle Freund became
photographers temporarily or began longer careers.
By the time Kertész left Paris in 1936, the city
was full of accomplished photographers competing
for jobs with illustrated magazines or working for
the fashion pages, when only ten years earlier
there had been but a handful.

Of all the photographers who took Paris as their
special subject, the one whose work and career
formed almost a mirror image of Kertész's was a
woman who arrived in the city from Amsterdam
in 1924. She was sponsored by Robert and Sonia
Delaunay and, with a wealthy friend of theirs, set
up a studio for fashion photography in the stylish
neighborhood of the Madeleine, only to abandon
it a short time afterwards to pursue a different
kind of photography. Germaine Krull was born in
1897 in Wilna, Poland, to a French father and a
German mother. She was raised in Paris, but left
for Munich in 1909 with her mother after her parents were divorced.[38] She studied at the Bavarian
Academy of Photography from 1916 to 1918. In
Munich she set up a studio, but in 1920 she moved
to Berlin and opened another. Between 1921 and
1924, she was a freelance photographer in Holland,
where she first became fascinated with photographing structural ironwork.

Figure 31
Ilse Bing,
Paris, by the Seine,
1931.

Krull's start in Paris was different from Kertész's. She spoke French and German, she had known the city as a child, she had contacts through the Delaunays with the artistic pulse of the city, and she had been professionally educated as a photographer. In the 1925/26 annual photographic salon, she entered a series of photographs of ironwork she had taken in Amsterdam's harbor with her Agfa Ikarette 6 x 6 cm camera, but they were not accepted. Delaunay consoled her by saying that he would exhibit them with his paintings at the Salon d'Automne of 1926. Krull took a small apartment in Montmartre and began to explore the streets of her neighborhood, as well as the quais of the Seine, with some of the same instincts that Kertész had when he first arrived in Montparnasse.

With the Delaunays, Krull attended a soirée hosted by a Rumanian couple for young journalists, artists, and musicians. There she met a young Rumanian, Eli Lotar (1905–1969), who had been born in Paris (of Rumanian parents), but raised in Bucharest, and who had just returned. They soon became a photographic team; at first, Lotar did much of the darkroom work and Krull the photography. In a short time, Lotar became a photographer in his own right and a partner to Krull.[39] After they separated in 1929, he worked with Boiffard, for the cinematographer Jean Painlevé, and with Joris Ivens, whom Krull had married in 1927. During the early years of Krull's partnership with Lotar, there was more time than work, and their days were filled with long walks in the streets of Paris, which often ended with an evening at Les Deux Magots, a small cafe across from the church of St. Germain des Prés. Kertész or Man Ray might be there, if they were not in Montparnasse at the Dôme. They met young cinematographers such as René Clair or Luis Buñuel, and painters such as Foujita, André Lhote, or occasionally Picasso.

One morning a young film director, Jean Dreville, seated himself at their table and told them of a new publishing venture. In a short time, they were introduced to Lucien Vogel at the *Vogue* offices across the Seine. Vogel was planning a new illustrated magazine to be called *Vu*, inspired by the German illustrated press. Years later, Krull remembered the meeting: "Vogel was a very dynamic and gifted man, who still had the refined lifestyle of the 'old French.' He was much older, but was fond of young people and open to everything new. He had seen my photographs of ironwork."[40] He wanted something exactly like it for *Vu* and assigned Krull to take photographs of the Eiffel Tower.[41]

Krull could not depict the famous landmark as a symbol of Paris—for her, as it had been for Moholy, it became instead a powerful machine— but nevertheless Paris opened up to her. Or, perhaps, Vogel opened Paris up to her, as she became the "accompanying eye" to Vogel's journalists. Her first assignment with Henri Danjou was to report on the colorful *clochards* who lived along the Seine between Notre Dame and the Pont Neuf and called themselves "seignors" or "philosophers." With another writer she photographed the produce markets of Les Halles, a subject that, like the *clochards*, the Seine and its bridges, or the rooftop view of Paris, had been treated by Kertész as well (see cat. no. 48, fig. 28). But these were and would remain attractive subjects for others too, such as Bill Brandt and Ilse Bing, or the Belgian artist and poet Michel Seuphor, whose view of the Pont Neuf must have been taken on the exact spot where Krull had been standing, or vice versa (see figs. 29–31). One should remember, however, that the types of assignments Krull and Kertész received, as well as the treatment of the subject and the layout, were determined in part by the editors and writers. In addition, smaller cameras encouraged a kind of peripatetic exploration of the city and its life, which Kertész had begun in Budapest.

Fig. 32
Germaine Krull,
100 x Paris (1929),
pp. 70–71.

Figure 33
Moï Ver,
Paris (1931), n. pag.

Krull recollected that Kertész in this period was "famous for his predilection for detail. His great photograph of the fork laying on the edge of a plate made him famous. He did not go 'out on the street,' that is, he found interest in the still, picturesque aspects of the city. A half-open window, a gas light over a poster advertisement, a child's toy on a bench: he belonged, nevertheless, to those who were acquainted with the new way of seeing."[42] This recollection is an accurate assessment of Kertész's singular ability to organize either scenes or interiors into compositions that have the craftmanship of a great still life, but it diminishes his personal sense of street life. Kertész's memory of Krull is that her interests in ironwork were not like his, but much of the rest of her photography borrowed from subjects that he felt he had been the first to photograph. The point, however, in comparing two similar photographers is not to determine who photographed a certain subject first, but rather to study the kind of artistic personality that emerged from the result.[43]

Man Ray, Abbott, Kertész, and Krull had all been working in Paris with little public exposure as photographers other than what appeared in magazines. As Krull had found out early on, their work was not acceptable to the established photographic salon. Both Abbott in 1926 and Kertész in 1927 had had small one-person exhibitions at the gallery Au Sacre du Printemps. Louis Jouvet, a friend of Krull's who had permitted her free reign in photographing dress rehearsals in his theater, Comédie des Champs Elysées, offered its use for an exhibition. The exhibition was officially called the "First Independent Salon of Photography," but was nicknamed the "Salon de l'Escalier" because of its novel location flanking the two flights of stairs where audiences gathered during intermissions. The organizing committee was composed of Lucien Vogel, René Clair, Florent Fels, Jean Prévost, and Georges Charensol, none of whom were photographers. The exhibitors were all working in Paris, although only a few were French: Abbott (who showed portraits), d'Ora (a fashionable photographer of society portraits), Laure Albin-Guillot (who had had success in various salons), George Hoyningen-Huené, Kertész, Krull (whose name appears as Krull-Ivens), Man Ray (who showed some "Rayograms"), Nadar (studio of Nadar, with work of father and son), and Paul Outerbridge (then working in Paris for *Vogue*). In addition, a small retrospective of the work of Atget, who had died a year earlier, was presented for the first time.

Besides the photographs that appeared in magazines like *Vu* and occasional exhibitions, the public saw the work of several of the leading photographers through books, many of which were about Paris. One of the differences between the careers of Krull and Kertész in this period from the late 1920s to the mid-1930s was that Krull had a good number of books of her work published, more than any other photographer in Paris. In 1927, perhaps because of the inclusion of her ironwork photographs in the Salon d'Automne, her first book, *Métal*, appeared. It gave her recognition in certain circles; she was welcomed by the publisher Eugène Merle as the "Walkure of Iron" at one of his soirées. Because the book was successful, new, and relatively daring, it gave her an instant identity and caught the notice of others. In 1929 Krull's *100 x Paris*, with a text in German, French, and English by Florent Fels, was published by Justh in Berlin (see fig. 32). The following year, her *Etudes de Nu* was published by A. Cavalas, and her landscape photographs accompanied a text by Gerard de Nerval in a book published by Firmin-Didot, *Le Valois*. In 1931 Gallimard published the monograph *Photographes Nouveaux—Germaine Krull*, in a series of tiny paperbound books that had already featured Man Ray. Firmin-Didot included her photographs in *La Route de Paris à la Mediterranée* with text by Paul Morand. That book also contained photographs by Kertész and others.[44] A similar book, *La Route Paris—Biarritz*, with Krull photographs only, was published by Jacques Hammont in the same year. In 1935, *Marseilles* was issued by Plon. In the same period, only three Kertész books were published, one of which appeared after he had left for America.[45]

Krull's volumes were among the many books about Paris that were illustrated by photographs and usually reproduced in rotogravure. In 1928, a year before *100 x Paris*, a book entitled *Paris* (in the Gesicht der Städte series edited by Justh) by the photographer Mario Bucovich was published in Germany.[46] Twenty-three of its 256 plates were by Krull. The foreword, in German, was by Morand. In 1930 the first book of Atget's photographs, *Atget, Photographe de Paris*, appeared. Prefaced with an essay by Mac Orlan, it reproduced one plate to a spread in collotype. In 1931 a strange and truly innovative volume entitled *Paris* was published by Editions Jeanne Walter. It consisted of an introduction by Fernand Léger, followed by montages and multiple exposures of Paris street scenes by a photograper known only as Moï Ver (see fig. 33).[47] In the same year, Ilya Ehren-

burg's *Moj Pariz* appeared in Russian with a dust-jacket designed by El Lissitsky and photographs by the author. Another introduction by Morand began *Paris de nuit*, Brassaï's beautiful classic, which was published by Charles Peignot in February 1933. Kertész's second book, *Paris*, did not appear until 1934. It is important to note that the order of the appearance of these books does not accurately reflect the order in which the photographers made their photographs; Kertész's book, for instance, was filled primarily with photographs taken before either Krull's or Brassaï's.

Krull's *100 x Paris*, like Bucovich's book, was basically a tourist's program, although dotted with innovative photographs of striking beauty. Both publications gave an overall sketch of the famous buildings and urban vistas from predictable vantage points, which occasionally transcended standard interpretations. They allowed one to carry away a miniature view of all the sights. The visual relationship of the single images on opposing pages was, for the most part, not considered in the layout in the Bucovich book and was too slight in the Krull book to announce itself. Kertész's book, on the other hand, was personal in almost every aspect.[48] The design of each spread was thematic: there were no photographs of the Louvre or the Panthéon, nothing of the grand boulevards, the monuments to French history, or the Opéra. It was not Paris in evening dress, but the city of the Seine with its *clochards*, its fishermen, its reflections against barges and mooring chains, or the atmosphere of rainy streets, the warm glow of a bistro at night, or the shadows of the chairs in the Tuileries or the Luxembourg Gardens. It was a book by a photographer who *was* "out on the streets" capturing private moments that might have occurred in between visits to the monuments listed in the guide books, as well as a few that a tourist could never have experienced at all. Pierre Mac Orlan's preface prepared the viewer for the work of a photographer who could "reveal the secret and public dramas that give a certain movement to the masses of stone, cement, and iron" and whose images of Paris are "easily completed by the silhouette of the Genius who naturally, but temporarily, inhabits them and gives them a human value."[49]

If the "Genius" of Paris was in Kertész's *Paris*, the *daemon* was in Brassaï's *Paris de nuit*. Both books were insiders' views meant for connoisseurs and tourists alike, but Brassaï's was strictly nocturnal, giving the reader a feeling of being led by his guide through dark streets and alleys spotted

L'homme de la police surveille la maison. Dans le ciel livide la pluie achève son offensive d'automne. La rue appartient au hasard d'un jour de roman.

LE QUAI D'ORLÉANS APRÈS LA PLUIE.

LE PONT-NEUF APRÈS LA PLUIE.

Ce vestige du passé de la ville, au tournant du pont, n'existe plus. Il a été enlevé par un collectionneur américain.

Figure 34
Brassaï,
Paris de nuit
(1933), pp. 17–18.

Figure 35
Kertész,
Paris (1934), n. pag.

here and there with enough light to reveal a florist shop window, a railyard, a pissoir, a carnival, a show at the Folies Bergères, black limosines, or just the details of wet paving bricks (see fig. 34).

Brassaï had moved to Paris in 1924 from Berlin, where he had gone from Budapest to study painting and sculpture.[50] He was born Gyula Halász, but later named himself after the village in which he was born, Brassov, in what is now Rumania. His native language was Hungarian, but he spoke German as well. When he first came to Paris, he spoke little French. In Paris he became a journalist in order to support himself. His clients were German and Hungarian newspapers, and it was only natural that once or twice he and Kertész worked together as a team before Brassaï himself became a photographer. When he did, around 1930, it was Kertész who taught him. Brassaï had always loved a secret underworld Paris that the camera had never seen, and he was intrigued to find through Kertész that photography at night was possible. From his first years in Paris, he lived by night, "going to bed at sunrise, getting up at sunset, wandering about the city from Montparnasse to Montmartre" in the company of Léon-Paul Fargue, Raymond Queneau, or Henry Miller.[51]

Miller recalled seeing some of his night photographs: "One day [when] the door was finally thrust open I beheld to my astonishment a thousand replicas of all the scenes, all the streets, all the walls, all the fragments of that Paris wherein I had died and was born again."[52] Brassaï was at the time not only a photographer but an aspiring painter and sculptor, as well as a journalist, and it is perhaps these multiple talents and his natural curiosity that brought him and Miller into a close friendship. The best description of Brassaï is provided in Miller's *Tropic of Cancer*:

> He was a good companion, the photographer. He knew the city inside out, the walls particularly; he talked to me about Goethe often, and the days of the Hohenstaufen, and the massacre of the Jews during the reign of the Black Death. Interesting subjects, and always related in some obscure way to the things he was doing. . . . We explored the 5th, the 13th, the 19th, and the 20th arrondissements *thoroughly*. Our favorite resting places were lugubrious little spots such as the Place Nationale, Place des Peupliers, Place de la Contrescarpe, Place Paul-Verlaine. Many of these places were already familiar to me, but all of them I now saw in a different light owing to the rare flavor of his conversation.[53]

But Paris at night had been Kertész's special photographic subject since 1925, and he remembers that when Peignot had first asked him about a book on the subject he told Kertész that he could not afford to pay a photographer much for it. At the time, Kertész was thirty-seven, had made a reputation for himself, and expected the kind of remuneration that had come to him from his magazine work. The offer went to his younger friend, who ambitious now to be a photographer took the opportunity, excused himself for several months from the company of the cafés on the boulevard Montparnasse, and, in order to increase his portfolio of night photographs of the city, began a frenzy of activity.

Paris de nuit was a critical success because of its incredible photographs and its introduction by a well-known author (Paul Morand). It served as a souvenir not only of common experiences like seeing the Arc de Triomphe lit up at night or the Place de la Concorde from the terrace of the Auto-mobile Club, but also of the more exotic fare of witnessing the *clochards* warming themselves under one of the bridges along the Seine, the cleaning of the Parisian cesspools, or an encounter with a streetwalker. Brassaï's appetite for the sensational was not fully satisfied in his first book. Bolder photographs of the Parisian *daemon* were printed in a second book, smaller in size and of a limited run. *Voluptés de Paris*, which appeared in 1935, included no photographs of any famous attractions, but rather those of lovers on benches or in bars, prostitutes, lesbians, floorshows, brothels, and stripteasers. Most of these images, taken in 1931 or 1932 (the same period as those for *Paris de nuit*), revealed a little too much of the other side of Paris for the mass audience. Not surprisingly, these photographs and others by Krull and

Roger Schall found other outlets as illustrations for the crime magazines *Détective* and *Scandale*.

For Kertész, such subjects were not attractive. His portrait of the city at night, like a de Chirico painting, was concerned exclusively with the mysteries and marvels of place and situation rather than those formed by sensation or notoriety (see fig. 35). Brassaï, too, had marvelous photographs of the abandoned streets of Paris evoking the sinister, but what clearly separated his work from Kertész's were his photographs of the characters that populated the underground life of Paris. But it was Kertész who had led the way. As early as 1928, even before Brassaï became a photographer, Mac Orlan described the character of Kertész's photographs: "Kertész seeks a fantasy of the street which while conforming rather more to Central European tastes, interprets the secret elements of light and shade for others to find romantic situations therein." [54]

Each photographer who photographed Paris claimed her as his own, and as a result, each was a little jealous of the others or of those who had the good fortune to find a publisher. Although they had different points of view, it cannot have pleased Kertész to see Krull's book on Paris appear first, although it was more a publisher's book than a photographer's. Four years later he had to deal with the appearance of Brassaï's brilliant book. Nor could it have been easy for him to read Henry Miller when he referred to Brassaï as "the eye of Paris" a few years later. [55] But pioneers and innovators like Kertész are not exempt from competition and have to suffer not only from the new territory they tame, but also from witnessing subsequent successes that they helped initiate, but which proceed from the talent in others.

VIII. Changing Paris, Changing Photography

In his book on Henry Miller, Brassaï described the Paris that Miller found upon his arrival in 1930 as a contrast to the one the author had glimpsed on a trip a few years earlier.

The face of Paris was not quite the same as in 1928. . . . The atmosphere of Paris had changed in two years. It was the crash of Wall Street . . . [that] put to an end the years of plenty and insouciance, of easy money, which had made fortunes for the great houses of fashion, the galleries, the travel agencies, and 20th-century courtesans. . . .

But there was still a space where a certain pleasure of living lingered, Montparnasse, as if the century's great catastrophe had spared it. How this corner of Paris encircled with showier real estate, but itself unpicturesque, without charm, and devoid of character, could have been the artistic center of the world, the ferment of all cultural and even social revolutions, remains a mystery. . . . In a world that was beginning to sour, even the middle-class down to the small shopkeeper, in the quest of pleasure and gaiety, was attracted by the atmosphere of euphoria, of liberty, and of nonconformity. [56]

Catalogue no. 96
Mrs. Hubbell, 1931,
from *Photographie*,
1931, no. 4;
photograph at right by
Germaine Krull.

Figure 36
Photographie, 1931,
nos. 8–9, photograph at
left by Lee Miller, at
right by Maurice Tabard.

The sense of an extended life that Montparnasse gave to Paris during the Depression is analogous to the spirit that photography lent to the pages of its magazines. The world appeared spirited, newly invented, and optimistic. Illustrative photography and photojournalism had gained a little more respect and offered a certain fame through credit lines. It was no longer a profession left only to immigrants. Although Abbott, Brandt, Miller, Lotar, and Krull left Paris between 1929 and 1933, French photographic talents had just appeared or were beginning to sprout everywhere to replace them. The names of Pierre Verger, Gaston Paris, René Zuber, Jean Moral, and Pierre Boucher appeared under photographs. They were not only French: Hug Block, Francis Kollar, Lucien Aiger, and later Erwin Blumenfeld appeared, as did the Hungarian women Rogie André, Ergy Landau, Nora Dumas, and Ylla.[57] The influx of photographers fleeing Hitler after 1933 assured that there would always be a large population of foreign photographers in Paris.

In the 1920s, outside the annual salons, there had been only scattered opportunities for the exhibition of contemporary photography in Paris. The 1930s provided a better fare. Each year at places like the Galerie de la Pléiade, a small group of photographers, including Kertész, displayed their photographs.[58] In addition, the Galerie d'Art Contemporain, the Plume d'Or, and the International Salon of Photography had exhibitions. As an active member of the Société des Artistes Décorateurs, Albin-Guillot exhibited her work in their annual expositions without much stir or company. In 1930, however, when the Deutscher Werkbund was invited by the Société to exhibit in a special section, there was plenty of the "new photography" to be seen in Paris. Photographs by Moholy, Herbert Bayer, Max Burchartz, T. Lux Feininger, Walter Finsler, Lotti Jacobi, Lucia Moholy, Peterhans, Robert Petschow, Renger-Patzsch, and Sasha Stone appeared alongside architectural renderings, lamps, jewelry, fabrics, furniture, and telephones. Paris had a firsthand look at the new German photography. It was during this exhibition that Moholy visited Paris and met Kertész for the first time.

In Paris the most important photographic exhibition of the decade was the "Exposition Internationale de la Photographie Contemporaine" of 1936 held at the Musée des Arts Décoratifs. The catalogue listed 1,692 photographs. Nearly every Parisian photographer of consequence was represented, as well as a selection from Germany, Russia, England, and the United States. There was a section devoted to scientific photography, as well as one on the history of photography, which had been assembled from the Société Française de Photographie, the Royal Photographic Society, and the private collections of Messieurs Gilles, Barthélemy, and Sirot, among others.[59] The exhibition lent prestige to photography, but the real currency of the photographic image still lay in publications and not with museums or galleries.

Not only did Paris of the 1930s produce an increasing number of books and exhibitions of photographs, but also an annual illustrated review of what was considered to be new. *Photographie* appeared in March 1930, the first special issue devoted to photography by Charles Peignot's deluxe magazine for typography, book design, and the graphic arts, *Arts et métiers graphiques*. It was impressive, but it was not the first of its kind: Alfred Stieglitz's *Camera Work* had grown out of an amateur publication into a handsome quarterly, the Photo-Club de Paris had their annual publication, as did the Pictorial Photographers of America, to name a few. Beginning in 1927 in Germany, *Das Deutsche Lichtbild*, an annual of the newest in photography—but restricted to photographers (including Munkacsi) working in Germany or Austria—became the model that others followed. Although it may have had German antecedents, *Photographie*, like *Vu*, was meant to have its own personality. It was the first international annual devoted to what was new in photographic imagery. The publisher collected work from leading photographers for the first issue, mostly through names and addresses supplied to him by Vogel, who was also on the advisory board of *Arts et métiers graphiques*. The first issue was beautifully printed in rotogravure and was prefaced by a long introduction by Waldemar George describing photography's history, character, and capacities. The photographs were reproduced one to a page with an accompanying credit but with no titles or editorial comments.

Photographers in Paris and Germany were well represented, as were the Americans Steichen and Sheeler. One could get an idea of the range of contemporary photography, as well as a feeling for developing clichés. An editorial innovation was presented in the second issue. The first ten photographs were portraits of the same woman, a Mrs. Hubbell, by Alban, Albin-Guillot, Hoyningen-Huené, Kertész, Krull, Lucien Lorelle (studio),

Man Ray, Lee Miller, Tabard, and André Vigneau, demonstrating the different styles and characteristics of each photographer (see cat. no. 96, fig. 36). In the later issues, however, the editors began to include uninspired photographs of animals, close-ups of objects and plants, or nudes. On one occasion, they published in the 1940 annual a photograph by Marie et Borel nearly identical to Kertész's 1928 winter view of the little park Vert Galant which had been published in the 1936 annual (see cat. no. 79, fig. 37).

Although it came close to being a "who's who of contemporary photography," it was not a perfect sample. The representation was complete enough, however, for one to wonder why photographs by Sander, Salomon, Man, Capa, Chim, Walter Hege, Freund, Francis Bruguière, or any Russians never appeared in any of the issues between 1930 and 1940. American photographers were generally represented well, considering it was a foreign publication for them, although no photographs by Stieglitz, Lewis Hine, or Walker Evans were ever reproduced. Although work by Henri Cartier-Bresson and Brassaï appeared in the third and fourth issues, respectively, they were represented by only a few photographs that did not permit the viewer to form any opinion about their talents. In general, the selections were weighted toward the photographer as illustrator.

Kertész had five photographs in the first issue, one of them being his famous *Fork* (cat. no. 65). Tabard and Parry, who worked for the publisher's family, had seven and six photographs respectively, Steichen seven, Man Ray three, and Krull only two. After the first issue, Kertész was represented by three photographs in the second and only a single photograph in the 1933–34 and 1936 issues. Similarly, he was well represented in the first two issues of *Modern Photography*, the English counterpart, which began in 1931, but not in the following issues.[60]

The increased visibility that photography had gained first through the pages of small magazines like *Der Querschnitt*, *Uhu*, *Variétés*, or art and literary journals like *Bifur*, *transition*, *Jazz*, *Broom*, or *Das Kunstblatt*, and then later through exhibitions or in the photographic annuals helped to display existing talents. These magazines did not assign specific photographs to be made. The use of photographs as illustrations in newspapers and magazines and especially in advertising had another effect. Although these publications presented their illustrations as the work of photo-

graphic innovators, the truth of the matter was that the harder economic times made photography that was truly independent and innovative less attractive. The usefulness of the photographer as illustrator forced many to bend to the will of the publishers and the readership in order to maintain their jobs. In the mid-1920s, photographers like Man Ray, Kertész, or Krull had no audience and were therefore left to photograph on their own.

By the 1930s, through the use of photographs in the illustrated press and advertising, an audience had been developed whose expectations and appetites were a powerful force in determining what was reproduced. What independent photographers remained often bifurcated their work; previous to this time there had been less of a distinction among nonamateur photographers between their professional and private work.

IX. French Photography

Although they were different with each issue, an explanation of the medium of photography was the subject of each of the essays that introduced an annual of *Photographie*. The first issue gave a long description of the medium under various headings: the origin of photography; characteristics of photography; photography as an end in itself; photography and literature; photographic conscience; Atget, photographer of Paris; modern magic; photography and publicity; scientific photography; and photography and imagination. The second issue was introduced by Philippe Soupault, who argued that photographs above all were aspects of the documentation of reality and therefore had to be judged by different standards than painting. In his conclusion he reiterated a common

sentiment that in order for photographs to be appreciated for what they are they had to rid themselves of their false "artistic" ambitions. André Beucler, writing in the next issue, declared that the fact that photography invents nothing is its power. The fourth issue printed an article by Louis Cheronnet, who pleaded for the establishment of a museum of photography that would be a comprehensive synoptic presentation of the artistic and scientific history of the medium.

Waldemar George's introduction to the first issue of *Photographie* was a lengthy accumulation of scattered notions about photography which had been emerging during the century. Although it is somewhat exhaustive, it is not the most critically illuminating. Paris had no Walter Benjamin who could in a sustained piece of writing define what photography had become under her encouragement.[61] In order to begin to understand what might be considered the French contribution to photography in this period, other than providing the inspiring environment of Paris for numerous foreign photographers, one has to consider French sources and French writers.

Perhaps the first article by a French author to reach the public on the emergence of photography as an art relating to the avant-garde was published just after the VIe Congrès International de Photographie was in session. It appeared as two pages illustrated by Man Ray photographs in 1925 in Florent Fel's new magazine *L'Art vivant*. Its author, the twenty-five-year-old Surrealist writer René Crevel, described in a fanciful literary manner photographers as prestidigitators who reveal that reality, forms, and colors are not so simply real as one would like to believe: "Painting is not photography say the painters. But photography is not photography either, that is to say it is not a copy."[62]

Almost all subsequent writers dealt with the fact that photography is not just a copy of that which is in front of the camera, as the common notion of it must have been. Nonetheless, the superior objective record of the lens continued to fascinate writers throughout the 1930s. In 1939 the poet Paul Valéry celebrated the centenary of photography: "Thanks to photography, the eye grew accustomed to anticipate what it should see, and to see it; and it learned not to see nonexistent things which, hitherto, it had seen so clearly."[63] Nearly a decade before this statement, Pierre Bost, in a concise and brilliant essay introducing a small, 1930 limited-edition book of twenty-four rotogravure plates entitled *Photographies modernes*, reminded the reader that we do not see in a purely optical way: "We never see the world in one way only, but rather with our hands, our ears, and our steps, and that because of the collaboration of all of our senses, we do not know the work of the eyes by themselves. The photographer's camera, which is an eye, justly superior to our eye, is nothing but an eye, but it discloses to us the pure visual image that we had forgotten since our first sight as newborn infants."[64] The pure visual image was not to be accepted unexamined, however. Bost warned of photography's ability to lie convincingly through light, its "amenable accessory." He too spoke of the photographer as a prestidigitator performing miracles. He incorporated in his idea of photog-

raphy a technique employed by the Dadaists: "The role of photography is to isolate that which is familiar in order to render it strange."[65] While he discussed photography as a transforming medium of seeming objectivity, Bost also made a crucial point about the importance of time. "Ephemeral truth? Yes. It is the strength of photography and at the same time the limit of its power. . . . It is said that photography is the only way by which we can know this instant, nearly approaching the unattainable and barely conceivable knowledge of the pure moment."[66] His essay was accompanied by one of the best selections of photographs of the period.

Although Bost referred to the moment of the photograph as an "ephemeral truth" (*vérité éphémère*), he was not the first to try to give it a name. Pierre Mac Orlan called it "the right moment" (*bon moment*) in a 1928 essay: "Photographic art, in its present state, may be divided into the two classes which are approximately the poles of any artistic creation. There is the plastic photograph and the documentary photograph. The second of these two categories is unconsciously literary, for it is no more than a depiction of contemporary life seized at the right moment by an artist clever at seizing this right moment." In another article printed the following month, Mac Orlan elaborated on what he meant by "literary." At the time, it was probably the most brilliant description in French of the power that the medium of photography had on the imaginative, literary viewer.

It is through the mediation of photography that we are permitted to seize the unreal forms of life, which demand at least one second of motionlessness in order to be perceptible. . . . The greatest field of photography, for the literary interpretation of life, consists, to my mind, in its latent power to create as it were death for a split-second. Any thing or person is, at will, made to die for a moment of time so immeasurably small that the return to life is effected without consciousness of the great adventure. But this photographic adventure is not lost. Others are present who read upon the fine countenances illuminated by Man Ray, Berenice Abbott, Kertész, and others rich destinies of which the shortest may not be contained in three hundred pages.[67]

Thus, the French imagination in photography was closely linked to a literary one, especially as it con-

Figure 38
Henri Cartier-Bresson,
Alicante, Spain, 1932.

Figure 39
Henri Cartier-Bresson,
Spain, c. 1932.

cerned what was called documentary photography. Mac Orlan reiterated it plainly in the first sentence of his introduction to the 1931 monograph on Germaine Krull: "Photography, which has influenced, more or less, a part of the German expressionist movement, seems to be determined to mix itself with the inspiration of lyric writers, who, alas, remain an enigma for the great public."[68] Most of the photographers in Paris from Man Ray on worked with or had close friends who were writers, journalists, or poets. Through reviews, introductions to books, exhibitions, and the photographic annuals, or for special articles in *L'Art vivant* or in its 1929 series "La Photographie est-elle un art?" writers expressed their views on photography.[69] But one can find close links to painting and film too. In his introduction to Moï Ver's *Paris*, for example, Léger stated: "It is incontestable that the cinema has opened the way, but the fact that photography 'keeps,' that it 'fixes' the image, appears to be just the opposite of the cinemagraphic fact, which is moving and successive by definition. A painter, for example, is much more apt to be able to make a beautiful photograph than a cinematographer, who is in the habit of fragmenting. . . . Like painting, photography looks for that which can last."[70] Léger went on to say that he felt photography should not borrow from the cinema or from literature. Other writers were saying it should not borrow from painting either. Even though there were extensive aesthetic influences from other art forms, photography in Europe and America was beginning to define itself and reexamine its powers, without isolating itself from its sister arts of literature, film, or painting. In France, however, the combination of influences favored literature.[71]

One of Crevel's younger friends was destined to become the greatest French photographer of the period, although his achievements would not be generally known to a large public until after World War II. Henri Cartier-Bresson (b. 1908) was a political radical who was not attracted to his family's textile business but rather to art, literature, and the intellectual activities of Surrealism. Sustained by a small income, he first studied painting with André Lhote and in 1928 went to Cambridge to study literature as well. Around 1930 he began to photograph. The Leica camera, which he, like Kertész, felt was made for him, became his constant companion from 1931 on. It accompanied him on his travels in Europe through 1932, and it was the camera that he used for some

Figure 40
Kertész,
Rue de Crimée, 1928.

of his best early photographs in Italy and Spain.

Cartier-Bresson was not interested in the sharp, static photographs of the members of Die Neue Sachlichkeit, nor by those of its conservative counterpart in Paris, Emmanuel Sougez. In fact, he knew little of the work of other photographers at the beginning of his interest in the medium. Consequently, he was relatively free of restricting influences of other photographers and could develop many of his ideas independently. One early influence, however, was the work of Munkacsi, which seemed fresh and original. Cartier-Bresson's genius for understanding the relationship that time had to photography did not result in Munkacsi's frozen-moment, stop-action images. They were rather Surrealist versions of Mac Orlan's "right moment" that caused a split-second death in the people and objects of the scene and which the viewer brought back to life through his imagination. He also acknowledged Kertész's general influence. However, unlike Kertész's notion of the arrested scene, Cartier-Bresson's visual ideas and calculated ambiguities allowed for nonnaturalistic interpretation if the viewer so chose (see figs. 38,39).

The "right moment" was not a particularly compelling expression. Cartier-Bresson's later term,

image à la sauvette, was more a photographer's description. Literally it means an image taken hastily or by impulse. A similar French phrase, *vendre à la sauvette*, means "sold on the street," and so Cartier-Bresson's term connoted a photographer who roamed the streets responding to that which changed and vanished in front of his eyes. Thus, it was subtly and intellectually, although indirectly, related to the interest in motion that Vertov had so strongly voiced about film, as well as to Moholy's later term "vision in motion." Even though *image à la sauvette* can mean an image taken "on the run," it has more to do with time, or more precisely with a timing that suspends time, than with the juxtapositions provided by mobility and positioning. In 1952 Cartier-Bresson's term became famous in English as "the decisive moment," the title of his first book. Although the translation was compelling, it did not suggest Cartier-Bresson's seed of coincidental ambiguity that was essential to his aesthetic and that had had an earlier germination in 1928 in such Kertész photographs as *Rue de Crimée* (fig. 40), *Meudon* (cat. no. 58), or *Rue de Lévis, Montmartre* (cat. no. 70).

The increasing sophistication of the aesthetic relationship of time to photography that Kertész helped to establish and its resulting emphasis on the power of representing simultaneity in one exposure was also part of Cartier-Bresson's vision. But the discipline of printing from the whole, uncropped image of the negative, that Cartier-Bresson came to insist upon, was wholly his own. Technically, the Leica and other 35mm cameras permitted the photographer not only the convenience of movement, but also some three dozen sequential exposures by which he could test his reflexes of perception against a scene in continual flux. The 24 x 36 mm negative was, however, not large in comparison to those of the standard reporter cameras of the period, which were 9 x 12 cm. Consequently, there was an advantage to using the whole negative from which to enlarge. The habit of cropping, practiced by most photographers including Kertész, implied that the photographer was starting with either a large or a fine-grain negative, neither of which the Leica provided. Intellectually, Cartier-Bresson's insistence on the use of the whole frame had a reason that was more fundamental to his aesthetic than to his technique. The viewfinder of the Leica was designed so that the camera acted nearly as an extension of the eye. Through the frame of the viewfinder, the photographer could observe the continually changing positions of objects and people in space almost as if he were viewing a film and had but to chose the frame he wished to print as a still. The simultaneity of independent events defined through the frame of the viewfinder was not unlike a kind of automatic writing that the Dadaists and the Surrealist poets had discovered a decade earlier. It was a matter of selection and removal.

X. Kertész in New York

By the fall of 1936, when Kertész was on his way to New York, the other photographers who had come out of Hungary were either establishing their careers, like Brassaï in Paris and Capa in the Spanish Civil War, or moving to America. Munkacsi had already arrived in 1934, and Moholy, who was in England at the time, was preparing to leave for Chicago, where in 1937 he would establish a school known as the "New Bauhaus." Both Moholy and Capa found ways to continue the work with which they had been identified. Munkacsi and Kertész, on the other hand, came up against the commercialism of America. Success was immediate for Munkacsi, who sold his talents to *Harper's Bazaar*, where they were initially invigorating; but soon restricted to the subject of fashion, the unpredictable spontaneity of his work began to suffer, surviving only in diminishing and isolated flashes. In publishing and photojournalism, it was no longer an age that fostered the independent photographer such as Kertész, Krull, and Man Ray had once been. For Kertész, success was a long way off. He met with bad luck, near financial disaster, and with a feeling of complete isolation. He felt as if he had disappeared from the face of the earth. He had to learn a new language and widen his circle again. This time, there was no welcoming café society that circulated his name and provided an introduction to the new culture. This time, he was forty-two years of age, farther from his native Hungary, and struggling on a new continent full of cold, hard cities for any photographer who thought he could sustain himself with the same wit and imagination that had been so readily received on the boulevard Montparnasse.

America had its own heroes of photography and its own history that was divided between the new commercial photographers and those who developed from a respect, bordering on reverence, for the subject photographed. The first group included those such as Steichen and Margaret Bourke-White whose credit lines were in *Fortune*, *Vogue*, *Life*, and *Look*, as well as in many other magazines. The second group consisted of Stieglitz, Strand, Weston, Ansel Adams, and Evans. The American photographs that were compatible with Kertész's view of the world were those being made —with the exception of Evans—by the photographers of the Farm Security Administration, which hired American photographers only. The photographers coming from Europe, like Alfred Eisenstadt, who had as much success at *Life* as any American, and Andreas Feininger, had to find their luck within the commercial system.

Outside of the commercial system, there was little help for the foreign photographer. One of Kertész's former connections in New York was Julien Levy, who had purchased a number of his photographs, along with those of his contemporaries, in the summer of 1930 and exhibited them in his gallery during the next few years. By 1936, however, Levy's most active period of collecting and exhibiting photography was coming to an end. There had been no collectors as it turned out, not for Atget, Man Ray, Abbott or any of the photographers of the "Salon de l'Escalier" or the Galerie de la Pléiade. Stieglitz was not able to help either. His gallery was now dedicated to a few American artists and only two photographers. At the time of Kertész's arrival, Stieglitz was exhibiting the work of Ansel Adams, three years later it would be Eliot Porter, and the last photography show he mounted was of his own work in 1941. He had known some of Kertész's European work through Zilzer, who had preceded Kertész to New York. During Stieglitz's only meeting with Kertész to see the set of nude distortions, for which there had been no publisher in Europe, he warned Kertész that if they were published in America the idea and technique would be copied immediately. Kertész replied that they were not as easy to make as they appeared, and he was the only one who could really succeed at it. Stieglitz only replied that Kertész did not yet know American photographers.[72]

Times were not easy anywhere. Scores of the best German and Eastern European artists and photographers, like their counterparts in other professions, found America to be the best solution in view of the political circumstances in Europe.

Kertész was again an immigrant who was forced to prove himself, but this time against more sophisticated competitors. His independence and integrity as an artist were at stake. His will not to start at the bottom of the ladder was as strong as his memory of the prestigious position he had achieved in Europe. The new odds seemed impossible and Paris like a dream slipped by. It was a time for courage and patience. This time, the strength he would draw from solitude would be tempered not only by his resolve to survive but by the bitterness of a cruel isolation.

Notes

1. Commandant Constant Puyo, "La Photographie d'amateur," in *VIe Congrès International de Photographie, Paris, 29 Juin–4 Juillet, 1925, Décisions, Procès-Verbaux, Rapports et Mémoires* (Paris: Société Française de Photographie, 1926), pp. 231–35.

2. The period between 1895 and 1910 was, without doubt, a fruitful time for photographic innovations: the rise of amateur photography occurred as Puyo noted; the Autochrome and other screen processes for color photography were introduced; the halftone screen and the intricacies of large-run rotogravure technique were perfected and used; the first single-lens reflex camera was marketed; numerous photographic papers attractive to the pictorial photographer were invented; cinematography began; x-rays were discovered; three- and four-color printing became commercially viable; wide-angle lenses were manufactured; panchromatic emulsions were introduced; and photographs were first transmitted over telegraph wires.

3. Quoted in Margaret Harker, *The Linked Ring: The Secession Movement in Photography in Britain, 1892–1910* (London: Royal Photographic Society and William Heinemann, Ltd., 1979), p. 134.

4. Puyo (note 1), p. 235.

5. The "Tourist Multiple" by Herbert & Hugesson of New York could take 750 exposures in the format of 18 x 24 mm and advertised: "Round the world without reloading." The French-made "Sept" could take snapshots, time exposures, or, with its motor-drive, motion pictures. Like a motion-picture camera, it had but one shutter speed. In addition, it could be used as a projector or an enlarger.

6. Light meters at the time were inaccurate and unreliable, so it was prudent to expose a strip of the same film under the lighting conditions to be employed by the cinematographer. For this, only a small hand camera was necessary.

7. "I took the double of the cinema width and saw that it worked very well, accordingly 24 x 36 mm resulted. Thus the origin of the Leica format. . . . I consider the 2:3 ratio to be the most beautiful and practical yet." Quoted in Urs Tilmanns, *Geschichte der Photographie, Ein Jahrhundert Prägt ein Medium* (Stuttgart: Verlag Huber, 1981), p. 276.

8. Tilmanns (note 7), pp. 275–79.

9. Kertész found that the Busch f2, originally designed for motion-picture cameras, was difficult to use at its widest aperture. Focusing was critical and the photographs it produced were generally soft because so much of the scene was beyond the lens's inherently narrow depth of field.

10. Kertész found the Rolleiflex, which appeared on the market in 1928, awkward for his purposes and therefore never used it.

11. Ullstein published not only the *Berliner Illustrirte Zeitung*, but also the popular magazines *Die Dame* and *Uhu*.

12. Tim N. Gidal, *Modern Photojournalism: Origin and Evolution, 1910–1933*, from the series *Photography: Men and Movements*, ed. Roméo E. Martinez, trans. Maureen Oberli-Turner (New York: Collier Books, 1973), pp. 15, 14.

13. Gidal (note 12), p. 19.

14. Edmond Wellhoff, "Sous la règle de St. Benoît," *Vu*, no. 109 (1930), pp. 337–40. This may be compared to the German article "Das Haus des Schweigens," *Berliner Illustrirte Zeitung*, no. 1 (June 1, 1929), pp. 35–37.

15. Puyo (note 1), p. 234.

16. László Moholy-Nagy, *Malerei Fotographie Film* (Painting photography film), 2nd ed. (Munich: Bauhaus Bucher: 8 [Albert Langen], 1927), p. 5.

17. The first edition of *Malerei Fotographie Film* (published in 1925 as *Malerei Photographie Film*) contains only one camera photograph credited to Moholy (one obviously taken in a studio, perhaps even by Lucia or someone else); the 1927 edition has six, several of which were undoubtedly taken in the summer of 1925.

18. Their first photograms were made on printing-out papers so that they could watch the progress of the picture and change it by adding or removing material. The same technique, but using developing-out papers, was discovered by Man Ray, who issued a privately published book of them entitled *Champs délicieux* with an introduction by Tristan Tzara in 1922. It is possible that this book made its way to Berlin in that year and into Moholy's circle.

19. For an excellent discussion of Moholy's work as a photographer and its relation to Dada, Surrealism, and Russian avant-garde art and film, see Andreas Haus, *Moholy-Nagy: Photographs and Photograms*, trans. Frederic Samson (New York: Pantheon Books, 1980). The original publication in German is *Moholy-Nagy: Fotos und Fotogramme* (Munich: Schirmer/Mosel, 1978).

20. Quoted in P. Adams Sitney, ed., *The Avant-Garde Film: A Reader of Theory and Criticism* (New York: New York University Press, 1973), p. 4.

21. Other exhibitors were George Grosz and Frans Masereel.

22. Similar subjects appeared in Krull's book *Métal* (Paris: A. Cavalas, 1927).

23. M. Meurer, *Ursprungsformen des greichischen Akanthus Ornaments und ihre naturlichen Vorbilder* (Berlin, 1896). This citation is drawn from the Afterword by Ann and Jürgen Wilde in the reissue of Karl Blossfeldt, *Urformen der Kunst* (Dortmund: Harenberg Kommunikation, 1982).

24. Karl Blossfeldt, *Urformen der Kunst* (The sources of form in art), introduction by Karl Nierendorf (Berlin: Verlag Ernst Wasmuth, 1928).

25. Friedrich Brockmann and Franz Wilhelm Seiwert.

26. Quoted in David Mellor, ed., *Germany, The New Photography, 1927–33* (London: Arts Council of Great Britain, 1978), p. 58.

27. He saw the book through his friend Anne-Marie Merkel. It was published by Kurt Wolff, who in the next year, 1929, would issue Sander's *Anlitz der Zeit* (The face of our time).

28. Fritz Kempe, "*The World is Beautiful*, A Model Book of Objects and Things," in *Albert Renger-Patzsch* (Paris, Cologne, and Boston: Créatis/Schürmann & Kicken, 1979), p. 8.

29. After *Das Chorgestuhl von Cappenberg* (The choir stalls of Cappenberg) was issued, other books on church architecture illustrated with photographs by Renger-Patzsch appeared: Wilhelm Wilhelm-Kästner, *Das Münster in Essen* (The minster of Essen) (Essen: Fredebeul & Koenen, 1929), and Werner Burmeister, *Norddeutsche Backsteindome* (North German brick cathedrals) (Berlin: Deutsche Kunstverlag, 1930). A classic series of books published by the Deutsche Kunstverlag with text by Pindar and photographs by Walter Hege began in 1925.

30. Walter Benjamin, "A Short History of Photography," in *Classic Essays on Photography*, ed. Alan Trachtenberg (New Haven: Leete's Island Books, 1980), p. 213.

31. Franz Roh and Jan Tschichold, eds., *Foto-Auge* (Photo eye) (Stuttgart: Akademischer Verlag Dr. Fritz Wedekind & Co., 1929). Werner Gräff, *Es kommt der neue Fotograf!* (Here comes the new photographer!) (Berlin: Verlag Hermann Reckendorf, 1929).

32. Ute Eskildsen, "Innovative Photography in Germany Between the Wars," in *Avant-Garde Photography in Germany, 1919–1939* (San Francisco: San Francisco Museum of Modern Art, 1980), p. 37.

33. Maria Morris Hambourg, "Atget, Precursor of Modern Documentary Photography," unpublished manuscript, 1983.

34. In Lartigue's albums one can find recorded a list of six cameras which he used between 1902 and 1905: a 13 x 18 cm *chambre en bois*, a 9 x 12 cm *jumelle à main* (a handheld camera), a Gaumont 4.5 x 6 cm (another small handheld camera), a folding Kodak 6 x 9 cm Brownie #2, and two stereo cameras. There are also records of personal technical successes: a record of a one-minute exposure in 1908 that captured a scene by moonlight, an overall view of Paris from the top of the Arc de Triomphe, and a night scene of fireworks taken in Monaco in April 1911.

35. Quoted in Maria Morris Hambourg, "A Biography of Eugène Atget," in John Szarkowski and Maria Morris Hambourg, *The Work of Atget*, Vol. 2, *The Art of Old Paris* (New York: The Museum of Modern Art, 1982), p. 29.

36. André Breton, "What Is Surrealism?" in *Theories of Modern Art: A Source Book by Artists and Critics*, ed. Herschel B. Chipp (Berkeley and Los Angeles: University of California Press, 1968), p. 411. The original article was published in 1934.

37. André Breton, "Surréalisme et la peinture," trans. David Gascoyne, in Chipp (note 36), p. 406.

38. She was born during a trip her parents had made from Germany to Poland.

39. In contrast to the Krull-Lotar partnership, Kertész always worked alone.

40. Germaine Krull, "Autobiographische Erinnerungen einer Fotografin aus der Zeit zwischen den Kriegen" in *Germaine Krull, Fotografien, 1922–1966* (Cologne: Rheinland-Verlag; Bonn: Rudolh Habelt Verlag, 1977), p. 123.

41. Krull's photographs of the Eiffel Tower were not reproduced in the premier issue of *Vu* as she remembered in an interview in 1977, but rather in the eleventh issue (May 30, 1928, p. 284).

42. Krull (note 40), p. 126.

43. Although Krull was well published in the late 1920s and in 1936, very few of her photographs survived World War II. She was forced to flee France for Brazil and was soon living in Africa. She never established another residence in France and most of her negatives and photographs were left with friends and publishers; only a handful have come down to us. It is therefore difficult to compare the career of Kertész with that of Krull, for her photographs were not well dated, nor are those that she may have taken outside of her professional career numerous enough to determine what may have been invented within the development that a large chronological sequence of photographs usually shows.

44. According to Kertész's memory, he was commissioned to photograph the same subject after Krull returned from the initial trip with too few photographs for the book. The book, in fact, shows that the publisher augmented the selection significantly with the work of other photographers: Aéro Michaud, Blanc et Demilly, Detaille, Henry Ely, F.F. (probably Florent Fels), Frost, Emmanuel Sougez, Spitzmuller, T.C.F., and Moï Ver.

45. Germaine Krull, *Marseilles*, text by André Suares (Paris: Librairie Plon, 1935). Other books by the same publisher were Kertész's *Enfants* (1933) and *Paris* (1934). These books took into consideration the design of the spread of photographs and the text and did not, as did many illustrated books of the time, present the photographs as single plates one to a page.

46. Mario Bucovich, *Paris*, preface by Paul Morand (Berlin: Albertus-Verlag, 1928).

47. Moï Ver, *Paris*, introduction by Fernand Léger (Paris: Editions Jeanne Walter, 1931). The photographs are not

presented as single plates one to a page, but rather the spread is designed as one unit.

48. André Kertész, *Paris*, text by Pierre Mac Orlan (Paris: Librairie Plon, 1934), n.pag.

49. Ibid. Although Mac Orlan used the word *demon* rather than the word *genie*, I have translated it as "genius" and reserved the word "daemon" to describe Brassaï's work in order to avoid confusing Brassaï's proclivities for the activities of the underworld with Kertész's infatuation with the appearance of the city at night.

50. Brassaï had lived with his family for a year in Paris in 1903 as a four-year-old child while his father was there studying.

51. Brassaï, *The Secret Paris of the 30's*, trans. Richard Miller (New York: Pantheon Books, 1976), n.pag.

52. Henry Miller, "The Eye of Paris," in *Max and the White Phagocytes* (Paris: The Obelisk Press, 1938), p. 245.

53. Henry Miller, *Tropic of Cancer* (New York: Grove Press, 1961), p. 171.

54. Pierre Mac Orlan, "La Vie moderne, l'art littéraire d'imagination et la photographie," *Les Nouvelles Littéraires*, Sept. 22, 1928, p. 1; also as the introduction to the catalogue for the exhibition "Une Exposition de photographie à la Galerie L'Epoque," Brussels, which opened on October 20, 1928. The exhibitors were Kertész, Atget, Abbott, Anne Biermann (Gera, Germany), Robert Desmet (Brussels), E. Gobert (Brussels), Krull, Lotar, E.L.T. Mesens (Brussels), Moholy-Nagy, Man Ray, and Robertson (Berlin).

55. See Miller (note 52), pp. 240–52.

56. Brassaï, *Henry Miller, grandeur nature* (Paris: Gallimard, 1975), pp. 12–14.

57. Rogie André specialized in portraits of painters; Landau in studio portraits, children, and nudes; Dumas in peasant life; and Ylla in animals.

58. The advertisement for the "Groupe Annuel des Photographes" in the May 15, 1933, issue of *Surréalisme au service de la révolution* listed these participants: (Ilse) Bing, Boiffard, Brassaï, (Georges) Bresson, Caillard, Cartier-Bresson, Derberny-Peignot, Nora Dumas, Ecce Photo, Florence Henri, Kaskell, Kertész, (François) Kollar, G. Krull, E. Landau, Lee Miller, Lemare, E. Lotar, Man Ray, (Jean) Moral, (Roger) Parry, Rosy Ney, (Emmanuel) Sougez, (Maurice) Tabard, Vandor, (André) Vigneau, Ylla, (René) Zuber, René Jacques.

59. The exhibition served as the model upon which Beaumont Newhall would base his 1937 landmark exhibition at The Museum of Modern Art on the history of photography, in which he included five photographs by Kertész.

60. *Modern Photography*, a special number of "The Studio," (London and New York: The Studio Ltd./William Edwin Rudge, 1931). This initial number contains an introduction by G. H. Saxon Mills.

61. Walter Benjamin was one of the few who recognized the greatness of Sander, in addition to that of Atget, Blossfeldt, Moholy-Nagy, and Krull.

62. René Crevel, "Le Miroir aux objets," *L'Art vivant* 1, no. 14 (July 15, 1925), pp. 23–24.

63. Paul Valéry, "The Centenary of Photography," in *Classic Essays on Photography*, ed. Alan Trachtenberg (New Haven: Leete's Island Books, 1980), p. 192.

64. Pierre Bost, *Photographies modernes* (Paris: Librairie des Arts Décoratifs, [1930]), n.pag.

65. Ibid.

66. Ibid.

67. Pierre Mac Orlan, "La Photographie et la fantastique sociale," *Les Annales politiques et littéraires*, no. 2321 (Nov. 1, 1928), p. 414.

68. Pierre Mac Orlan, *Germaine Krull* (Paris: Gallimard, 1931), p. 3.

69. The series of one-page articles entitled "La Photographie est-elle un art?" (Is photography an art?) written by Jean Gallotti ran through the 1929 issues of *L'Art vivant* and discussed the work of Atget, Albin-Guillot, Kertész, Man Ray, Krull, Lotar, and Alban in that order. In 1930 a series of general articles on photography with illustrations was written by Carlo Rim, and in 1931 a series by Florent Fels. Short illustrated articles by Jacques Guenne on Nora Dumas, Ergy Landau, Dora Markovich (Dora Maar), Georges Saad, Roger Schall, and Ylla were written between 1933 and 1934.

70. Moï Ver (note 47), n.pag.

71. The literary influence, as well as the influence of Kertész's and Cartier-Bresson's work, continued into the next decade in the careers of Robert Doisneau and Edouard Boubat.

72. The meeting must have taken place in the first years after Kertész's arrival since, as Kertész remembers, they spoke in French.

André Kertész: The Making of an American Photographer

Weston J. Naef

When André Kertész arrived in New York with his wife, Elizabeth Saly, on October 15, 1936, via the S.S. *Washington*,[1] the worst of the Great Depression was not yet over. The November elections occurred two weeks after their arrival, and they saw Franklin Delano Roosevelt returned for his second term. Kertész was surprised to discover that America was divided between the employed and the unemployed, a situation not unlike what he had just left in Europe. He saw lines of men who showed up daily at the state unemployment offices hoping for work. Lower Broadway was still filled with people selling apples to survive. Many artists, writers, and photographers had jobs in Roosevelt programs like the Works Progress Administration, which included the Federal Art Project, Federal Writers' Project, and Federal Theater Project, as well as two ancillary undertakings that in an incidental way employed photographers, namely, the Resettlement Administration and the Farm Security Administration.[2] Any other photographer who had a job was in all likelihood employed by publishers Condé Nast, William Randolph Hearst, and Henry Luce, or eked out a living as a free-lance stringer for the news services. It was not easy to keep food on the table if making photographs was one's only source of income.

The Kertészes took up residence in the Hotel Beaux-Arts, which still stands today at 307 East 44th Street. There, Kertész made one of his first American pictures, a self-portrait (cat. no. 112). They took all of their meals in coffee shops and small restaurants on Lexington and Third avenues near the hotel, but Kertész made no photographs at these places, and so we have less of a feel for his daily routine than in Budapest and Paris, where cafés form a continuous subject. He walked the streets prospecting for photographs during the waning days of 1936, though few prints made then have survived in his possession. Kertész was deeply affected by the poverty and suffering he saw; and, with his income for the present assured by a weekly paycheck from Keystone Studios, he vowed to himself that in America, money and art would take equal position among his priorities. The word "mercenary" is perhaps too strong to be appropriate here, but it touches upon one aspect of Kertész's personality and cannot be ignored when measuring his art. He moves continuously between pleasure and necessity.

I.

Among the often-repeated lines in Kertész's very skimpy published biography is the statement that he arrived here with a contract from Keystone Studios.[3] No one has seen this contract recently—if indeed it exists—but its contents are essential to establishing Kertész's situation upon arrival. The following may be inferred: a contract sufficiently attractive to lure a person across the Atlantic would normally guarantee an income in return for an exclusive right to the employee's creative output for a certain period. Kertész recalls this amount to have been $80 to $100 per week. Today, however, he asserts that the contract was unfair because it required him to relinquish all artistic freedom in exchange for a salary that was ample, but not regal. This "Faustian pact" placed him at the beck and call of the picture agents at Keystone, who had exclusive right to utilize his material in exchange for making their best effort in finding assignments and in creating the opportunities to photograph through which income would be generated from anticipated sales. When he finally did get an assignment, he was asked to do what he had never done before: to work in a traditional photographic studio making photographs of products, commercial portraits, and even figure studies from models. Kertész remembers seeing his work displayed in the elevators of the Saks Fifth Avenue store to promote products.[4] He recently recalled this

Figure 1
Kertész,
Self-Portrait with Elizabeth and Friends at the P M Gallery,
New York, 1937.

period with some bitterness: "In the beginning it was, 'we need you.' Arrive [in New York] and find nothing [no assignments]. They say 'Patience, Mr. Kertész, we're preparing things for you.' I don't need preparation, only shooting. Weeks go by [there are no jobs] and I am confused. Then [when an assignment came], they just want commercial things, not reportage."[5] The fact that very few photographs in his files today date from 1936–37 testifies to the way uncertainty and change can paralyze creativity.

By the late spring of 1937, Kertész began to realize that he had made a great mistake in immigrating to America on the basis of the Keystone Studios contract, because he had come to be a reporter and had never imagined that Keystone would confine his work to studio set-ups. Six months had elapsed and nothing of consequence had been accomplished. Between May 15 and July 15, Kertész had to devise ways to turn the coming sixteen months into something valuable so that, if all else failed, he could at least return to Paris with the raw materials of a book on New York.[6] During the course of the spring, he cast his eyes over the horizon of possibilities. He observed from a distance certain American photographers to see what they were doing, and he looked closely at the American publishing scene. He saw that American photographers were essentially applying themselves to two types of subjects: those things of interest to persons who comprised "café society," and those that addressed the current national condition or were of general topical interest. Pictures of the former type appeared principally in magazines devoted to style and fashion and were created by photographers charged with creating the visual fictions required to sell products and entertain readers. Pictures of the latter type were made principally by documentarians and reporters for whom the quest for truth was uppermost. Among the latter group were, of course, photographers who depended upon spot news and made it their job to be in the right place at the right time. These photographers, with the exception of Weegee (whom Kertész did not know personally until much later), generally did not concern themselves with photographic style or attitude. For the photographer in quest of spot news, the subject had to be centered, in focus, close-up, and well-lighted; the news photographer was an assembly-line worker charged with making the same photograph over and over again with mechanical reliability. Photojournalists were another breed entirely. They produced interpretive picture essays (see figs. 6, 7) that in the highest form expressed what they felt about the subjects they were asked to observe. Photographers recognized that they were of two social classes, one slightly blue-collar, the other philosophical and intellectual. Artist-reporters like Berenice Abbott, Walker Evans, Margaret Bourke-White, and Kertész were charged with using artistic license to make each new subject fresh and interesting, to make it appear as though it had never been photographed before—and might never be again.

The only photograph from 1936 to enter Kertész's published oeuvre—the numerous anthologies based upon his own choices—represents a crippled dwarf of a woman whose crutches are mysteriously shrouded by her overcoat (cat. no. 114). A curious thing about the photograph is that the scene does not look like New York. The woman is a Paris street-type, the treelike stanchions of the elevated railway give the impression of a Paris boulevard, and the sidewalk is full of atmosphere that one associates more with Europe than with America in the 1930s. Our image of the city of this period is the one represented in Abbott's *Changing New York*, where in picture after picture (see fig. 2), bright sun, clean air, and sharp edges contrast with the softness in Kertész's work. Abbott favored frontality, symmetry, and pyramidal hierarchy of elements, while Kertész preferred diagonality, asymmetry, and the ambiguous juxtaposition of figure and ground.

When, during the winter of 1937, Kertész began to look around at the work of American photographers so as to understand himself better, one of those he looked to was Abbott, who was then preparing her own chronicle of New York. Kertész had known Abbott in Paris, where she had worked as an apprentice to Man Ray from 1923 to 1926 and then on her own until 1929. After she returned to New York in 1929, Abbott became obsessed with architecture, a subject that she explored independently until 1935, when the Federal Art Project division of the WPA absorbed her project and set about creating an archive on the architecture of New York (see fig. 3). Abbott was engaged to direct work on a series called "Changing New York," which finally resulted in the aforementioned book of the same title, and it was during 1936 that a great many of her own photographs of this subject were made.[7] Abbott

Figure 2
Berenice Abbott,
Christopher Street,
New York, 1949/50.

Figure 4
Walker Evans,
Pouchatoula, Alabama,
1936.

Figure 3
Berenice Abbott,
Department of Docks,
Pier A, New York,
1936.

embarked upon her project with a strong memory of Eugène Atget, whose photographs she had come to know very well in Paris, and her ambition was to realize a documentation of New York comparable to what Atget had produced for Paris. The key word in Abbott's vocabulary was "documentary," by which she meant "to reach the roots, to get under the very skin of reality," in order to create a picture in which "the form . . . must grow out of a clear understanding of the meaning of the thing photographed."[8]

Kertész, who had seen Atget's photographs at the Salon de l'Escalier (see Phillips, p. 36), rejects Abbott's emphasis on the word "documentary" in favor of "naturalism," which he has sought in his own work. Indeed, there are fundamental differences between Abbott and Kertész: Abbott is at heart a formalist, in that for her, content is the result of an interlocking network formed by the structural elements of the picture. Kertész, the naturalist romantic, wished the content to emerge from a web of relationships that are as much psychological as they are structural. Nevertheless, some of Kertész's Paris work, such as *Mondrian's Glasses and Pipe* (cat. no. 21), demonstrates absolute mastery of the formalist vocabulary. More at the center of his attitude, however, is *Satiric Dancer* (cat. no. 25), in which a rigorous formal system is amplified by the emotional impact of the figure. Abbott's highest aim was to delineate clearly the surface of the thing photographed; Kertész's first goal was to express his *feeling* about the subject.[9]

Kertész has said that he never met Walker Evans, the American photographer with whom he really had more in common than with anyone else on the photography scene in New York in 1936. Evans had spent a year in France in 1926–27, and he was honored in the year of Kertész's arrival in America by a small exhibition at The Museum of Modern Art ("African Negro Sculptures"). Evans, like Abbott, relied upon the government for employment. The period from late 1935 through early 1936 was a highly productive time for him: he created a dozen images that are among the most often reproduced in his oeuvre, including overviews and details made in Easton and Bethlehem, Pennsylvania, tenant farm families in Alabama, as well as *Pouchatoula, Alabama* (fig. 4), and *Mainstreet, Vicksburg.*

Evans and Kertész shared a love of the commonplace and a respect for the photographer's role as one who both arrests chance events and builds compositions through an interlocking network of

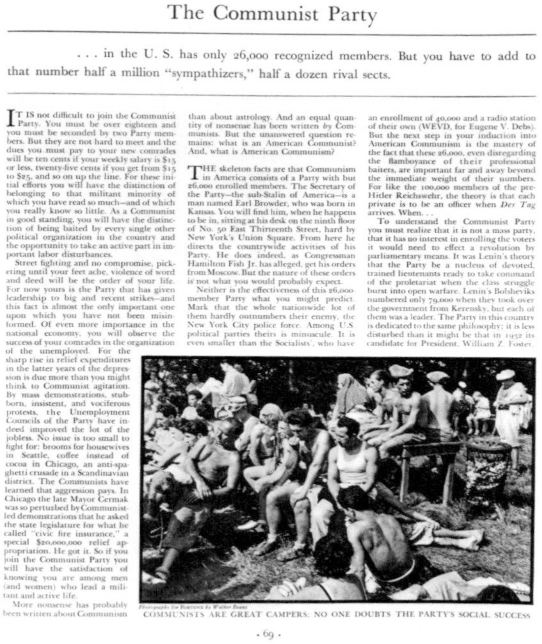

Figure 5
Fortune,
Sept. 1934, p. 69,
photograph by
Walker Evans.

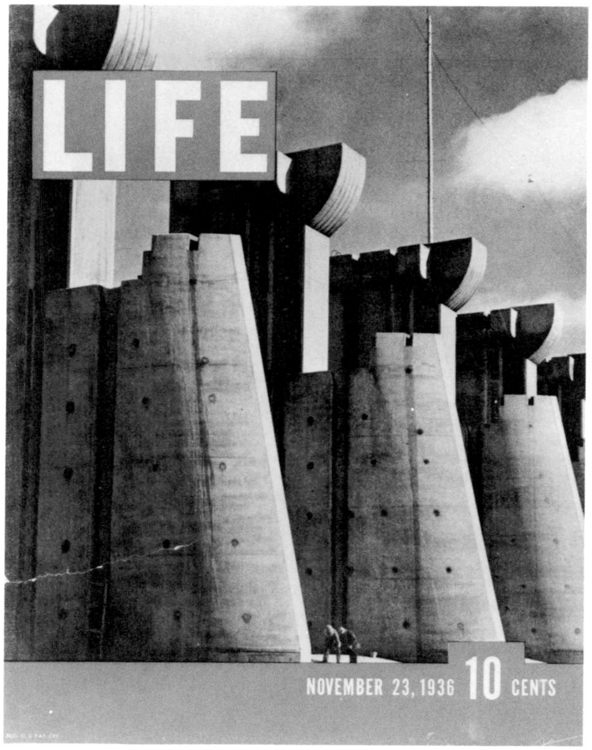

Figure 6
Life 1, no. 1
(Nov. 23, 1936),
cover photograph by
Margaret Bourke-White,
*Fort Peck Dam,
Montana*.

The Communist Party

. . . in the U. S. has only 26,000 recognized members. But you have to add to that number half a million "sympathizers," half a dozen rival sects.

COMMUNISTS ARE GREAT CAMPERS. NO ONE DOUBTS THE PARTY'S SOCIAL SUCCESS

· 69 ·

NOVEMBER 23, 1936 10 CENTS

shape and form. Evans, like Abbott, almost always photographed his subjects head-on, in bright sun, and on clear days, while Kertész preferred an oblique approach to observe his subjects silently and without their being aware of his presence. Both were reporters of the human condition who pursued their quarry with a rigorous sense of form. They also shared a belief in the virtue of experiment, an understanding that the machinery of photography is fundamental to its idea, and a high disdain for fussy technical purism. Both had high regard for the printed page as the ideal vehicle for presenting photographs, and both eventually became wedded in the 1940s to particular publications—Kertész to *House and Garden* and Evans to *Fortune* (see fig. 5)[10]—relationships that continued until the 1960s. Both men also felt their careers and reputations to have been atrophied by their publishing associations.

Kertész, Abbott, Evans, and many other photographers who were not newshounds but rather interpreters of experience, faced one major problem: editors and publishers seemed to be at a loss to know what to do with photographs that had deep emotional content or with photographers whose work was complex and whose perceptions operated on many levels of understanding. For this and other reasons, illustrated magazines were in great turmoil as tastes and needs changed and as editors and publishers devised ways to cope with new possibilities. Condé Nast's *Vanity Fair*, which for two decades was the foremost showcase for photography in America, ceased publication early in 1936. A few months later Henry Luce created *Life*, the first issue of which, dated November 23, appeared only one week after Kertész's arrival in America. Three months later, in February 1937, *Look* was established in direct competition, published in the unlikely location of Des Moines, Iowa. That very month *Coronet*—under the editorial direction of Arnold Gingrich—was founded in Chicago. Between them, *Life*, *Look*, and *Coronet* created a revolution in American journalism by adopting the practices of European picture magazines (see Travis, pp. 60–63). Heavy emphasis was placed on photographs as the principal illustrations. All three magazines challenged the dominance of the Condé Nast and Hearst enterprises in the area of mass-market illustrated periodicals.

Jack M. Willem, who called this the "picture boom of the 30's," published in 1942 an intensive market study of the types of pictures that were most popular with the public.[11] His research deeply influenced such newcomers as Luce's editors. Willem asked 50,000 men and women to select their preferences of photographs reproduced in newspapers. In doing so, he accumulated a file of 15,000 halftone reproductions marked as to preference. His findings were as follows: topmost were pictures of scenery and travel; second, pictures of places and objects in the news; in third and fourth places were science and animals, with "Leg-Art" fifth, and children sixth; after that were categories labeled "Personalities," "Persons in the News," "Historical pictures," "Society," "Fashions," etc., down to sports pictures, which ranked at the bottom. The conclusion one may draw is that most serious photographers of this period desired instinctively to photograph subjects other than those which the market researchers had decided that people really wished to see. The issue became quite simple: was the public to be given what artists create, or were artists going to be asked to make what people wanted to see? The distinction being drawn was essentially that between fine and commercial art, an issue that was never very far from Kertész's own mind. Photographers who supplied what art directors ordered resembled commercial illustrators of the prior epoch, while those who pursued their work out of inner necessity stood a chance of becoming artists. Very early on Kertész had gained a reputation for doing things his own way. But his attitude was not welcomed at the fledgling newsweeklies, where team players, rather than creative free-spirits, found success. The editorial policy at *Life*, for example, is typical of the prevailing attitudes toward photographers and their work.

The role of photography at *Life* is worth exploring in some detail, because the policies there had such a direct effect on the course Kertész's own art would take, and because it had such a strong influence on the course of photography in America in the 1930s and 1940s. The cover of the premier issue of *Life* was designed around a reproduction of Margaret Bourke-White's photograph of a dam at Fort Peck, Montana (fig. 6), a picture that fell into Willem's second level of preference, "objects in the news." The magazine's masthead named as staff photographers, in addition to Bourke-White (at the head of the list), Alfred Eisenstadt, Thos. D. McAvoy, and Peter Stackpole. Inside may be found a much less homogeneous mix of images than that suggested by Bourke-White's arresting cover and the accompanying feature picture-essay. Indeed, the magazine's edi-

torial policy, stated with unabashed candor on page three, in an article entitled "Introduction to this first issue of *Life*," explains why this is so:

If any Charter Subscriber is surprised by what turned out to be the first story in this first issue of LIFE, he is not nearly so surprised as the Editors were. Photographer Margaret Bourke-White had been dispatched to the Northwest to photograph the multimillion dollar projects of the Columbia River Basin. What the editors expected —for use in some later issue—were construction pictures as only Bourke-White can take them. What the Editors got was a human document *of American frontier life which, to them at least, was a revelation.*

Having been unable to prevent Bourke-White from running away with their first nine pages, *the Editors thereafter returned to the job of* making pictures behave with some degree of order and sense. *So there follow, not far apart, two regular departments: Life of the American Newsfront, and the President's Album. The first is a selection of the most* newsworthy snaps *made anywhere in the U.S. by the* mighty picture taking organization of the U.S. press (*emphasis added*).[12]

The editorial statement focuses our attention on the vast chasm that separated the picture-makers from the wordsmiths and picture-arrangers. The editors admitted surprise that Bourke-White's picture-essay was as good as it was. The phrase "their first nine pages" is very telling for it leaves no ambiguity about whose wishes would dominate the contents of what would soon grow to be the foremost magazine in the world devoted to photographs. If any party to the creation of the first issues of *Life* was guilty of taking liberties ("running away"), it was the editors, who manhandled the pictures to suit their own purposes. Take, for example, Bourke-White's barroom scene that runs across two pages (fig. 7). It is laid out to give the panoramic effect of being from one negative, but, in fact, two separate negatives are joined and figures are repeated with different gestures and expressions, most noticeably those of the blond child, who is the only person to show recognition of having been startled by the preceding burst of flash.

MONTANA SATURDAY   NIGHTS: FINIS

Figure 7
Life 1, no. 1
(Nov. 23, 1936),
pp. 16–17,
photographs by
Margaret Bourke-White.

Many readers protested that I had placed the baby on the bar. This I would never have done, even if I had thought of it. I might go so far as to place a baby in an empty baby carriage, if a picture demanded it, but any time I photograph anything as startling as a baby on a bar, it has to be there to begin with.[13]

The difference between Kertész and Bourke-White, as well as many others who did photographs on assignment to satisfy editorial needs, is that she would *sometimes* rearrange a subject; Kertész *never* would.[14] The guiding principal of his art was naturalism, and it was contrary to his style and character to alter his subjects to suit editorial needs.

In order to comprehend properly the role of the photographer in the service of the printed page, we must try to put ourselves in the position of Bourke-White in 1936 and, by extension, that of all other photographers in the same service, including Kertész. She was made acutely aware that text editors did not take pictures seriously, and that there was an enormous gap between them and the photographers. Each day she faced colleagues who thought of photographs as "snaps," as something equivalent to peanuts—each image identical in its message and force—as things to be devoured by the handful, with no apparent desire to acknowledge the style and personality of the individual photographer-artist. Picture editors at *Life* and *Look* were nervous whenever they worked with artists like Bourke-White. They

preferred to deal with the anonymous product of the "mighty picture-taking organization of the U.S. press," by which they meant the agencies that figured prominently on the page listing the sources of the photographs reproduced. Such agencies as Pictures, Inc., International, Ewing Galloway, and Wide World sent forth each week to publishers around the world dozens of images produced largely by free-lancers who were brought by luck face-to-face with a celebrity or a newsworthy event, and who relinquished the right to have themselves credited with the pictures once they sold the copyright to the agency. For *Life*'s editors, photographs were like parts on the factory assembly line; they were useful components in the creation of a product: "Because we know how pictures, well handled, step up a publication's reader interest (and consequently its advertising pulling power) we think *Life* will prove a sensational success," so the publishers advertised to potential buyers of advertising space in the magazine.[15] Someone at *Life*, probably Henry Luce, emulating Condé Nast, placed Bourke-White's name high on the magazine's masthead. But soon the initial high-minded philosophy was eroded by the editors' quest for authority and dominance. Bourke-White's position was far from secure; she was not granted the rights, freedoms, and privileges that photographers who worked for Nast and Hearst enjoyed.[16]

If at *Life* the editors assumed their wary posture toward photographers out of the fear and envy generated by Luce's high regard and respect for photographs and their makers, at *Look* the attitude was one of ignorance and contempt for the integrity of photographs. A typical cover from 1937 (see fig. 8) is sufficient to indicate the sensationalist character of its contents. Essays that interwove text and images, such as Bourke-White's Fort Peck suite, were not even considered part of *Look*'s format at its inception. Its photographs came directly from the files of agencies, and were rarely, if ever, credited to the maker, but rather to the agent who supplied the picture.[17]

It was into this milieu that Kertész was trying to find his own place in the spring of 1937. Kertész today recalls reading the editorial statement in the first issue, but he had already sensed intuitively the enormous difference between the way pictures were selected in Europe and the way the American weeklies had decided to go about it.[18] The arrival of Kertész in New York at this particularly fertile moment in the history of illustrated journalism

Figure 8
Look 1, no. 6
(May 11, 1937), cover.

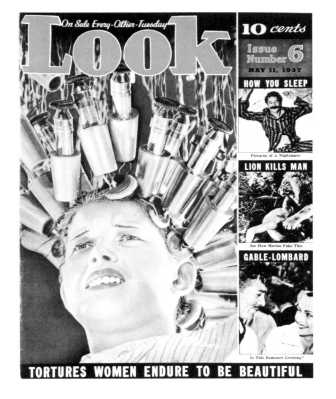

would, by objective analysis, appear to have been the ultimate manifestation of good luck for him. Between 1928 and 1936 in Paris, Kertész had helped to define what it was to be a professional photojournalist, an occupation that did not even exist before the invention in France and Germany of publications imitated by *Life*—the illustrated

newsweekly stuffed with halftone reproductions of photographs.

In Paris Kertész had elicited the admiration of his peers from the very beginning. In 1934 Pierre Boucher commented to Maria Giovanna Eisner at an opening reception for one of Kertész's first shows, "Not one of us here is fit to hold a candle to him."[19] Eisner later wrote that Kertész, then forty years old, "was respected and admired, with almost the veneration that youth is supposed to have for old age." When he arrived in New York two years later, he was already considered a "European Old Master."

Perhaps it is too much to expect for history to take a direct course, for, if this were the case, Kertész would have been invited immediately to work side-by-side with Bourke-White and Eisenstadt at *Life*. Whether he would have accepted the invitation is another matter. The process through which *Life*, in fact, elected not to hire Kertész, was not, in all likelihood, a decision made in a single stroke by one person, but rather was a collective decision that materialized gradually between mid-1937 and mid-1939. It was, in any event, made final to him in 1939, after he was finally invited to work on a project photographing the New York waterfront, a piece of reportage that never found its way into print. But in order not to get ahead of ourselves in the story, we should focus on what Kertész did with himself between the summer of 1937 and the invitation by *Life*.

II.

Kertész abrogated his Keystone contract in the spring of 1937, so far as can be deduced from alterations of his wet stamps and from his change in address and telephone number. Once freed from Keystone, he was able to pursue various avenues, the most logical being the network of friends and acquaintances from Paris who had landed in New York for the same reasons he had. The first person to approach Kertész was Alexey Brodovitch, who had emigrated in 1930 and who had spent the years 1930–34 as the head of the advertising design department at the Pennsylvania Museum School of Industrial Art. In 1934 Brodovitch was spotted by Carmel Snow, William Randolph Hearst's editor-in-chief at *Harper's Bazaar*, and was invited to become art director there, charged with the assignment of redesigning the layout and typography of the publication.[20] Brodovitch had curious working habits and was permitted to spend

only half-days at the office, with the balance of his time dedicated to industrial and poster design.[21] Already in the 1920s, uniform book typography had begun to be abandoned at *Vogue*, the publication considered most experimental in this regard, and Brodovitch carried this direction at *Harper's Bazaar* to its logical extreme by abandoning the use of any set recurring patterns in the layout.[22] Brodovitch also had an exceptionally good eye for photographs and was one of the few people in his business who could discern mediocre from exceptional work. He had known Kertész in Paris, recognized that a talent had landed in his lap, and immediately put him to work, coincidentally about the same time that another Hungarian who had a big reputation in Europe, Martin Munkacsi, also began working for *Harper's Bazaar*.

Sometime in February or early March 1937, Brodovitch gave Kertész the first assignment to be

Figure 9
Harper's Bazaar,
no. 2694 (Apr. 1937),
pp. 116–17, photographs
by Kertész.

published under his name in America. He was asked to visit the Saks Fifth Avenue department store to photograph what takes place after closing time. Thirteen photographs were reproduced under the title "5:30—The Curtain Falls" (see fig. 9). According to Kertész, Brodovitch was responsible for the layout, which placed the pictures butted edge-to-edge on the diagonal, leaving a void at the center for text, which was placed also on the diagonal. Utilizing the charm and wit for which he was noted in Europe, Kertész elicited the cooperation of employees, from president Adam Gimbel, shown striding out of the store in mid-step with a dress-box in hand, to a charwoman sweeping. The subjects range from a suggestive still life, "The Abandoned Glove Stand," typical of the understated visual humor for which he was noted, to the playful "Spooks on the Third Floor," showing a clerk with a sheet over her head, and to carpenters caught during a break in their work examining the price tags of ladies' coats. Most impressive of all are the tight compositions involving arrested motion that he realized of clerks draping cloths over shoes and other objects. In this suite of photographs for *Harper's Bazaar*, Kertész demonstrated his remarkable ability to survey a complex organism and to render it in pictures for which the text is largely an ornament. Kertész was accompanied by an editor, who offered suggestions as to desirable subjects, but the most striking images are those that manifest his own sometimes sideways, sometimes backward glance at the environment.

Travel is fundamental to Kertész's manner of working. His mind is charged by new places and situations. His life has truly been an odyssey for which photographs are the journal. Budapest, Paris, and New York are the landmarks on this chart. In Europe he often traveled from cities to the surrounding suburbs and countryside. In the United States, however, for six months he did not budge from Manhattan; then in June 1937 Brodovitch gave him the opportunity.[23] He went by car with an editor to the Philadelphia suburb of Haverford, an enclave of deeply rooted families. There he photographed the children of Mr. and Mrs. Nicholas Luddington, who were to be the models for various lines of children's fall apparel. The results of this session appeared in the August issue[24] and resemble Kertész's work of the Paris period. The pictures relate directly to his first book, *Enfants* (1933). In his Haverford pictures, his goal was to represent the children not looking like professional models, but rather in the most natural possible poses and activities.

When five- and six-year-olds are dressed up, it is usually for family events—church, a visit to grandmother's, or perhaps a wedding—and in the course of an afternoon, they end up spending a lot of time hanging around, waiting for something to happen. Kertész, in a deceptively simple strategy, allowed the Luddington children to do what they would inevitably do while waiting—to engage in self-devised amusements. Slyly and discretely Kertész arrested their moments off guard. None more perfectly represents this attitude than a photograph published with the caption "On the Dashboard" (cat. no. 122), showing the Luddington boy hanging from the door handle of a shiny new black Chrysler Imperial. Kertész thought enough of this picture to retain an example in his own archives; such was not the case for much of his work of this period. It is almost certain that Carmel Snow or Brodovitch had *Enfants* in mind when they asked Kertész to undertake this assignment, because elsewhere in the same issue of *Harper's Bazaar* are reproduced *Little Girl in a Tub* and *Brushing Teeth*, from the 1933 book. About those pictures Jean Nohain wrote in his preface to *Enfants* that "the 'children' of Kertész live with prodigious intensity and we are astonished when we think of the patience and skill necessary to accumulate so many types, attitudes and expressions."[25] Brassaï thought so highly of this aspect of Kertész's work that he made a point of singling it out in his 1963 "homage" to his old

Figure 10
Kertész,
*The German
Ambassador V. Hoesch
with the Novelist
Dr. Walter Harich
and his Wife*, from
Die Dame 57, no. 11
(Feb. 1930), p. 18.

friend: "He was capable of traveling miles to take photographs of children and animals, and to work at this for hours and hours."[26]

During the fall of 1937, Kertész was employed as well by Louis Marie Bude, art director of *Town and Country*, a sister Hearst publication to *Harper's Bazaar*, to do some society portraits and to photograph the Smithtown (Long Island) horseshow.[27] These assignments indirectly related to Kertész's European work, though he may not have found them exciting. In Paris, for example, he had made candid pictures at social events such as the diplomatic reception which appeared in the German publication *Die Dame* under the title "Ein Deutsches Ballfest in Paris" (fig. 10).[28] The principal difference, however, was the experimental, caught-off-guard posture of the Paris subjects, who were treated from a distinctly non-hieratic point of view. Kertész even saw some of his more peripheral Paris work reproduced here.[29]

There was a deeper logic to Kertész's association with *Harper's Bazaar*, *Town and Country*, and, in 1938, with *Vogue*. The reasons have to do with the role played by publications devoted to style and fashion in the history of photography in New York between 1917, when Alfred Stieglitz discontinued *Camera Work* along with the Photo-Secession Galleries, and 1945. *Vanity Fair* inherited from *Camera Work* the mantle of being the most distinguished publication in America committed to the regular presentation of photographs. Its publisher, Condé Nast, inherited from Stieglitz the role of principal benefactor to photographers, a benefactor, however, with motives different from Stieglitz's, but nevertheless a

genuine claimant as heir.[30] The far-reaching influence of the Nast publications on the evolution of photography in America has yet to be thoroughly investigated, and one of its most interesting chapters will surely be how Nast replaced Stieglitz as the chief sponsor and patron of photographers long before Kertész was even on the scene. Nast began to whittle away at Stieglitz's franchise on photography in 1914, when he stole Baron de Meyer away from Stieglitz's sphere of influence. De Meyer, who was given shows at the Photo-Secession Galleries in 1907, 1909, and 1911, was the last person from the pictorialist generation in whom Stieglitz had invested energy. It was Nast, however, who persuaded de Meyer to move from Paris to New York to become the principal photographer for *Vanity Fair*, which made him the first photographer in America assigned to a position of celebrity at any magazine. After the arrival of de Meyer, the hand-drawn illustration disappeared in favor of near exclusive reliance on photographs for editorial uses. While advertisers continued to use drawings to convey a direct sales pitch, photographs were elevated to an important role as the bearers of the principal editorial information. De Meyer worked for Nast until 1923, when William Randolph Hearst, through Carmel Snow, in a game of catch-up with Nast, stole de Meyer for *Harper's Bazaar*. Once Nast had replaced de Meyer with Edward Steichen, protégée and cofounder with Stieglitz of the Photo-Secession, Steichen's visability in *Vanity Fair* soon earned for him the title "the world's greatest living photographer."[31] This sequence of events points to the key ingredients that distinguished Nast as a benefactor of photography: he was the first person to organize commercially oriented publications around photographs as the central element of content, and to pay higher salaries to the photographers than they ever thought it possible to earn. Nast also believed that photographs were the result of talent, craftsmanship, and thought, and he rejected the claim of those who denigrated photography as a mechanical product. Nast treated his photographers with enormous respect and friendship, and made it clear that they were fundamental to the publications as he conceived them. This attitude did not go unnoticed in the world of publishing. It was in the spirit of Nast that Henry Luce, in founding *Life*, placed more emphasis on documentary photographs, in contrast to posed portraiture and the elaborately staged *tableaux vivants*

necessary for Nast's subjects. Luce, however, had insufficient conviction actually to place the photographers above the editors in either the social or the corporate hierarchy of his magazine as Nast did. Likewise inspired by Nast, William Randolph Hearst encouraged his editors in the same attitude toward photography.

When, in the summer of 1937, Kertész had to move in one of several commercial directions to maintain his income—studio portraiture, product advertising, or fashion photography—it was the last of these that seemed most promising. Naturally Kertész first looked to his friend Brodovitch and to Hearst publications, where he was attracted to the warm and welcoming embrace being extended to photographers. Shortly thereafter, in 1938, another of Kertész's European acquaintances, Mehemed Fehmy Agha, who had been editor in Berlin of German *Vogue* until it folded in 1929, arrived on the New York scene and was hired as art editor for *Vogue* by Nast through Edna Wollman Chase, *Vogue*'s editor-in-chief. Agha and Brodovitch became twin legends in the world of publishing; between them they had more influence on the look and contents of illustrated publications of the late 1930s and 1940s than any other two people. Moreover, it was in the light (or per-

haps the shadow) of two competing geniuses at layout and design that *Life* was born, where no midwife of equal experience was present.

With the support of Brodovitch and, initially, of Agha, Kertész's situation improved enormously from the dark days of late 1936 and early 1937. Between 1937 and 1939, however, he was given no assignments that provided him with the opportunity to appear in his own, most favorable light. He did come into contact with some distinguished families like the Luddingtons of Haverford and the William Vanderbilts of Newport, Rhode Island, where Kertész went to photograph for *Town and Country* some artifacts returned by Vanderbilt from various marine expeditions. Meanwhile, he saw his colleagues involved with projects more central to their own art than those with which he was spending his time. Kertész did not know that Brassaï was represented by an article on ballet dancers in the October 1937 *Harper's Bazaar*, but he did notice that certain photographers who had emigrated about the same time—like Martin Munkacsi, Andreas Feininger, and Alfred Eisenstadt—had begun to carve niches for themselves in styles they had pioneered in Europe, while he felt trapped in a dead-end street. Munkacsi was especially successful with his staged action pictures of models outdoors that sometimes have very eccentric compositions. One photograph of a model posed before the Statue of Liberty (fig. 11), made with the camera tilted to give the effect of the statue tilting, is typical of Munkacsi's style.[32] His gimmicks are diametrically opposed to the classic naturalism that was Kertész's unwavering hallmark. At this point Kertész realized that magazines of fashion were so concerned with tricks, illusions, and artifice that his pictures would always look understated, go overlooked, and be misunderstood in the context. He knew he had to look in other directions for the proper outlet for his particular mix of style and talent. Kertész began to think that *Life* might have something to offer after all. About this time he engaged a salesman whose job it was to contact publishers on his behalf; in 1939 he was finally invited to do a project for *Life*.[33] Kertész put his heart into the undertaking in a way that surpassed anything he had yet done in this country; the surviving pictures are important testimony that he wished to impress the editors with his versatility and ability to treat a very complex subject comprehensively.

The invitation to try an assignment for *Life* can be compared to the types of things Kertész was

Figure 12
Kertész,
*Self-Portrait on
Moran Co. Tugboat,*
1939.

first asked to do for the Condé Nast and Hearst publications; these had been conservative assignments in which Kertész effortlessly replayed a style and attitude that he had pioneered in Paris. They did not invite nor even permit experiment, and they were an elementary challenge for the photographer simply to work at his maximum power of observation. Kertész had been asked to engage in something that artists are often required to do: to rework old, familiar ideas of a favored style or period.

The *Life* assignment was another matter. Kertész was asked to devise, in collaboration with the editors, a project that would utilize both his talents and the magazine's formidable corporate resources to realize something very special. Today, Kertész calls it the "Tugboat" assignment (see cat. nos. 150–53, 161–63), but the range and character of the surviving pictures suggest that the project must have been broader in scope, including the waterfront in general and its various transportation systems.[34] The waterfront was a subject at the commercial heart of the urban corpus—yet, something so decentralized, so amorphous, and so complex that it defied encapsulation in a series of photographs. Despite its daunting aspect, Kertész decided to give it a try. This assignment was especially difficult in part because of an effect in photography called the rule of "inverse proximity." This simply means that the closer to

home, the more familiar a subject is to either the photographer or the audience, the harder it is to treat. From the point of view of the audience, the general rule is that the more remote a subject is from common experience, the greater is its appeal. In the waterfront series, Kertész was working with a subject that was very close at hand for him, as well as for most people in the New York metropolitan area. It was, therefore, a resistant motif that offered him the challenge to be original and inventive. The most that Kertész could hope to contribute to such a subject were his feelings about it. The problem was whether the audience, accustomed to being visually spoon-fed by the editors' selection of hot news subjects, would have the sensitivity to recognize and ultimately appreciate the visual sonnets of a poet whose message was intended for the heart through the eyes.

Kertész accepted the fact that he would have the best chance of accomplishing his goal if he utilized all of *Life*'s resources. He knew the subject must be observed from above, from the sidelines, and from the inside out. To do this, he first obtained access to a dirigible, which took him past the Empire State Building (see cat. no. 161) on the way to the Hudson River piers (see cat. no. 151) and trainyards. He also entered the inner sanctums of the boats themselves (see fig. 12) in order to comprehend the human element, and he wandered on foot to the dreary edges of the water around the meadowlands of Hackensack, New Jersey (see cat. no. 163). Kertész envisioned a complex visual narrative that ranged from high to low, from the inside and from the outside—leavened by his own powers to observe and to interpret.

There is nothing European about this series. We do not get the feeling in it that he replayed the style and attitude he formed in Paris. He faced the toughness, dynamism, and complexity of New York without sacrificing the human and interpretive element that so greatly distinguishes his European photographs. The waterfront series was an artistic and personal breakthrough for Kertész, and it will surely stand as one of the most accomplished essays in the early history of American photojournalism. About the challenge given to him by *Life*, Kertész has said, "I have the feeling that they wanted [me] to reinvent documentary photography, denying the European experience."[35] Kertész tried his best to do this by taut formal compositions with strong human content from which sentimentality is totally lacking.

The waterfront essay was never published in *Life*. This rejection came as a demoralizing blow to Kertész and was among the forces that turned him back into the Nast and Hearst spheres of influence. Kertész today believes that his waterfront suite never ran in *Life* because the advent of the war in Europe made other types of stories more attractive to the editors. However, thumbing through old issues of the magazine proves there was room for lighthearted articles that focused on subjects at home. There was perhaps another reason: Kertész has said that he was told by a *Life* editor "You are talking too much in your pictures." The statement is perplexing because all intelligent pictures talk, that is, they have a visual message that can be deciphered. Moreover, the conventional understanding of *Life*'s goals was to talk through the pictures reproduced there. One may ask why *Life*'s editors would reject the work of an acknowledged master. The editor responsible for this statement may have been trying to indicate that, with Bourke-White and Eisenstadt on the staff, *Life* had too many picture essayists and not enough photographers to pick up anecdote and spot news, which were very necessary types of pictures for the patchwork quilt that the editors with gluepots and snappy captions whipped into shape as a magazine. Kertész, however, took the comment in a very personal way and believed it was his particular manner of talking with pictures that was unacceptable. He failed to realize that editors did not really like any pictures that made their own jobs more complicated; they wished to avoid situations where a limited number of images were presented in a sequence fixed by the photographer. The older generation of photojournalists used film and printing paper sparingly by today's standards, and both Bourke-White and Eisenstadt were encouraged to make more exposures than they would have if left to their own devices. Bourke-White has expressed what this meant to her own working procedure and what she would not have done if the choice had been hers alone:

Usually, whenever practical, I try to make a point of covering, even if briefly, something representative of the editors' story ideas, and then to follow up with the pictures that seem to have the greatest photographic possibilities. And usually also, I make a very strong point of taking a few general shots to show what the all-over scene is like. Very frequently these general shots are not

photogenic and may never see print, but I feel that part of the photographer's function is to supply the people back home who are doing the writing and the editing, with every scrap of information that may help them, and frequently this information is conveyed better on a few sheets of film that may be unremarkable as pictures, than in a folio full of written notes.[36]

Kertész, by comparison, was sparing to the extreme, often returning with a dozen or so finished prints from a project.[37] If the pictures were to be used to tell a story, then he wished the story to be told as much as possible in the language of photography: light, atmosphere, point of view, and the other ingredients that constitute the syntax of camera art. Kertész, however, also wished the images to represent as fully as possible the sole manifestation of how he felt about the things he observed without the overlaid ingredient of someone else's words. As Ben Lifson has noted, "Kertész decided as the result of this experience that he and his decision was their loss since few photographers in the world were as well equipped as he to alter the course of photojournalism."[38]

The role of language—the ability to understand and be understood—cannot be ignored as a force in Kertész's life. During the eleven years he spent in Paris, Kertész became reasonably fluent in French; recently, however, he has said the following about receiving an assignment from Lucien Vogel, founder and editor of *Vu*: "When Vogel gave me a subject for a story in Paris, I said, 'Look Vogel, my French is not good, it's difficult for me to express myself.' [Vogel replied] 'Kertész, forget it. Your pictures talk for you.'"[39] Today Kertész continues to speak mainly through his pictures, and his verbal language is a mixture of French and English with imperfect, but understandable grammar. It is unlikely that he ever wrote or spoke either French or English better than he does today. Kertész is a man with no fluent spoken language except his native Hungarian. Despite the intelligence of his ideas, his diction and pronunciation impede easy comprehension except by the most experienced listener. His photographs became both a visual language and a replacement for the verbal facility he lacked. Because Kertész literally talks with his photographs, there was perhaps a greater reason for retaining his selection and sequence than with other photographers who sometimes supplied the raw materials for picture captions.

A FIREMAN
GOES TO SCHOOL

T HIS man walking across a ladder 35 feet in
the air is training to become a member of
New York City's fire department. He must go
through a 60-day student period in the instruction school before qualifying for actual
duty with the fire fighters.
Candidates also must pass a civil service
examination before becoming firemen. They
are paid at the rate of $2,000 a year while in
training, as well as during a probation period
of three months, which follows. It will be three
years before this student is a first-grade fireman, earning $3,000 a year. The fire chief gets
$11,500 a year.

8-Hour Day

The New York fire department has added
1,800 members since Jan. 1, 1937, to keep its
force at full strength while shifting from a
12-hour to an 8-hour day. The city has 8,761
active firemen. They may retire on half-pay
after 20 years.
The firemen's training school was established in 1882, has a teaching staff of a battalion
chief and 16 assistants. The two primary purposes of the school are to teach the men the
technique of fire-fighting and to get them in
tiptop physical condition.

Fireboats Help

New York's per capita cost of fires in 1937
was eighty cents, the lowest in many years.
The total fire loss for the year was $5,980,000.
About a third of all calls turned in are false
alarms.
The city has 362 fire stations. Nine fireboats
help protect the waterfront. From five to nine
men are killed each year fighting New York's
fires, and hundreds are injured.

(Erney Prince photo)

Page 21—LOOK—Oct. 25, 1938

Continued on Next Page

Figure 13
Look 2, no. 22
(Oct. 25, 1938), p. 21,
photograph by Kertész.

A purist, Kertész soon came to be comfortable
only in situations where his photographs were the
essential content of the publication and the words
acted like ornaments. An inveterate naturalist, he
disdained photographs inspired by the desire to
fictionalize reality. When he looked around for a
potential employer whose needs meshed with his
own style, he found that very few existed. One
incident in particular prejudiced him totally
against the newsweeklies as employers. Kertész
picked up the October 25, 1938, issue of *Look*,
where he found to his surprise seven photographs
that he had made in March 1937 reproduced with
a credit to Erney Prince (see fig. 13). Prince was
the nephew of Alexandre Garai, director of the
Paris Keystone agency, and the person who had
pursuaded Kertész that America needed him.
Look obtained nearly all of its photographs from
agents in the early years and practically never
credited an individual photographer, but Kertész
did not understand or accept this fact of life, and
this incident soured him completely on the possibility that his future was with the weekly publications aimed at a general audience.

He gravitated quickly toward publications with
specialized audiences like *Coronet*. Of pocket-sized
format, it offered in each issue the astonishing
number of thirty to forty, one-to-a-page reproductions of photographs. The contents on the title
page were divided into "Textual Features" and
"Pictorial Features," an arrangement that placed
equal importance on texts and illustrations.
Coronet was perhaps the only periodical in
America that wanted "talking pictures," and in
an editorial comment under that very heading
made the following statement of policy:

> *We become less and less inclined to talk about the
> photographs as we become more and more con-
> vinced that* the best photographs talk for them-
> selves, *speaking in a language of their own, and
> that* the less there is left to say about a picture,
> by way of explanation, after looking at it, the
> better it is as a picture (*emphasis added*).[40]

This was an attitude 180 degrees from that taken
by *Life* and *Look*, where photographs were
required to have interpretive analysis. In later
issues of *Coronet*, Arnold Gingrich made statements of policy that were far more liberal in their
acknowledgment of the role of photographs than
those of his colleagues at other publications. "The
photographs that appear in Coronet are there
solely because they happen to be the most interesting examples of their art form available. They
are selected on face value, without ulterior intent
to instruct, cajole or edify."

Gingrich asked Kertész to submit work early in
1937, and in the May issue reproduced the first
photograph by Kertész to appear alone on a page
as a work of camera-art in an American publication. It showed a circular brass horn hung over
a rush-seated chair, an image that had never been
reproduced before and apparently never has been
since. *Coronet* was the first *American* publication to
reproduce Kertész's work, all but one from the
Paris period, and all presented in the context of
mostly European photographers. Coincidentally,
there were also many Hungarians, a fact that

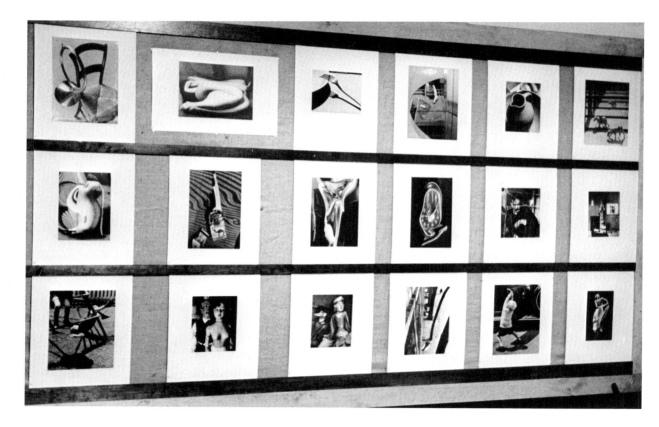

was accepted with the following editorial note: "Can we help it if the best photographs seem consistently to be produced by Hungarians?"[41]

In his December 1937 issue, Gingrich published a monographic feature of Brassaï photographs. Almost the entire picture section was devoted to someone whom Kertész had introduced to photography, and to whom he had handed over his list of clients when he left France in October 1936. The *Coronet* editor's comment on Brassaï could have been composed for Kertész: "He is abnormal only in the rare normality of his vision. We hold no brief against beautiful liars but Brassaï tells the simple truth so eloquently that he would be foolish to resort to trickery."[42] With a philosophy like this, *Coronet* would have been an ideal employer, but the problem was that it did not have a single photographer on its staff. Instead it relied on the work of artist–photographers around the world who supplied images through agents on a "pay-for-what-is-printed" basis. Many photographers received compensation for one-time use, but none of them were given expense accounts and high salaries as were the staff photographers at the houses of Nast, Hearst, and Luce. *Coronet*, as ideal as it appeared in theory, was not the pot of gold at the end of the rainbow, but it was a

charming and respected showcase for some of the best photographers in the late 1930s, and it was sufficiently admired to breed an imitator: *Lilliput*, founded in London, edited by Stefan Lorant, Kertész's old friend and former editor of the *Münchner Illustrierte Presse*.

Kertész found that building a reputation was a step-by-step process, especially when the basis for the reputation was to be the *how*, rather than the *what*, of making pictures. Kertész wished to develop a circle of admirers whose basis for judgment was: "Is this a beautiful picture," not "what is the subject of this picture." An important event in this context was his first American exhibition, which took place in December 1937 in the gallery of *PM* magazine, a trade publication established in 1935, addressed to "advertising production managers, art directors, and their associates." At the PM Gallery, located at 525 West 37th Street, Kertész hung sixty works (see figs. 1, 14),[43] twelve of which were credited as assignments for *Harper's Bazaar* or *Town and Country*, or noted to be "fashion" or "advertising"; the balance consisted of images of Paris. A short note in *PM* announcing the show stated that Kertész, fresh from eleven years in Paris, was "a pioneer among modern photographers."[44] This event was very important in bringing his work to some of the important figures in the world of art and photography. The mailing list of *PM* included the following influential individuals: Harry Abrams, Joseph Albers, Will Bradley, Alexey Brodovitch, Frederick W. Goudy, Walter Gropius, Paul Outerbridge, Edward Steichen, and Kate Steinitz —all of whom followed *PM*'s activities with enough interest to attend its gala birthday dinner at the Architectural League, September 22, 1937.[45]

Albers and Gropius, of course, were former Bauhaus instructors who had come to America after the school's Berlin studios were closed in 1933. Shortly after the dinner that brought them together in New York, the New Bauhaus American School of Design opened on November 9 in Chicago with László Moholy-Nagy as director. Photography played a very big role in the New Bauhaus curriculum just as it had in Germany, and an understanding of its principles was considered essential for artists and designers.[46]

How did the sudden influx of Bauhaus artists which coincided with Kertész's arrival influence his acceptance by Americans? The question cannot be answered with certainty because it involves the often murky process of tastemaking. What is clear is that the Bauhaus alumni were very rapidly assimilated into American culture and that they began immediately to influence decisions that concerned the arts of design. If we are to judge by the New Bauhaus curriculum in Chicago, formalism was the key underlying aesthetic ingredient. Surrealism was its stylistic antithesis and, in the politics of art, was the antagonist to form-follows-function.

It was, however, in the direction of Surrealism that Kertész's work was headed. He did not leave behind in Paris his oblique interest in Surrealism. The year the American Bauhaus was formed, Kertész produced the first of his American pictures that have been included in every anthology of his work since, and it has a strong Surrealist posture. *Arm and Ventilator* (cat. no. 120), made at the corner of 8th Street and Fifth Avenue in December 1937, shows the arm of a repairman at work on a drugstore ventilator. *Lost Cloud* (cat. no. 118) is probably the most often reproduced photograph incorporating the Empire State Building ever made. What gives these two images staying power is that they represent certain invisible forces at play with nature; they are pure manifestations of the power of chance and accident in the creation of a work of art.

In the same way that the tugboat series was a manifesto on naturalistic photojournalism, *Arm and Ventilator* and *Lost Cloud* are manifestoes of a kind of naturalistic Surrealism and were addressed to the growing gallery and museum audience that existed in America for Surrealism. Exactly one year prior to *Arm and Ventilator*, a widely publicized show of paintings by Max Ernst had been installed at the Julien Levy Gallery, where in 1932 Kertész had been represented in a group show devoted to European photographers, long before relocating to America was a serious thought. In the pages of *Harper's Bazaar*, it was announced, "The surrealists are exulting America [and] their opening gun is to be fired by Max Ernst."[47] That statement, attributed to Julien Levy, was quoted as the caption of a photograph by Man Ray of his large painting of a woman's lips hanging on a wall above a sofa upon which a woman stylishly reclines. Even though Kertész has said that he is not a Surrealist, he cast his lot with them in 1937 when it came to a choice between Bauhaus formalism and the compromised aesthetics of the managers at the newsweeklies. The significant differences in style and taste represented in these publications is indicated by the choice of *Life*'s editors to feature the painting of John Stuart Curry in their inaugural issue. In the art of museums Kertész felt more comfortable with a taste that leaned toward Max Ernst, but his heart always leaned toward folk art and handicrafts.

Kertész's Paris network was gravitating to New York, and the balance now stood at two allies in the Nast offices, and one, Brodovitch, with Hearst, which made it possible for him to receive assignments from both organizations. During 1939 and 1940 he divided his time almost equally between *Vogue* (Nast) and *Town and Country* (Hearst), while also selling individual pictures to *Coronet* (independent). In these two years he had not a single assignment from *House and Garden* (Nast), which in 1938 had given him more work than *Vogue*. Kertész was deftly playing the field, gaining an education in the mechanics of American magazine publishing, and discovering for himself how the art of photography could be made to jibe with the business of photography. Assignments from various clients led Kertész to experimental work in new directions. For example, the portrait of an unnamed stage designer (cat. no. 140), who is represented with a transparency projected across his face, expresses the man's role as an innovator in the use of projections as an element in scenography.

The art of photography was given far more distinct definition in 1938 than it had since the middle of the nineteenth century. In January Edward Steichen retired from his position as principal photographer for the Condé Nast publications, a position he had held ever since he was called to replace Baron de Meyer in 1923.[48] This change did not significantly alter the house preference for drama, glamor, and fictionalization in its photographs, but the absence of Steichen did tend to place the other Condé Nast photographers on a more equal footing. Kertész favored this change since he felt distance from Steichen's fictionalized tableaux, and he disdained the American photographer's preoccupation with high society.

Two events at New York's Museum of Modern Art focused attention on the character of photography as art. One was Beaumont Newhall's exhibition "Photography 1839–1937" in March 1937 to commemorate the centenary of photography, and the other was Walker Evans's landmark show and publication *American Photographs*, which took place in October 1938. Kertész was represented in the historical survey by five images, including *Distortion No. 172*, an American building façade from rural Connecticut, and several works from the European period.

Kertész attended the Evans exhibition, and he was sufficiently impressed with what he saw that he set about the self-assigned task of creating his own interpretation of small-town America as best he could through visits to villages in Connecticut, New Jersey, and the Hudson River Valley. A single aesthetic decision set him apart from Evans, and Abbott as well. He refused to confront his subjects head-on, and categorically rejected the frontal viewpoint. Instead, Kertész systematically chose to look up (see cat. no. 118) or down (see cat. no. 124) at his subject, or to regard it obliquely (see cat. nos. 128, 132, 135). In choosing these points of view, Kertész seems to have been saying that he is a stranger looking with fascination at unfamiliar subjects for the first time. In character these works are reminiscent of the first photographs that Kertész made from his hotel window after arriving in Paris from Budapest (see Phillips, fig. 1). He shared with Evans the desire to preserve the word "documentation" from fashionable vulgarization, and a deep commitment to the idea of letting the photographs be the principal expression of what is going on in the photographer's mind.

Between 1939 and 1945 one issue began to crowd out all others in Kertész's mind, and that was to supply in his pictorial diary an answer to the question: what is America? In one way or another, he had asked the same question of himself in approaching Hungary and France, and the body of photographs from both of his earlier places of residence amounts to a definition of national character as manifested in certain faces, places, and objects that caught his attention. His interest shifted from the exterior corpus of the city of New York, which had been a principal subject between 1936 and late 1938, to the quest for symbols of a broader American sensibility. He found them in images like the Armonk, New York, schoolhouse of 1941 (see cat. no. 167). Kertész attempted to express as well something of himself in these photographs and often teasingly challenged the viewer to answer the question: what's wrong here? In this case, the schoolhouse is set behind an enormous, looming tree stump that is the focus of attention.

A slightly later, untitled picture (cat. no. 168) is a photograph with carpentry as fine as that which went into the clapboard house represented. Here the humanizing element of an otherwise very abstract picture is the pair of homemade benches on either side of the door that demonstrate the differences in style between the cabinetmaker and the folk artist. Kertész had set about defining America for himself well before the exhibition "Image of Freedom" was installed at The Museum of Modern Art in November 1941. This show consisted of photographs by sixty-five amateurs and professionals from sixteen states. Kertész's Armonk schoolhouse was reproduced in the museum's *Bulletin*[49] and, when purchased for the museum for the price of twenty-five dollars, it became the first Kertész photograph to enter the collection of an American art museum.

There may have been confusion in the minds of some over the difference between the commercial photographer, which Kertész in some ways resembled, and the fine artist. But there was no doubt in his own mind that he belonged in this show, which also included such camera-artists as Imogen Cunningham, Wright Morris, Eliot Porter, Charles Sheeler, Aaron Siskind, Frederick Sommer, Brett Weston, and Minor White—individuals whose names are now as entrenched in the history of photography in the twentieth century as is that of Kertész. No photographers from the Nast or Hearst stables except Kertész were included in this show, the balance of which consisted principally of work

Figure 15
Kertész,
Sari Dienes, c. 1930.

by amateurs rather than professionals. Despite his *curriculum vitae* to the contrary, Kertész always considered himself an amateur and advised others to do the same. "I am an amateur and intend to remain one all my whole life long," he had said to Jean Vidal in 1930. "For this very reason I refuse all the tricks of the trade and professional virtuosity which could make me betray my canon."[50] The Möbius strip of continuity that connects amateurs and professionals in the art of photography is a subject worthy of a book-length treatment. It would certainly involve an exploration of the hypothesis that amateurs are granted freedom from the demands of paying clients and have only self-assigned goals to accomplish, while professionals are at the beck and call of those who commission their services. The supremacy of amateurism is premised on the idea that high art requires maximum freedom, and that because amateurs have more freedom they are more likely than professionals to produce high art. It is no coincidence that the vast majority of great photographers from Julia Margaret Cameron to Ansel Adams started their careers as amateurs. In America Kertész may have been classed by the tastemakers as an amateur—which worked to his detriment in the world of publishing, where client-oriented professionals dominated the scene. In the 1930s the rule of thumb was that amateurs used miniature (Leica-style) cameras, while professionals used large ones. The conflicting demands upon Kertész when he arrived here are documented in the 1936 self-portrait (cat. no. 112), where he is shown proudly holding the latest model view camera.

III.

The two years that André Kertész and Elizabeth Saly had agreed would be their sabbatical in New York expired on October 15, 1938. It is unlikely that they ever sat down deliberately to make the decision whether to stay in America or to return to Europe. Events in Europe and the wave of immigrants coming in this direction made it clear that it was inadvisable for them to return. Kertész has never said that he and his wife actually did wish to return, only that if they had wanted to return to France, they did not have the money to do so.

Kertész tried very hard to ingratiate himself with Americans who were influential in the creation of illustrated books and magazines. Frank Crowninshield, editor-in-chief of *Vanity Fair* from its founding in 1914 to its closing in 1936, had remained in the employment of Condé Nast after the magazine's demise and continued to be one of Nast's closest confidants. In 1938 or 1939 he saw a few of Kertész's Paris Distortions and liked them so much that even before meeting the photographer he proposed to do a limited-edition portfolio of them. Crowninshield's introduction to Kertész's work came through Sari Dienes, a woman Kertész had known and photographed in Paris (see fig. 15). Kertész was pleased at Crowninshield's interest, because in the early 1930s he had assumed Condé Nast's job of bringing new photographers into his prestigious circle. Unfortunately, Crowninshield died before they could meet, but it was indirectly through him that Kertész commenced a new series of distortions (see cat. no. 159). He used the same distorting mirror he had brought from Paris, and in one image replaced the female torso with a clock. The finished picture was reproduced in a striking design under the title "Vogue's-Eye View of Holiday Time" (fig. 16).[51]

The Americanization of Kertész was proceeding in a way not unlike that of other aspiring immigrants. He did not, for example, choose to live in New York's Hungarian enclave, situated on Manhattan's commercial Lexington Avenue between 68th and 78th streets, but about 1941 moved from his first residence, the Hotel Beaux-Arts, in the French enclave on the West Side, to a rooming house in Greenwich Village. The Village was as close to the experience of small-town America as it was possible to have in Manhattan. Just when his life seemed to be headed in a clear and positive direction, several devastating events occurred in Kertész's professional life in 1940–41 which, on top of other factors that had materialized, caused total paralysis of his creative instincts.

In November 1940 *Coronet* published its fourth-anniversary issue with a special section entitled "*Coronet*'s Most Memorable Photographs."[52] Kertész was represented by but a single work, labeled by the editors "Thunder on the Left [Bank]." Originally used in the May 1938 issue, it was neither a very fair representation of Kertész nor a proper acknowledgment of how consistently he had been shown in those pages. The editorial slight to Kertész may be placed in perspective by the fact that the now-forgotten Ernő Vadas (also of Hungarian origin) was represented by five

"ABSOLUTE time...was abandoned by the relativity theory," said Albert Einstein. We're abandoning absolute time, too. For time is out of joint. It's been pushed around, knocked silly. Super-speed plays havoc with it. A transatlantic air service, once something only dreamed, is about to annihilate crossing time. And *you* can tamper with time.

Stretch time out and take a jaunt to Finland, with its scrubbed door-steps, *voileipäpöytä* (the native smörgåsbord, as you'll discover on page 97). Laze down on Hawaii for a session of surf-riding—or shoot down on the China Clipper. Or perhaps let this year's trip be to Rome, where a new tempo has replaced "dolce far niente."

Boil time down to a minimum, and span the States by plane. Take up fishing (where and how is told on page 32), flying in a few hours to the hide-outs of sailfish or salmon.

Save time on an all-too-short week-end by packing your bag with non-wrinkling, non-crushable clothes that bob up fresh after hours in a suitcase. (You can see these on pages 100 and 101.)

Keep pace with time by reading, in this issue, the psychiatrists' de-glamourized, scalpel-sharp analysis of why women wear screwy hats, red toe-nail polish, and other frivolities.

Turn back the clock to Victoria's time, when women flounced around in demure prints like those now made up, paradoxically, into beach clothes. (These are on pages 78 and 79.)

And bide your time for a special occasion to come forth in one of the beautiful evening dresses, in twilight shades of violet, sketched on page 65.

Figure 16
Vogue,
May 15, 1938, p. 38,
photograph by Kertész.

selections. This was a signal that Kertész was perhaps not doing something right in the cultivation of his professional life in America. His photographs possess a quiet authority and an understated perfection of composition that cause them to be easily overwhelmed by more aggressive and illustrational pictures—a type favored by Arnold Gingrich, *Coronet*'s editor. Kertész understood intuitively the difference between himself and other photographers, but nevertheless apparently had great difficulty understanding why his less-talented Hungarian colleagues were being accorded more welcome treatment at *Coronet*, where the Hungarian style was as well appreciated as anywhere in America. (The Hungarian "style" was typified in the work of Ernő Vadas, Hein

Gorny, Imre Révész-Biró, and Gyula Halberg by an attraction to human interest subjects that often borders on sentimentality.)

Kertész granted *Coronet* permission to reproduce three more pictures of his that they had in their files, but thereafter submitted no more work for their consideration. His form of reply to the editor's slight was to withdraw—the beginning of a pattern that was to be repeated over and over again in his relationships with publishers.

At this time Kertész had every reason to believe that the house of Nast, through Agha and Vogel, was very favorably disposed toward him. He hoped this new alliance would be cemented by a new friendship with Frank Crowninshield. However, the June 15, 1941, issue of *Vogue* was for Kertész an omen of what lay ahead for him with this organization: the entire magazine was devoted to the art of photography in general, and to *Vogue*'s contribution in particular, in order to honor Condé Nast. About this piece of history, Crowninshield wrote:

> I think it can be said that, because of the extraordinary group of staff photographers which Vogue and Vanity Fair gathered together for more than twenty-five years (Vogue, throughout the whole period, and Vanity Fair during its existence of twenty-two years)—those magazines have attained a unique distinction among the periodicals of the world. The photographers developed by them have, in the pages of the Nast Publications, solved new esthetic problems—instigated major changes, and augmented the horizons of photography generally. . . . Mr. Nast's interest in photography has been persistent, knowledgeable, and profound.[53]

Crowninshield proceeded to chronicle step-by-step the incidents as they happened from the hiring of Baron de Meyer in 1913 and Steichen in 1923, to the arrival of Kertész's contemporary George Karger in 1937; Karger took the place in this list that should have been accorded to Kertész. Sixteen photographers were discussed and their portraits reproduced with a short biographical statement. Kertész was not among them, even though he had been a contributor to the magazine. Was his omission from this roster of photography celebrities willful or accidental? The latter appears to be the case. The choices were made largely by Crowninshield, who naturally directed his attention to the *Vanity Fair* years, making his cutoff date for newcomers 1937—a year when Kertész did most of his work for the Hearst publications; he did not begin regular work for Condé Nast until the January 1938 article, "La Fondue,"[54] about buying cheeses at Bellows, Inc., New York. Bad luck rather than ill will seems to have been the cause of Kertész's exclusion from a roster of names of photographers destined for short-term commercial success.

Certain of the Nast photographers that Crowninshield profiled, such as Hoyningen-Huené, Anton Bruehl, Horst, and Charles Sheeler, worked in a style diametrically opposite to that of Kertész, and their presence in (or absence from) such a roster is not particularly relevant to him. Others, Kertész's friends or acquaintances from Europe, such as Cecil Beaton and Man Ray, form the basis of comparison. But the inclusion of photographers who were much younger than Kertész and whose craft had itself been learned from what he had done for *Vu* in Paris offers good reason to believe that he was being ignored by those who should have known better. Remy Lohse, Roger Schall, and George Karger were exemplified as the path breakers and problem solvers of a photojournalistic style that was invented by Kertész. More than anything else, however, the oversight in *Vogue*'s special issue failed to reflect the fact that between 1936 and 1940 Kertész had been the photographer for more than thirty articles in *Vogue* and *House and Garden*. He had every reason to feel discouraged; he surely wondered if Agha, Vogel, and Crowninshield did not know enough to act forcefully in his behalf, who did? Incidents such as these implanted the seed of anti-Americanism that has influenced his relationship with this country ever since.

On top of these events, an unexpected blow was dealt by the government. The war in Europe escalated and the success of German U-boats in menacing the transatlantic shipping lanes resulted in a national security edict to curb the flow of information that would be helpful to the Germans in their offensive against supply ships. Kertész and his wife both held Hungarian passports and were considered enemy aliens by the United States government. Aliens were advised to be very careful about photographing any subject that may have had national security value.[55] Kertész took this advice very seriously because at this time he and Elizabeth wanted desperately to become naturalized American citizens. Elizabeth was growing more and more involved with a cosmetics business she

had founded with an old Paris friend and fellow Hungarian, Frank Tamas. Cosmia Laboratory succeeded in duplicating fashionable Paris scents at a time when European products were difficult to obtain here. Elizabeth became engrossed in the increasingly profitable business, which supplied an assured source of income that equaled what Kertész himself earned from his own profession. This was an additional source of tension for him, although what he most regrets about Elizabeth's enterprise is that it took her away from a promising career as an artist.

By the late spring of 1941, Kertész was in a deeply despondent frame of mind. Shortly after being fingerprinted at the New York Public Library, along with hundreds of others whose birthplaces caused them to be designated as enemy aliens, he stopped accepting magazine assignments altogether. Between April 1941 and June 1944, nothing of Kertész's was reproduced in an American publication; he withdrew almost completely from the world of photography until 1944.

Kertész continued to observe the rising stars of others, such as Feininger, Eisenstadt, and Munkacsi. Munkacsi was continuously featured in *Harper's Bazaar*.[56] Kertész saw a deepening competition between the editors at Nast and Hearst publications to be the first to discover or present certain photographers, who, for the first time since the 1850s in France, were being treated like celebrities. George Platt Lynes, for example, was given an exhibition at the prestigious Pierre Matisse Gallery, directed by the son of the French painter, which was an important outpost for European art in New York. *Town and Country* featured in November 1941 a monographic portfolio of his photographs that were presented not as magazine illustrations but rather as examples of camera-art. An editorial note stated, "As the first magazine to have recognized the talent of George Platt Lynes, we are proud to offer a variety of his unpublished celebrity portraits before his show at the Pierre Matisse Gallery."[57] As early as December 1937, *House and Garden* reproduced five Paul Strand photographs one-to-a-page as works of art, and in June 1941 Edward Weston's work was seen on the pages of *Vogue* for the first time. The hard-edged, concrete realism of Strand and Weston were the antithesis of the picture-style *Vogue* normally favored. Kertész himself questioned why this should be the only style of photography that Americans considered high art.[58] He began to perceive that the real world and the world as he had begun to shape it in his own mind were both being turned upside down and inside out. His natural solution—indeed, the only solution—to such profound upheaval, was to withdraw.

The *Vogue* incident demonstrates the extreme temporality of magazines devoted to style and fashion, and Kertész began to gravitate toward architecture and interior decoration as subjects of personal interest. Brodovitch, who now became Kertész's key ally in the world of New York magazine publishing, stated the paradoxical similarity between his job and Kertész's perfectly when he said, "I deal temporarily with temporary things. . . . Fashion is a butterfly, here today and gone tomorrow."[59] The raw materials of Kertész's art are very temporary things, but his art is directed toward an opposite goal—to stay what is fleeting, to arrest and make permanent a chance encounter, to give materiality to the immaterial. Kertész had spent his life attempting to give temporary things some permanence. He became very aware that America was then ruled by markets concerned with the present only insofar as it may affect the future. This was a very different attitude from what he had been taught as a child, since Europeans consider the present as a legacy from the past and come to understand the present by looking back. Kertész had great difficulty in accepting the American sense of temporality, and he began to wonder how his own artistic growth could occur under the conditions that were being presented to him. There is no doubt that if he could have returned to Europe in 1941 Kertész would have done so. The Germans, however, were occupying Paris, and only a fool or a madman would have gone if motivated by pride alone.

At the bottom point of his depression, on New Year's Eve 1942, an unexpected glimmer of recognition materialized. In response to a picture he saw reproduced, a newspaper reporter named John Adam Knight, of whom Kertész knew nothing, wrote the following article in the *New York Post*:

> *It was a great day for American photography when André Kertész landed on our shores—a greater day than many editors, critics and museum curators realize yet. Not having a flair for self-advertising, he is being "discovered," but slowly. Yet it is almost certain that in the years to come his work will be as much admired and appreciated as that of Hill, Atget, Stieglitz, Steichen, Weston, Strand and Hine."*[60]

Knight's comment is extraordinary: the list of names of respected photographers with whom history would indeed place Kertész is perfectly correct.

On the subject of the cessation of his photographic activity in 1941, Kertész has remained silent, except for acknowledging the government's war regulations. Still, there are signs of a discontented life. For example, the Kertészes changed their place of residence several times. The first move out of New York's French Quarter on 44th Street to a rooming house on East 12th Street, about 1941, was necessitated by an unpleasant incident that resulted in the Kertészes being locked out of the Hotel Beaux-Arts. It was also at this time that Kertész experienced the first signs of a hearing loss along with a recurrent vertigo that made it difficult to work in the darkroom. His physicians advised him to give up making his own prints. About 1943 the couple relocated to an apartment house on East 20th Street, then to an apartment at 31 East 12th Street (from which cat. no. 186 was made). They remained there until moving in 1952 to apartment 12–J at 2 Fifth Avenue, which has become famous as the location from which Kertész's often-reproduced photographs of Washington Square were made.

IV.

When Kertész and his wife were sworn in as naturalized citizens of the United States of America in the early summer of 1944, it was as though he were released from a cage. Catalogue numbers 170–72 represent his first work after becoming naturalized. Soon Kertész was in a frame of mind that permitted him to solicit assignments from the mass-market publishers for the first time since 1941.

He remained, however, from his own personal point of view, on the outs for the time being with both the Condé Nast and Hearst publications. He had, therefore, just one big-league alternative; he could try his hand somewhere in Henry Luce's empire other than *Life*, and there he really had just two choices: *Fortune* or *Time*. *Time* was not a

Figure 17
Kertész,
Factory Worker, 1944,
from *Fortune*,
July 1944, p. 134.

Figure 18
Kertész,
*Chemical Cleaning of
Winery Walls*, from
Les Cathédrales du vin
(1937), n. pag.

serious alternative for reasons that were given by Cecil Beaton, whom Kertész had met and photographed early in 1938 (see cat. no. 139):

> Time *invented a new technique of writing which gives even triviality a general importance, and by which it is possible to be rude with such seeming innocuousness that by now its editors are generally surprised at the resentment it sometimes inspires. A particular form of provocative and personal title-description has been created by* Time. *Under the photographs we read:* "*Conductor Reiner loves Spaghetti," "Professor Alma Neill, her rats got stiff necks too," "Cinemactor [sic] Smith, shaggily impressive.*"[61]

Fortune, then, was the logical place for Kertész to turn, for as Beaton commented in the same context, "*Life* shows what we can see, *Fortune* analyses what we cannot see. *Life* shows the outward scene, *Fortune* shows 'the forces behind.'" It is unclear why Kertész did not go to *Fortune* earlier. Founded in 1930, it was lavishly illustrated by top photographers with many one-to-a-page gravure reproductions. Bourke-White earned her reputation there and only later went to *Life*.

Fortune was a natural client for Kertész. He was never very interested in merely describing surfaces; it was his ability to penetrate to the structural essence of his subjects that gives the waterfront series their strength. Immediately after becoming naturalized, Kertész was invited by Peter Piening, the magazine's Bauhaus-trained art director, to travel to Chicago and other "smokestack America" cities. In Akron, Ohio, he photographed a factory where enormous tires for earth-moving equipment were manufactured. His photograph of a worker at his machine (fig. 17) has all of the compositional complexity of his best work. The picture suggests that Kertész respected this proletarian subject the same way Lewis Hine had. One of Kertész's last European projects was a suite of pictures published under the title *Les Cathédrales du vin* (1937), where one of his concerns was to express the contrast in scale between workers and the enormous fermentation vats that surround them (see fig. 18). In the Akron series he was able to work in the classic American style of treating industrial motifs naturalistically, heroizing the situation without idealizing it. In the fall of 1945, he did another assignment for *Fortune* on leather-workers William and Elizabeth Phelps at work, an

article for which Walker Evans also contributed illustrations, including one in color.[62] Kertész was not aware of it, but the editors of *Fortune* were considering the possibility of adding a serious photographer to the permanent staff. The nod was given to Evans, who had been a free-lance contributor there from 1934 to 1941. He made his debut as a staff member in the December 1945 issue with a suite of photographs entitled, "The Boom in Ballet." The principal difference between Evans and Kertész at this point in their careers was that Evans was abandoning former picture-making strategies, while Kertész was refining old ones to even higher powers of expression. Evans discarded the view camera in favor of the Leica, while Kertész put aside his Leica and explored the view camera. Comparison of their respective ballet pictures of 1939 and 1945 reveals that in 1945–47, Evans was deeply preoccupied with facial expression and bodily gesture to the near exclusion of all else. For example, in *Alicia Markova Rehearsing "Giselle"* (fig. 19),[63] the figures are isolated by a burst of flashbulb illumination using the classic technique of the newspaper photojournalist. The facial expressions captured are truthful to the 1,000th-of-a-second time in the day of those persons, but are not typical of them as individuals. In his *Ballet Dancer* (cat. no. 157), Kertész delineated the performer in a highly typical pose and gesture, placed in a context that was totally under his control. Unhappy with the expression of the dancer, he printed only the bottom half of the negative. In 1937 and 1938 Kertész was also very interested in the gesture and expression of anonymous figures (see cat. nos. 125, 130, 131), but he fastidiously built them into compositions that bear the signs of his own architecture. Evans, in his studies made on the streets of Chicago in 1946, cast aside the photographer's prerogative of structuring a pictorial framework around his subject in favor of shot-from-the-hip candidness, exemplified by page 118 of the February 1947 issue of *Fortune* (fig. 20).[64] Evans and Kertész in 1945–46 were headed along divergent paths: Kertész was set on demonstrating that the rational mind of the photographer counted, while Evans was demonstrating that the art of photography has a deeply irrational aspect.

There is no denying that in late war-time New York, photography was an extremely competitive world in which Kertész saw himself moving sideways, while others, some of less certain talent, were rising in visibility. Most of the newcomers,

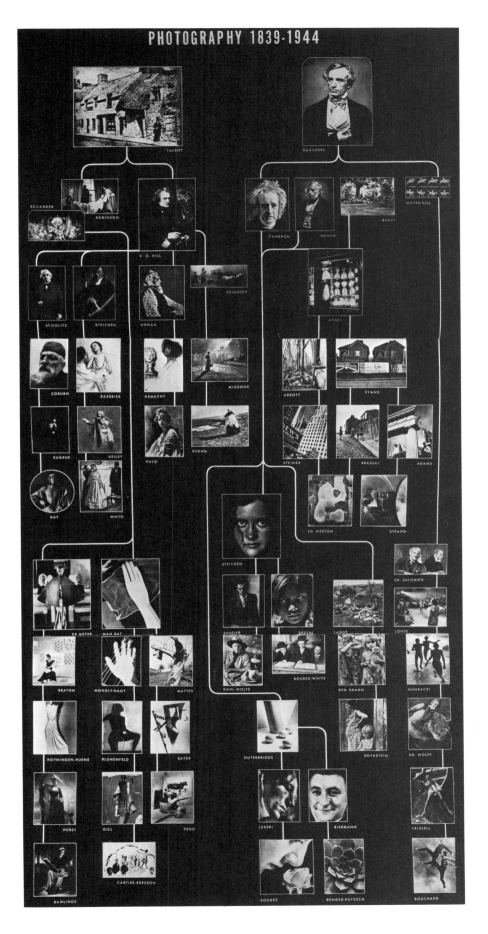

PHOTOGRAPHY 1839-1944

like Karger, Lohse, and Schall, were Europeans, while two of the youngest photographers on the *Fortune* staff, Irving Penn (whom Kertész knew and whose work he admired)[65] and Richard Avedon,[66] were Americans. In November 1944 final confirmation of Kertész's apprehension was delivered in that month's *Harper's Bazaar*, where Agha had just gone to work after resigning from *Vogue*. Agha's first project was to prepare a reprise of the special issue devoted to photography that had appeared in *Vogue* in November 1941. Agha's creation for *Harper's Bazaar* was entitled "Horseless Photography," and it featured an elaborately designed, three-page, fold-out diagram bearing the apparently definitive masthead "Photography 1839–1944" (fig. 21). The diagram was in the form of a genealogical chart that presented in two branches thirty photographers believed to be descended from William Henry Fox Talbot and thirty-one descendants of Louis Jacques Mandé Daguerre. Kertész was not listed anywhere, even though he should have been included in the line descended from Atget that included Abbott, Evans, Ralph Steiner, Ansel Adams, and Brassaï (who had yet to set foot in this country and was known here only through reproductions). Or, alternatively, Kertész could have been placed along with Henri Cartier-Bresson at the foot of the descent from Talbot. Agha's genealogy altered the history of photography, perhaps in just one way: it confirmed that Kertész was destined to be an outsider in America, and was to be thwarted in his sincere quest for admission to the fraternity of photographers acknowledged by their peers here to be undisputed masters of the art. Certain patterns were beginning to repeat themselves; the Agha article was the final confirmation. Kertész deserved a position among the inner circle, yet found himself at the edges time and again. In retrospect it is evident that he exemplified Agha's guiding idea as well as any photographer working in America at that time.

In his essay Agha gave the following rationale for his guiding idea:

> *Photographers should not worry about art and should stop thinking of their work as machine made painting: the mobile designers did not get anywhere until they stopped thinking of their cars as horseless carriages. . . . Some like to think of Talbot as the father of all the artistic "machine painters," and of Daguerre as the patron saint of all the scientific "straight" photographers.*[67]

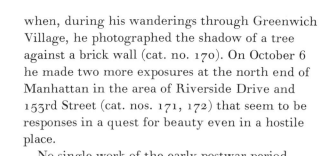

CONTINUED ON NEXT PAGE ▶

Figure 22
House and Garden 86
(Dec. 1944), pp. 56–57,
photographs by Kertész.

Agha was creating a new lineup in the team of players that had dominated American photography for several decades. About Stieglitz he wrote, for example, "It is difficult to see the real Stieglitz through the haze of fifty years of glory. Only late in life, in his photos of clouds and of Georgia O'Keeffe, does he grow to the stature which might have justified the adoration that surrounded him long before."[68] Kertész was observing a general realignment of values about photography, with an old order giving way to a new one. He personally felt more kinship with the self-expressive work of Stieglitz than he did with the sales-oriented style created by the Condé Nast and Hearst stables of photographers. Kertész wished to be a part of the new order, but he had deep sympathies with the old one.

Kertész's photographs of the mid-1940s are full of melancholy. With war raging in Europe and in the Pacific, there were many external reasons why that state of mind should be. His photographs began to display an emotional bent that has its roots in his Hungarian work more than in what he did in Paris. There is hardly a trace of the Constructivist side of his artistic personality. Mood rather than form became his chief concerns at this time. Nowhere else in the body of Kertész's work is his assertion "I photograph what I feel" more observably manifest in a single series of pictures than it is in those he made in July and August 1944 (see cat. nos. 170–73). A highly introspective melancholy surfaces in the pictures on August 6

when, during his wanderings through Greenwich Village, he photographed the shadow of a tree against a brick wall (cat. no. 170). On October 6 he made two more exposures at the north end of Manhattan in the area of Riverside Drive and 153rd Street (cat. nos. 171, 172) that seem to be responses in a quest for beauty even in a hostile place.

No single work of the early postwar period better exemplifies this than a study of a figure carrying a model schooner from Conservatory Pond to the boathouse in Central Park (cat. no. 173). Kertész has often reproduced this photograph under the title *Homing Ship*, a phrase that may be a metaphor of his own buried homesickness. He rarely gave symbolic or suggestive titles to his pictures; usually they are descriptive only of date and place. Kertész's artistic personality is equally divided between the urge to create symbols and the desire simply to observe and arrest chance occurrences for future regard. *Homing Ship* was made within two days of the fifth anniversary of the Kertészes' arrival on these shores, and a few months after they had become naturalized citizens. The idea of returning permanently to Europe was by now a remote possibility. *Homing Ship* is an instance of symbolic autobiography, but it also has fine carpentry to lead the eye to the subject. The reflection of the tree takes the eye to the gently curving stone curb that carries us to the row of benches and finally to the deep background. Through compositional elements that are instinctive rather than calculated, Kertész engaged the observer in the process of perception.

Not much more than a month after *Homing Ship* was created came the break that Kertész had waited nearly ten years for. Wolfgang Fyler, art editor of *House and Garden*, invited him to do an assignment that recalls the sort of thing he once did for *Vu*: a Christmas confection consisting of a toymaker's shop, a woman with her dog, and a child with toys at the Museum of the City of New York which appeared under the title "Blessed of St. Nicholas" (fig. 22).[69] During the balance of 1945, Kertész did several more free-lance assignments for *House and Garden*, all of which were room interiors or still-life arrangements (table settings) made with a tripod-mounted, four-by-five camera.

Kertész had an intuitive feeling for the ways in which architecture, both interior and exterior, could be used to lock in the elements of a composition. He had already demonstrated this in his

Figure 23
Kertész,
*Model with Room
Designed by
Grace Meyercord*,
1938.

Constructivist pictures of 1937–38 (see cat. nos. 124, 129, 132, and 141). He seemed genuinely to enjoy the intellectual game of creating a seamless continuity of shapes across the surface and visual pathways into the space represented. He also seemed to enjoy the many opportunities for ironic juxtaposition. Already in the 1938 *House and Garden* assignments, he recognized directions in which this could take him. In 1938, for example, he had been asked to photograph Grace Meyercord with the miniature living room and apartment model that she had designed for the Kaplan Furniture Company. The serenity and relaxation he was able to instill in the figure and the improbable juxtaposition of scale resulted in an image that has more lasting interest than the design work it pictured (see fig. 23).

Kertész's good fortune continued throughout 1945. Drawing upon the enormous amount of pent-up nostalgia for prewar Paris, he accomplished what no other photographer of his standing was able to achieve: a handsomely designed and reasonably well printed picture book. *Day of Paris*, a volume of one-to-a-page photographs issued at great financial risk by the publisher, J. J. Augustin, with long descriptive captions written by George Davis, appeared at a time when few photographer's monographs were being issued. Reproduced there, for the first time in America,

are numerous photographs of the Paris period that are now fundamental to his oeuvre.

The book was designed by Kertész's old friend Alexey Brodovitch; his layout for *Day of Paris* gave each photograph a quarter-inch white border and included a few photographs bled across two pages in a manner that avoids any diminishment of their character. Today Kertész finds the design so satisfactory that he feels it could be reissued in the same format. One American reviewer called the photographs "purely philosophic,"[70] which is as fine a two-word description of Kertész's style as has ever been stated.

In January 1946, shortly after Alexander Liberman was installed as art director of *House and Garden*, Kertész was offered, and accepted, a contract to work exclusively for him there. Kertész has never disclosed the salary but suggests that it was very ample. The copyright for any photographs published in the magazine became the property of the publisher, although Kertész retained the negatives. He was to be credited on every page where his photographs were reproduced—a condition that the editors religiously observed, and through which the published works can be unambiguously identified today. When one leafs through the pages of *House and Garden* of the 1940s, a caption with his name only confirms one's first impression that a particular picture is by him. Kertész's work jumps from the page because of his skill in choosing subjects, viewpoints, lighting, and the dozen other subtle decisions that comprise a well-designed photograph.

The decision to work exclusively for *House and Garden* meant that there would be less variety in the subjects of his photographs, but while the subjects were less diverse, Kertész gained the opportunity to travel extensively at the company's expense. Between 1945 and 1949 he traveled throughout the New England and Middle Atlantic states; he was given privileged access to the homes of substantial old families such as those of Winthrop Rockefeller, Arthur A. Houghton, and Dewees Dilworth, as well as show-business celebrities like Cole Porter. In 1949 he was sent even farther afield, to Pittsburgh, Chicago, and various cities in Texas. He was also given the opportunity in 1949 to return to Europe, where he traveled through England for the first time, photographing country houses. The highlight of this venture was a brief return to Paris. This visit, curiously enough, did not yield pictures that have so far entered his body of work, and it may be deduced that he felt he had little new to say in pictures about his former home, a kind of backhanded compliment to New York and the life he had created for himself here.

The number of Kertész photographs reproduced in *House and Garden* is astounding: more than 3,000 have been identified from the years 1945 to 1962, and the count is incomplete.[71] This may be reckoned as the largest body of photographs in one publication by a significant photographer of the mid-twentieth century. By way of comparison, during the twenty-one years that Walker Evans worked for *Fortune*, 372 of his photographs were published in the magazine, according to a recent count.[72]

A central question cannot be ignored. It has been said by some, including Kertész himself, that twenty years of his creative life were wasted in this employment. Is it possible that a photographer of Kertész's enormous visual intelligence could spend twenty years of his life and fail to produce memorable photographs in the course of that work? The answer is that he applied the same taste, intelligence, and good humor to his *House and Garden* photographs (see cat. nos. 176, 177, 183, 184) as he did to all other work. The points of view were chosen with great care and the objects in the room were subtly altered by the addition of a book, the opening of a door, the repositioning of a chair, or the use of light to give plasticity to the objects and a strong sense of space to the room.

The work Kertész produced in New York between 1936 and 1946 is united by at least one thread if no other, and that is the fastidious attention to detail. In photographing still lifes, interiors, and gardens, Kertész became so compulsively attentive to minor decisions that he was famous in the administrative corridors of Condé Nast Publications. He worked closely with one editor in particular, Brooke Astor, who took an immediate liking to him and greatly admired his perfectionism; because of this admiration, Astor had the patience to endure what were often hours of preparation on location while the light or the weather became perfect for Kertész to realize the pictorial idea he had in mind.[73] He exerted such a powerful and charismatic influence that Astor wrote the following about her association with him in her autobiography:

We were fortunate in having really great photographers; some of them were fashion photographers who only photographed for H & G occasionally, as it bored them. They preferred live models rather than empty rooms. However, André Kertész was a photographer who rejoiced in whatever his camera could catch. We often worked together, and sometimes I grew impatient when he would insist on waiting all day to photograph a garden to catch the afternoon shadows, or the angle of a book left carelessly on a chair—his signature. With his unerring eye for just the right object and his total dedication to perfection, he taught me a great deal.[74]

Examining a few of the photographs that Kertész made for *House and Garden* leads to a better understanding of their character and their relationship to his prior work. In the fall of 1946, he was asked to go to the home of Joseph B. Platt in Little Compton, Rhode Island. Platt was a consulting editor at the magazine, and this connection made Kertész's visit particularly easy, in that he did not have the usual first hurdle of this type of work, which was to establish a friendly relationship with the owner of the property he photographed. We sense that Platt's and Kertész's tastes may have been very similar, judging from the game room of the house, where Kertész found a carved wooden relief of a fat circus angel hanging on the wall above a watchmaker's sign in the shape of an outsize pocket watch (see cat. no. 176). When taken out of their original context, first by the collector and then, in a second layer of interpretation, by the photographer, the objects assume a lively new appearance. It was the talent to give life to immobile subjects that earned Kertész the great reputation he had at *House and Garden*. Each element represents a seriously considered decision, and none is more important than where he chooses to place his camera. The viewpoint puts the table in the picture as a diagonal element that meets the comparably oblique line established by the stone wall on which the angel hangs. Kertész worked hard to minimize frontality and to realize complex diagonal compositions that lead the eye from foreground to background by an interlocking network of elements (see cat. nos. 161, 162).

Kertész showed unswerving consistency in his assignment work of this period, as is evident, for example, in a single component in the complexion of his style—the love of outsize objects and the great respect he had for the power of decontextualization in creating new forms of cultural meaning. When he visited the apartment of the *couturier* Mainbocher in the winter of 1948, he saw an improbable juxtaposition of a zebra-skin rug and a shelf of what are known to librarians as "elephant" folio books (see cat. no. 183). Kertész loves books of all varieties, and he has often included one or more in his pictures as a form of signature. The opportunity to encounter a rank of books suspended in air on their sides like some odd still-life arrangement delighted the photographer, and he built the subject he was assigned to take around the strangely arranged foreground element; the architecture of the shelves, the doorframe, and the framed picture on the left wall form an network of lines that lead to the nominal center of interest, the bedroom.

Two months later another odd collection of objects in the apartment of Charles G. Shaw caught Kertész's eye (see cat. no. 184). In one room an outsize sign for a Paris glove shop is the center of interest around which the objects are placed. The apartment was chock-a-block full of Shaw's collection of carvings representing American Indians, like the one barely visible on the top shelf here. Kertész was entranced by these examples of folk art, an interest nurtured during his childhood in Hungary.

Kertész has always tended to distinguish in conversation between his assignment work and certain "private" work he did at odd moments during the course of an assignment, perhaps en route to a location, or on the return. The two photographs discussed above (cat. nos. 183, 184) show how blurry the line may have been between what was genuinely private and that which was central to the editorial content of an assignment. The *House and Garden* assignments increased Kertész's interest in architectural subjects of all varieties, but because works of 1937–38 already demonstrate a strong natural inclination in this direction, this cannot be called a significant departure.

Kertész made a photograph in the spring of 1947 of the Manhattan Bridge observed from Brooklyn down a narrow street through an overhead passageway (cat. no. 179). It is the most often reproduced picture by Kertész made during his *House and Garden* period, and for good reason. Its elements equal in drama and complexity his Eiffel Tower views of the Paris period. We see here, however, the repetition of certain threads established in the published architectural work: the use of an outsize motif, here the clock with Roman numerals (which recalls the clockface in cat. no. 176), and the reliance on an interlocked web of

architectural elements to tie the picture together.

The ambiguity between a private element and for-hire assignments in Kertész's work is perhaps most evident in a picture he made from the back window of a house located on the Vanderbilt-Morgan row that faces the East River from a prime vantage point on Sutton Place at 57th Street. In a private moment Kertész chose to point his tripod-mounted, four-by-five camera out a servant's window to observe the unromantic vista to be had when facing west toward the Manhattan span of the Queensborough Bridge, where a pair of now-demolished gas storage tanks on York Avenue between 60th and 62nd streets dominated the background (see cat. no. 180). Such lean industrial subjects bear little relationship to the objects of high value inside the residence, but Kertész chose here to turn his back on fine art and look out the window to observe two types of American folk art: ironwork and sheet-metal work. In the foreground are the sculpted shapes of tin chimneys, and in the background is the creation of anonymous steelworkers who thought they were just constructing the framework of a gas storage tank, but which for Kertész becomes an abstract sculpture. Thus, the photographer established unexpected but archetypal connections between industrial architecture, the folk art collected by Joseph Platt (cat. no. 176), the oversized books collected by Mainbocher (cat. no. 183), and the sculpture collected by Charles Shaw (cat. no. 184).

Between 1948 and 1952, according to Kertész, he was responsible for transforming the look of *House and Garden*. He made photographs that are not mere records of the surfaces and appearances of what he observed, but rather intelligent, highly structured visual poems addressed to places, objects, and spaces. Kertész's ability to project his feelings onto the homes and objects he was asked to photograph is a talent that was valued by owners and editors alike. Interiors that have been orchestrated by professional designers often lack in their actuality the warmth and humanity that Kertész was able to impart to the rooms through his carefully designed pictures.

Kertész went about his work striving for balance, for the articulation of revelatory details, and for a quality of light and viewpoint that give the objects a presence without apparent artifice. He left nothing to accident in his interiors and still lifes; he made compositional decisions according to the principal of including only what was necessary to reveal the subject perfectly. He wished each picture to have its own individual character and to stand on its own as a photograph, deserving attention for reasons independent of the character of the subject illustrated. The natural effects he sought are exactly opposite the hyperbole and fiction that had become the trademark of the *Vanity Fair* style, exemplified in the work of Baron de Meyer, Steichen, and Hoyningen-Heuné. Their picture-fictions were aimed at making one believe that set-ups that existed for only a few hours in the studio are a true reflection of life. Kertész scorns those who invent the subjects of

their pictures, and he believes that the noblest task of the photographer is to observe intelligently subjects that exist before the photographer arrives. Cecil Beaton is among the few who understood, appreciated, and articulated the high merit of this aspect of Kertész's work:

> *Kertész had no pretentions about his contribution to photography, and those brilliant "interiors" for which he was renowned, taken for the Condé Nast publications, are not among those he chose to put into his book*, André Kertész: Sixty Years of Photography.[75]

V.

Kertész's initial deep infatuation with imparting plasticity and visual intelligence to the spaces and possessions of other people did not last forever. By the early 1950s he was spending too much of his time in this pursuit, and he was being transformed in the process into something resembling a mad philosopher. The pleasure of making a chance discovery while wandering through the streets of Greenwich Village or of observing the horizon of streets and buildings, however, had never left him. In the spring of 1950, for example, he passed a watchmaker's shop on Christopher Street and made an interpretation of it (cat. no. 185) in ignorance of Berenice Abbott's image of the same site exactly contemporaneous (fig. 2). He created his negative, transforming the figure into a transient shadow. In the photograph he intelligently utilized the improbable juxtaposition of a shabby delivery cart whose spoked wheels provide a counterpoint to the face and hands of the clock.

Kertész's day-in-day-out exposure to decorative objects that represented taste and rarity redirected what he chose to observe as he prowled through the streets. Moving from objects that had been blessed with the benediction of good taste, or that had been arranged for purposes of style rather than of function, he began to focus on the types of objects and structures that were totally opposite in nature and feeling. Typical of this pendulum-like shift in his focus is a series of studies of water towers positioned on the roofs of New York buildings (see cat. no. 186). They are objects of totally functional design whose purpose is to boost the water pressure on the upper floors of buildings above five stories in height and to hold water for fire-preventive sprinkler systems. Made utilizing craftsmanship that goes back to the nineteenth

century, these silolike shapes are a form of folk art not dissimilar to the sheetmetal forms and ironwork found in catalogue number 180. In executing this suite Kertész also utilized a type of photographic equipment that he did not customarily have the opportunity to use in the *House and Garden* work, the telephoto lens. In certain Paris pictures he had used a primitive, long focal length lens that he had specially altered to fit on his camera, so this was not a significant departure from past practice.

Certain Kertész photographs of the early 1950s demonstrate a distinct longing for the freedom to prospect more regularly through the streets of New York for suitable subjects than his demanding *House and Garden* schedule allowed. Catalogue number 187 is a very tough-minded and self-consciously inquisitive picture that in its bare elements is more like certain Paris images of twenty-five years earlier than anything he had done recently in New York. A figure observed on a flight of stairs was a favorite Paris motif, and at first glance one believes that this *is* Paris and not New York. Kertész, however, never commenced a photograph in Paris with such an uncompromising and prominent foreground element as the grotesquely out-of-focus railing seen here. He continued to experiment both in his free time and while traveling for *House and Garden*, although opportunities to do so on assignment seemed to become fewer. One notable example of a personal experiment made on assignment is a composition created in a cellar in Williamsburg, Virginia (see cat. no. 188). This picture of a room shrouded in mystery is comparable to that of the Poughkeepsie station (see cat. no. 124) in its power to arrest one's attention for reasons that defy explanation. Part of the attractiveness of this image lies in the simultaneous convergence of tactile and optical elements. We appreciate the photograph not only for what we see, but also for what we read into it from our own individual experiences.

Possibly the most significant event that influenced Kertész's work at this time was his move to a new apartment; in 1952 Elizabeth and he relocated to a brand new building at 2 Fifth Avenue. It had a balcony and windows overlooking Washington Square Park, with other views facing west and slightly north. Kertész passed many hours contemplating both the stationary and the passing scene that could be observed from his windows. Two styles emerge in these pictures, one Constructivist, and one situationalist. Certain images display the love of building a composition, piece by piece, like a theoretical jig-saw puzzle that is assembled line by line, shape by shape, and where everything we see is necessary to the image before us (see cat. no. 189). Others, such as catalogue numbers 190 and 191, are the result of a flash of the mind, and cause us to marvel at how well a chance occurrence has been arrested. *Washington Square, Winter,* of 1954 (cat. no. 192), is a picture made from a stationary position by a photographer awaiting an event like a hunter stalking his quarry. We recognize the utter necessity of the walking figure, without which the photograph would be banal. In a picture like this, we well understand what Kertész meant when he said to Joseph Platt in 1946, "Everything in photography is my specialty."[76]

Hilton Kramer has written something about Kertész's Hungarian photographs that is true of all of his work:

> *Like many young and aspiring artists, before and since, Kertész lived a divided life, shuttling between arid routine and precious hours of release. The tensions inherent in this situation— between the office and the street, between city obligations and country pleasures, between the bourgeois household and the private world of the darkroom . . . —form the essential subtext of every one of these early pictures.*[77]

Kertész's life, it seems, was spent continuously fighting an inner battle between the divergent pressures of his own work and what he was asked to do by others. He appears to be an artist who is motivated by the conflicting forces of life itself, and who assumes a personal responsibility for

giving order to this conflict, without which his art as we see it could not exist.

Was New York, considered as a collection of streets, buildings, objects, and their owners and inhabitants necessary for the creation of Kertész's art? Apparently so, and, furthermore, it may be postulated that in Paris his will to create had already begun to weaken by 1933. This was a time when fewer and fewer artistic advances were being made and when ideas that he formed a decade earlier were being repeated continuously. His move to New York was essential for further artistic growth to occur. Growth of any kind does not come without a certain amount of pain, and it is the pain, however essential it was to his art, that Kertész remembers most vividly today.

Surprisingly, the first unambiguous recognition that Kertész had made a major contribution to art came not from New York but from Chicago. Kertész was asked by Carl O. Schniewind, Curator of Prints and Drawings at The Art Institute of Chicago, to select approximately fifty photographs for display at the museum between June 7 and July 14, 1946. According to Kertész, the show consisted of mainly European work, but New York photographs were also included. Kertész has said that the show was the most important event that had happened to him since his arrival in this country. But even today he remembers that it was not reviewed in the local newspapers.

André Kertész lives today at the age of ninety in the same few rooms he has occupied for the last thirty years. The photographs he made in Hungary and France between 1912 and 1936 have gained for him a reputation somewhere between hero and prophet. The work he has made in New York, except for a dozen or so often-reproduced images (cat. nos. 114, 116, 118–21, 124, 158, 159, 173, 179, 188, 192), is generally not as well understood as is the European work. This is in part because, for reasons of his own creation, Kertész's fame abroad was cultivated by certain myths that he did not discourage. Prophetic artists have rarely entered history books admired for their power to generate truth about their own lives; rather, they are revered for their awesome ability to project an aesthetic sensibility forward in time. Kertész is exemplary of this rule, for we know more about the personal and intellectual lives of photographers half his age and a fraction of his fame than we know about this man. He has entrusted his biography to no one, and our knowledge of his life is but a schematic diagram.

Kertész has lived in New York longer than in any of the other places he has called home, but when he is asked, "Are you considered a prophet at home?" he replies, "No, I am just a voice speaking in the wilderness." His self-image is that of someone who has been ignored or misunderstood most of his creative life, and this fact is central to an understanding of his art.

Notes

1. U.S. Department of Justice, Immigration and Naturalization Service, *Petition for Naturalization*, no. 21263, Oct. 21, 1937. Elizabeth here recorded her family name as Saloman.

2. For a survey of the photographs made under various public programs, see Hank O'Neal, *A Vision Shared: A Classic Portrait of America and Its People, 1935–1943* (New York, 1976).

3. Anna Fárová, *André Kertész*, adapted by Robert Sogalyn (New York: Paragraphic Books, [1966]), p. 20.

4. André Kertész to Weston J. Naef, Jan. 1983. Much information in this essay was gathered through a series of interviews between the author and Mr. Kertész in 1983 and 1984.

5. Ben Lifson, "Kertész at Eighty-Five," *Portfolio* 1, no. 2 (June–July 1979), pp. 58–64.

6. In the last months of 1936 and the first part of 1937, Kertész began assembling photographs for a book on New York. The project was rejected by two publishers.

7. The New Gallery of Contemporary Art, *Berenice Abbott: Documentary Photographs of the 1930's*, exh. cat. by Michael Sundell (Cleveland, 1980), p. 6.

8. Berenice Abbott, "Civic Documentary Photography," quoted in Sundell (note 7), p. 4.

9. Denes Devenyi, "Kertész: Denes Devenyi Interviews the Father of 35mm Vision," *Photolife*, Jan. 1978, p. 12.

10. Wellesley College Museum, *Walker Evans at "Fortune," 1945–1965*, exh. cat. by Lesley K. Baier (Wellesley, Mass., 1977).

11. Jack M. Willem, "Popular Picture Subjects," in *The Complete Photographer: A Complete Guide to Amateur and Professional Photography*, known as *The Encyclopedia of Photography*, ed. Willard D. Morgan, vol. 8 (New York: National Educational Alliance, Inc., 1943), pp. 2933–34.

12. "Introduction to this first issue of *Life*," *Life* 1, no. 1 (Nov. 23, 1936), p. 3.

13. Margaret Bourke-White, "Assignments for Publication," in *The Complete Photographer: A Complete Guide to Amateur and Professional Photography*, known as *The Encyclopedia of Photography*, ed. Willard D. Morgan, vol. 1 (New York: National Educational Alliance, Inc., 1942), p. 312.

14. In "Paradox of a Distortionist," *Minicam Photography* 2, no. 12 (Aug. 1939), Arthur Browning quoted Kertész: "I see and plan each subject differently. Lighting, pose, and composition are kept true to life. . . . I try to give an honest, unbiased representation of what I see" (p. 41).

15. See *Life* 1, no. 1 (Nov. 23, 1936), p. 72.

16. Bourke-White (note 13) described her procedure as follows: "The usual procedure on receiving an assignment is to talk to everybody involved before leaving. This usually includes at least two editors, and in the case of a magazine such as *Life*, and sometimes three or four. It may include a writer, a researcher, who may have been engaged previously in collecting data, and once in a while an art editor who may have some special idea of layout, although this more often comes after the work is done" (pp. 312–13).

17. Erney Prince and his uncle Alexandre Garai were responsible for Kertész's decision to leave Paris for New York on what was described as a sabbatical of 18 to 24 months, after which time Kertész intended to return to Paris. But when Prince's relationship with the Keystone agency dissolved in the spring of 1937, Kertész began prospecting for his own assignments. It appears that he was also represented during this period by various free-lance picture representatives, including a man named Miller. On this topic, see Colin Ford, *André Kertész: An Exhibition of Photographs from the Centre Georges Pompidou, Paris* (London: Arts Council of Great Britain, 1979), p. 22; Carole Kismaric, *André Kertész* (Millerton, N. Y.: Aperture, 1977), p. 7; Fárová (note 3), p. 20; and Bela Ugrin, "Kertész's Photography in Full Bloom," *Houston Post*, Jan. 2, 1983, sec. G, pp. 12–13.

18. The practice of European picture editors such as Lucien Vogel has been characterized by John Szarkowski in *André Kertész, Photographer* (New York: The Museum of Modern Art, 1964): "The editors of that time were inclined to regard the photographer's work as a finished product, not as the raw material to be used in developing a story. Basic editing was done by the photographer himself, who would deliver those photographs which seemed to him to tell the story. On the average, Kertész recalls, if ten pictures were submitted, eight would be used" (p. 6).

19. Quoted in Maria Giovanna Eisner, "Citizen Kertész," *Minicam Photography* 7, no. 10 (June 1944), p. 28. Eisner also stated that Kertész "is one of our great photographers . . . yet strangely enough, [he] is something of a 'forgotten man' here in America," (p. 28).

20. George Herrick, "Alexey Brodovitch," *Art and Industry* 29, no. 173 (Nov. 1940), pp. 164–69.

21. Brodovitch was both a creative artist and an observer of the work of others, as shown, for example, by the exhibition and catalogue he organized and produced, *New Poster* (Philadelphia: The Franklin Institute, 1937).

22. Herrick (note 20), p. 165.

23. A photograph from this session in the possession of Merloyd Lawrence bears a *Harper's Bazaar* wet stamp indicating that the photograph was received from Kertész on July 1, 1937.

24. See "Peas in a Pod," *Harper's Bazaar* 70, no. 2698 (Aug. 1937), pp. 60–63.

25. See the introduction to Kertész's *Enfants* (Paris: Librairie Plon, 1933) by Jaboune (Jean Nohain), quoted by Brassaï in his essay, "My Friend André Kertész," *Camera* 42, no. 4 (Apr. 1963), p. 7.

26. Brassaï (note 25), p. 7.

27. See "These Disarming Women in Furs," *Town and Country* 92, no. 4181 (Oct. 1937), pp. 76–81, and "The Smithtown Horse Show," *Town and Country* 92, no. 4181 (Oct. 1937), pp. 82–83.

28. See "Ein Deutsches Ballfest in Paris," *Die Dame* 57, no. 11 (Feb. 1930), p. 18.

29. In 1934 Paris *Vogue* had printed his treatment of holiday relaxation in the Loire under the title "Sieste en Plein Air"; now, this piece was translated and reprinted in New York *Vogue*.

30. The role of Condé Nast in the evolution of American photography was described in a special issue of *Vogue* entitled "Vogue's Eye View of Photography" (June 15, 1941). Within that issue, Frank Crowninshield specifically addressed the role of Nast in "Vogue . . . Pioneer in Photography," pp. 27–30, 72. See also Caroline Seebohm, *The Man Who Was Vogue* (New York, 1982), pp. 9, 152, 204–05, 232–33.

31. Steichen's years with Condé Nast are described by Margaret Case Harriman in an essay written in honor of Steichen's retirement from the staff of *Vogue*. See "Steichen," *Vogue*, Jan. 1938, p. 37.

32. See Munkacsi's photographs in "Freedom of the Dress," *Harper's Bazaar*, no. 2696 (June 1937), pp. 46–47.

33. In 1936, at the suggestion of Rudolph Hoffman, Kertész engaged the services of a man named Miller to present his work to potential clients. Miller arranged the invitation from *Life*.

34. See *The Compass* 18, no. 8 (1942), pp. 6–7.

35. Devenyi (note 9), p. 13.

36. Bourke-White (note 13), p. 313.

37. Fárová (note 3) recounted Kertész's recollection of his rejection by *Life*: "Kertész did not succeed with his reportage in America, because he was told 'your pictures talk too much.' Editors, he found to his dismay, were not interested in his original and individualistic approach. 'What they wanted,' Kertész remembers with a wry shrug, 'was to have a photographer go out and shoot twenty or thirty rolls. Then the editors and the writers would sit down with hundreds of pictures and push them around and put their story together like a picture puzzle. They wanted documentary photography. That wasn't me'" (p. 22).

38. Lifson (note 5), p. 66.

39. Ibid, p. 61.

40. [Arnold Gingrich], "Talking Pictures: Pondering the Problem Presented by the Captioning of Photographs," *Coronet* 2, no. 1 (May 1937), p. 55.

41. [Arnold Gingrich], "Talking Pictures: Program Notes on a Few of the Photograph Pages in This Issue," *Coronet* 2, no. 4 (Aug. 1937), p. 55.

42. B. G. [Bernard Geis?], "Talking Pictures: About Brassaï, Who Tells the Truth and Nothing But the Truth," *Coronet* 3, no. 2 (Dec. 1937), p. 119.

43. The PM Gallery produced a small brochure entitled "André Kertész: An Exhibition of Sixty Photographs." The show ran from Dec. 1 to Dec. 15, 1937.

44. "P M Shorts," *P M* 4, no. 4 (Dec. 1937–Jan. 1938), p. 82.

45. "P M Birthday Party," *P M* 4, no. 2 (Oct. 1937), pp. 36–37.

46. László Moholy-Nagy, "Education and the Bauhaus," in Richard Kostelanetz, *Moholy-Nagy* (New York: Praeger, 1970), pp. 163-170.

47. "The Surrealists," *Harper's Bazaar*, no. 2689 (Nov. 1936), p. 62.

48. Harriman (note 31), p. 37.

49. Beaumont Newhall, "Image of Freedom," *The Bulletin of the Museum of Modern Art* 9, no. 2 (Nov. 1941), pp. 14–16.

50. Fárová (note 3), pp. 7–8.

51. "Vogue's-Eye View of Holiday Time," *Vogue*, May 15, 1938, p. 38.

52. [Arnold Gingrich], "An Anniversary Presentation of Coronet's Most Memorable Photographs, November 1936–November 1940," *Coronet* 9, no. 1 (Nov. 1940), pp. 111–42.

53. Crowninshield (note 30), p. 27.

54. "La Fondue," *House and Garden* 73 (Jan. 1938), pp. 44–45.

55. See the remark by Kertész in Paul Hill and Thomas Cooper, *Dialogue with Photography* (New York: Farrar, Straus and Giroux, 1979): "It was impossible to go back once I was here. And later the war came, and by then I was an enemy alien, fingerprinted [in the main Reading Room of the New York Public Library]. They thought I was a spy if I walked in the streets with my camera" (p. 41).

56. Martin Munkacsi, who immigrated to the United States in 1934, succeeded in obtaining regular assignments from Hearst Publications almost from the day of his arrival. He was blessed with the success that Kertész was denied. See John Esten, "Martin Munkacsi," in George Walsh, Colin Naylor, and Michael Held, eds., *Contemporary Photographers* (New York, 1982), pp. 544–46.

57. See "Lions Through the Lens of Lynes," *Town and Country* 96, no. 4230 (Nov. 1941), pp. 64–65.

58. Kertész's withdrawal from the mass-market publications is documented by the absence of reproductions of his work. He asserts that he did not stop working entirely, but rather eked out a livelihood from highly specialized publications such as *Cue* and *The Compass*. Very few reproductions have been traced to document this activity.

59. Herrick (note 20), p. 164.

60. John Adam Knight, "Photography," *New York Post*, Dec. 31, 1942.

61. Cecil Beaton, *Cecil Beaton's New York* (Philadelphia and New York, 1938), p. 66.

62. See "The Small Shop," *Fortune* 32, no. 5 (Nov. 1945), pp. 158–61.

63. Wellesley College Museum (note 10), cat. no. 5.

64. Wellesley College Museum (note 10), cat. nos. 11, 13, 14.

65. Irving Penn commenced work for *Vogue* in 1943 at the invitation of Alexander Liberman. So far as can be ascertained, his first reproductions appeared under the title "Sea Harvest" in the Aug. 1, 1943, issue, pp. 66–67.

66. Richard Avedon commenced work for *Harper's Bazaar* and *Junior Harper's Bazaar* in 1944. His first reproductions appeared under the title "I wore the prettiest dress . . ."; see *Harper's Bazaar*, no. 2795 (Nov. 1944), pp. 108–10.

67. M. F. Agha, "Horseless Photography," *Harper's Bazaar*, no. 2795 (Nov. 1944), p. 67.

68. Ibid, p. 71.

69. See "Blessed of St. Nicholas," *House and Garden* 86 (Dec. 1944), pp. 56–58.

70. Elliott Paul, "A Mood from the Dim Past," *Saturday Review of Literature* 28 (May 19, 1945), p. 10.

71. Margaret Kress, "André Kertész in *House and Garden*," unpublished research, 1983.

72. Wellesley College Museum (note 10), p. 6; the count was made by Lesley K. Baier.

73. Brooke Astor to Weston J. Naef, Jan. 27, 1984.

74. Brooke Astor, *Footprints: An Autobiography* (New York, 1980), pp. 219–20.

75. Cecil Beaton and Gail Buckland, *The Magic Image: The Genius of Photography from 1839 to the Present Day* (Boston: Little, Brown and Company, 1975), p. 146.

76. "André Kertész," *House and Garden* 90 (Nov. 1946), p. 141.

77. Hilton Kramer, "Introduction," in André Kertész, *Hungarian Memories* (Boston: New York Graphic Society and Little, Brown and Company, 1982), p. ix.

Plates

Note. The following photographs have been reproduced to the actual size of the exhibited print: cat. nos. 1–6, 8–9, 11–13, 15–17, 19–39, 41–42, 44–54, 56–63, 65–66, 69, 71, 73, 84–86, 102–06, 108–10, 118, 124, 126, 130–31, 139, 150, 185, and 188.

Catalogue no. 1
The Eiffel Tower, 1925

Catalogue no. 2
The Fountain in the Place de la Concorde, 1925

Catalogue no. 9
Pont Louis-Philippe, 1925/26

Catalogue no. 3
Notre Dame at Night, 1925

Catalogue no. 4
Behind the Hôtel de Ville, 1925

129

Catalogue no. 5
Quai d'Orléans, Fishermen Behind Notre Dame, 1925

Catalogue no. 6
Boulevard Malesherbes at Midday, 1925

Catalogue no. 11
Lajos Tihanyi, 1926

Catalogue no. 12
József Csáky, 1926

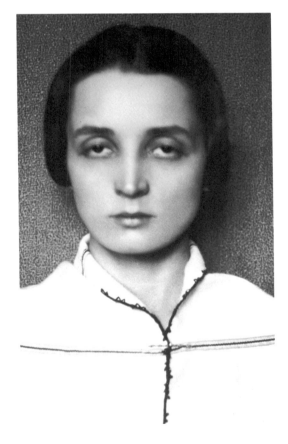

Catalogue no. 13
Anne-Marie Merkel, profile, 1926

Catalogue no. 15
Mlle. Jaffe, 1926

Catalogue no. 16
Miss Gundvor Berg, 1926

Catalogue no. 14
Anne-Marie Merkel, 1926

Catalogue no. 17
Chairs, the Medici Fountain, 1926

Catalogue no. 18
The Stairs of Montmartre, 1926

135

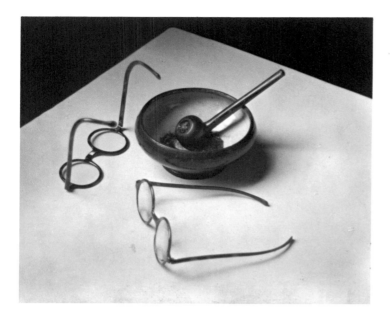

Catalogue no. 21
Mondrian's Glasses and Pipe, 1926

Catalogue no. 22
Chez Mondrian, 1926

Catalogue no. 23
Mondrian's Studio, 1926

136

Catalogue no. 24
Mondrian, 1926

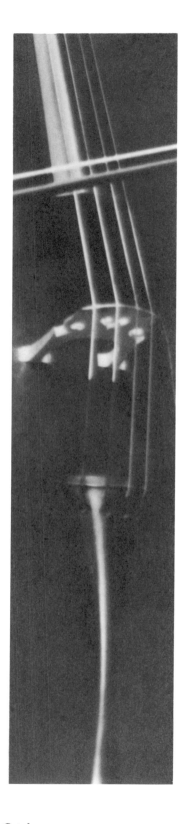

Catalogue no. 19
Cello Study, 1926

Catalogue no. 20
Quartet, 1926

138

Catalogue no. 26
Magda Förstner, 1926

Catalogue no. 25
Satiric Dancer, 1926

139

Catalogue no. 28
Wall of Posters, 1926

Catalogue no. 27
Quai d'Orsay, 1926

Catalogue no. 36
Woman on Stairs, 1926/27

Catalogue no. 37
Young Woman with a Curl of Hair, 1926/27

Catalogue no. 39
Portrait of a Young Yugoslav Bibliophile, 1926/27

Catalogue no. 38
Portrait of a Young German Doctor, 1926/27

Catalogue no. 46
Primel, 1927

Catalogue no. 30
Clowns of the Fête Foraine, 1926

Catalogue no. 29
Fête Foraine, 1926

Catalogue no. 31
Caretaker's House, 1926

Catalogue no. 32
Boats on the Seine Outside Paris, 1926/27

Catalogue no. 33
Seuphor on the Pont des Arts, 1926

Catalogue no. 73
St. André des Arts, 1928?

143

Catalogue no. 41
The Studio Cat, 1927

Catalogue no. 34
Zadkine in His Studio, 1926

Catalogue no. 35
At Zadkine's, 1926

Catalogue no. 66
African Sculptures, 1928

Catalogue no. 42
Tristan Tzara, 1927?

Catalogue no. 49
Chairs, the Tuileries, 1927

Catalogue no. 44
Montparnasse, Square Jolivet, 1927

Catalogue no. 56
Smokestacks at Night, 1927/28

Catalogue no. 45
Bistro, 1927

Catalogue no. 47
Les Halles in the Early Morning, 1927

Catalogue no. 48
Siesta, 1927

Catalogue no. 50
Mrs. Rosskam, 1927

Catalogue no. 52
Paul Dermée, 1927?

Catalogue no. 51
Pierre Mac Orlan, 1927

Catalogue no. 53
Still Life in Bookshop Window, 1927?

Catalogue no. 57
Mr. Titus, Editor and Publisher, Rue Delambre, 1928

Catalogue no. 54
Hands and Books, 1927

L'ÉLÉGANCE DU MÉTIER

LE FORT DES HALLES   LA CRÉMIÈRE   LA MARCHANDE DES HALLES   LE TUEUR

LE CHEF   LE MOTOCYCLISTE   PHOTOS   KERTESZ   LE MÉCANICIEN   LE BOUCHER

N° 264   VU   P. 504   N° 264   VU   P. 505

Catalogue no. 55
L'Elégance du Métier, 1927/28

Catalogue no. 75
Street Work, 1929

155

 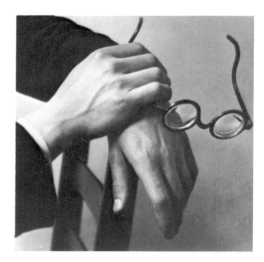

Catalogue no. 59
Paul Arma, 1928

Catalogue no. 60
Paul Arma's Hands, 1928

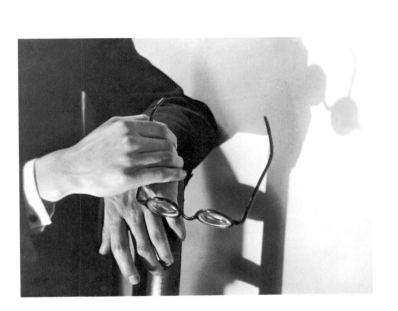

Catalogue no. 61
Paul Arma's Hands and Shadows I, 1928

Catalogue no. 62
Paul Arma's Hands and Shadows II, 1928

157

Catalogue no. 63
Ropes, 1928

Catalogue no. 64
In Les Halles, 1928

Catalogue no. 65
Fork, 1928

160

Catalogue no. 74
Study of People and Shadows, 1928?

Catalogue no. 67
Ady's Poem, c. 1928

Catalogue no. 68
Still Life in Ady's Room, c. 1928

162

Catalogue no. 69
In the Chartier Restaurant, c. 1928

Catalogue no. 70
Rue de Lévis, Montmartre, c. 1928

Catalogue no. 58
Meudon, 1928

Catalogue no. 71
Rue de Médicis, c. 1928

Catalogue no. 72
The Luxembourg Gardens, c. 1928

167

Catalogue no. 76
Boy Archer, 1929

168

Catalogue no. 77
Alexander Calder, 1929

Catalogue no. 82
Shadows of the Eiffel Tower, 1929

Catalogue no. 83
Clock of the Academy, Pont des Arts, and the Louvre, 1929

Catalogue no. 84
The Seine from Lady Mendl's Apartment, 1929

Catalogue no. 81
Paris Chimneys, 1929

Catalogue no. 86
Clayton "Peg Leg" Bates, 1929

174

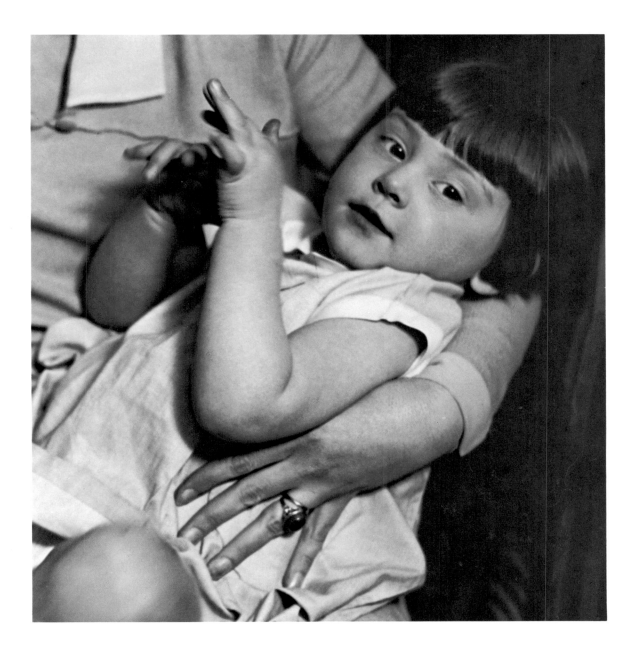

Catalogue no. 85
Child in Mother's Arms, 1929

Catalogue no. 91
The Daisy Bar, Montmartre, 1930

Catalogue no. 90
Tuileries Gardens, 1930

Catalogue no. 95
Elizabeth and André, 1931

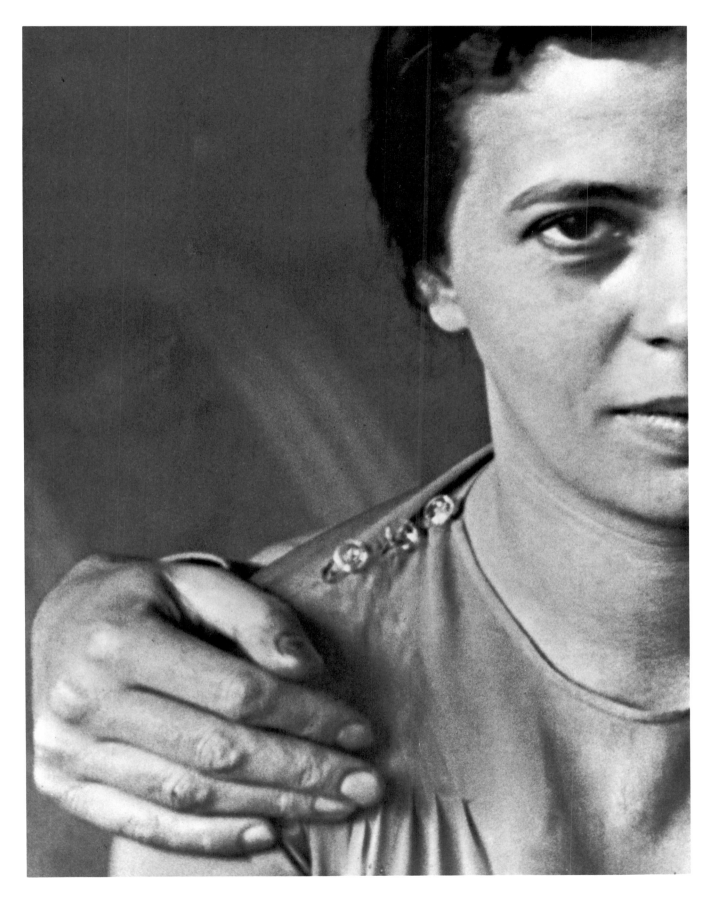

Catalogue no. 94
Elizabeth, 1931

Catalogue no. 99
On the Teeter-Totter, 1931

VU

NOËL

Des enfants émerveillés, émus ou craintifs, se sont approchés de la vitrine d'un magasin de la rue de Marbeuf pour parler au Père Noël qui y est venu tout exprès pour eux.
Photo Kertesz.

23 DÉCEMBRE 1931
4ᵉ ANNÉE - Nᵒ 197
PARAIT LE MERCREDI
PRIX : 2 FRANCS
LUCIEN VOGEL, DIRECTEUR

Catalogue no. 97
Father Christmas, c. 1931

181

Catalogue no. 89
Distortion Portrait of Carlo Rim, 1930

Catalogue no. 87
At the Fortune Teller's, 1929

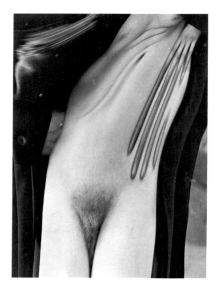

Catalogue no. 106
Distortion #72, 1933

184

Catalogue no. 105
Distortion #68, 1933

Catalogue no. 102
Distortion #17, 1933

Catalogue no. 103
Distortion #31, 1933

Catalogue no. 104
Distortion #20, 1933

188

Catalogue no. 107
Distortion #91, 1933

189

Catalogue no. 108
Distortion #164, 1933

Catalogue no. 109
Distortion #167, 1933

Catalogue no. 100
Chez Kisling, 1933

Catalogue no. 101
Eiffel Tower and Iron Bridge, 1933

193

Catalogue no. 111
On the Boulevards, 1934

194

Catalogue no. 110
Place Saint Sulpice, 1934

195

Catalogue no. 112
Self-Portrait in the Hotel Beaux-Arts, 1936

Catalogue no. 113
At The Metropolitan Museum of Art, 1936

Catalogue no. 114
Crippled Woman, 1936

Catalogue no. 118
Lost Cloud, 1937

Catalogue no. 119
Third Avenue, 1937

Catalogue no. 116
Clothes Lines, 1937

Catalogue no. 117
Sutton Place, 1937

Catalogue no. 121
Bronx, New York, 1937

Catalogue no. 124
Poughkeepsie, New York, 1937

Catalogue no. 136
Man with Spaniel on Leash, 1938

Catalogue no. 137
Rockefeller Center, 1938?

Catalogue no. 115
Distortion with Vase, 1936

Catalogue no. 159
Melancholic Tulip, 1939

Catalogue no. 120
Arm and Ventilator, 1937

Catalogue no. 148
Hand Holding Mushrooms, c. 1938

Catalogue no. 122
Nicholas Luddington, Jr., 1937

Catalogue no. 123
Merloyd Luddington, 1937

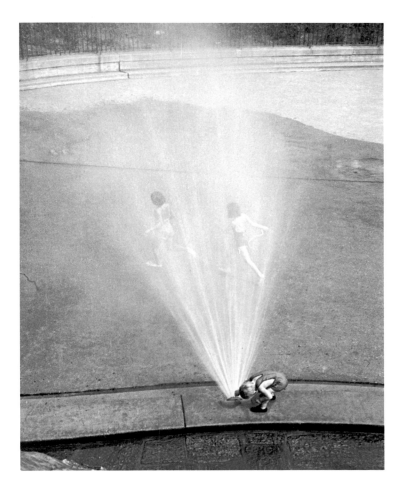

Catalogue no. 156
Children in Playground with Sprinkler, 1939

Catalogue no. 142
Children in an Art Gallery, 1938

Catalogue no. 125
Men Seated on Bench, 1937

212

Catalogue no. 138
Washington Square, New York, 1938

Catalogue no. 126
The Lake, Central Park, Near Bow Bridge, c. 1937

Catalogue no. 130
East River Pier Around 23rd Street, c. 1937

Catalogue no. 131
New York Public Library Plaza, c. 1937

Catalogue no. 132
Steps of the New York Public Library, c. 1937

215

Catalogue no. 128
From 85 Fifth Avenue, c. 1937

Catalogue no. 134
Apartment Houses in the Bronx (?), c. 1937

Catalogue no. 127
Elevated Train Platform, Bowery (?), 1937

Catalogue no. 133
The East River from 42nd Street, c. 1937

Catalogue no. 135
Ornamental Sphere on the North Tower of the Hippodrome, c. 1937

Catalogue no. 129
Third Avenue Elevated at 43rd Street, c. 1937

Catalogue no. 144
Beekman Terrace, 1938

Catalogue no. 149
Great Danes, c. 1938

Catalogue no. 160
Carousel Horses, Shelburne, Vermont, c. 1939

219

Catalogue no. 139
Cecil Beaton, 1938

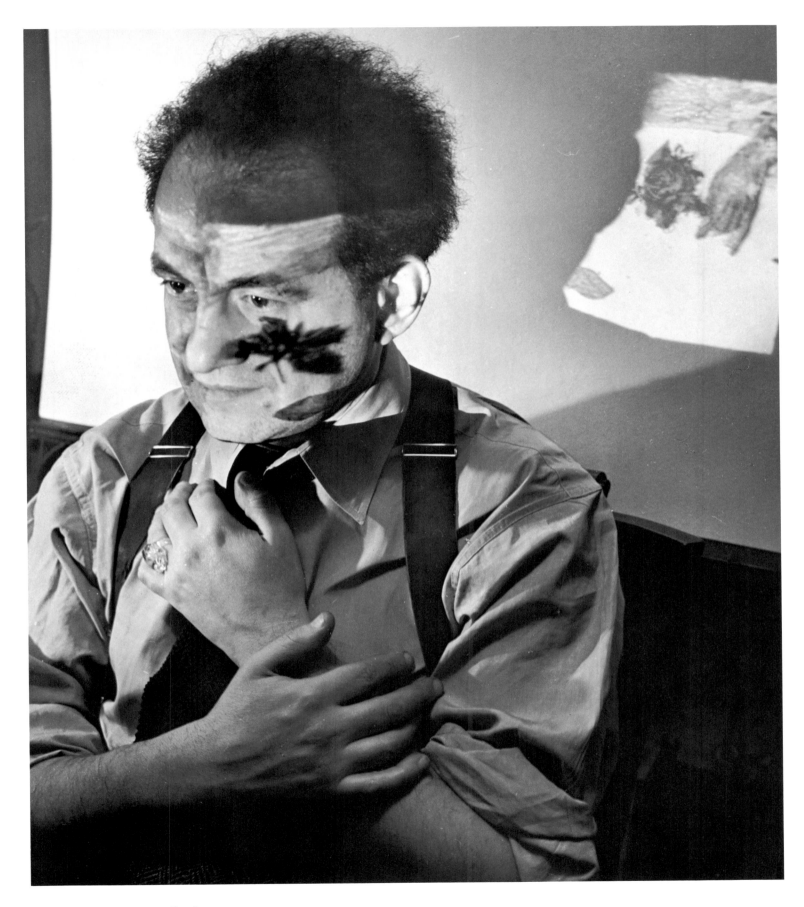

Catalogue no. 140
The Set Designer, c. 1938

Catalogue no. 158
Female Torso with Plaster Relief, 1939

Catalogue no. 147
Model Jumping Stones, c. 1938

Catalogue no. 157
Ballet Dancer, Roof Garden of Rockefeller Center, 1939

Catalogue no. 143
44th Street and the East River, 1938

223

Catalogue no. 145
Model Inspecting Tea, 1938

Catalogue no. 146
Model and Delivery Man, c. 1938

224

Catalogue no. 154
Sixth Avenue, New York, 1939

Catalogue no. 155
Sixth Avenue, 1939

Catalogue no. 150
Workmen on Waterfront, c. 1938

Catalogue no. 152
The Tugboat Eugene F. Moran, New York Harbor, c. 1938

Catalogue no. 165
Waterfront Buildings, c. 1939

Catalogue no. 164
Near Coxsackie, New York, 1939?

228

Catalogue no. 162
Weehawken, New Jersey, 1939?

Catalogue no. 153
Bridge and Ship's Stack, 1938

229

Catalogue no. 163
Weehawken, New Jersey, 1939?

Catalogue no. 166
Pilings, Weehawken, New Jersey, 1941

Catalogue no. 151
New York Harbor, c. 1938

Catalogue no. 141
Midtown Manhattan, 1938

Catalogue no. 161
The Empire State Building, 1939

Catalogue no. 167
Armonk, New York, 1941

234

Catalogue no. 168
Richfield, New Jersey, 1941

Catalogue no. 175
Ashfield, Massachusetts, Church Spire, 1945

235

Catalogue no. 170
Shadow of a Tree, 1944

Catalogue no. 169
Rye, New York, 1941?

236

Catalogue no. 186
Rooftop Water Tanks, New York, 1951

Catalogue no. 187
Stairs, Railing, Shadows, and Woman, 1951

237

Catalogue no. 173
East Walk of Conservatory Pond, Central Park, 1944

Catalogue no. 174
Washington Square, New York—After the Rain, 1945

Catalogue no. 171
Riverside Park Near 153rd Street, 1944

Catalogue no. 172
Hudson River, Henry Hudson Parkway, and Riverside Park, 1944

Catalogue no. 182
River Walk of Carl Schurz Park, 1948

Catalogue no. 181
Queensborough Bridge at Night, 1948

Catalogue no. 188
Williamsburg, Virginia, 1951

244

Catalogue no. 178
Crucifix and Light Bulb, 1947

Catalogue no. 183
Book-lined Hallway, Mainbocher Apartment, New York, 1948

Catalogue no. 177
Chair, Lamp, and Sculpture, 1947?

Catalogue no. 176
Game Room, The Joseph B. Platt Residence, 1946

Catalogue no. 180
Manhattan Span of the Queensborough Bridge, 1947.

Catalogue no. 179
Overhead Crosswalk with Clock, 1947

Catalogue no. 184
My Little Indians, 1948

Catalogue no. 185
Watchmaker's Shop, Christopher Street, 1950

Catalogue no. 189
Greenwich Village Rooftops, Day, c. 1952

Catalogue no. 190
Greenwich Village Rooftops, Evening, 1954

253

Catalogue no. 191
Homage to Robert Capa, 1954

254

Catalogue no. 192
Washington Square, Winter, 1954

Notes on the Catalogue

All measurements of image size are given in millimeters, height before width. All inscriptions are in the handwriting of André Kertész, unless stated to the contrary. All photographs were printed by the photographer, unless otherwise indicated. All titles not set in italics have been supplied by the authors. It is accepted that a print was made during the period of occupancy at the address stated on the stamp. Prints without stamps are considered to be contemporaneous with the negative unless otherwise stated. The date given is that of the negative and has been established by the authors with the photographer. In those cases where an exact date of the negative has not been established through an inscription or a published source, an estimate of the date has been made. A date with a circa represents a less certain opinion than one with a question mark, which is accurate within one year. Two dates separated by a slash indicate that the photograph was taken in one of those two years.

The mounting materials Kertész used to present his photographs varied from the cockled-surface paper described below as vellum to a common poster board. Because many of the mounts have been trimmed down, destroying the original proportions intended by the photographer, mount measurements have not been included in the catalogue entries. It seems, however, that an untrimmed vellum mount intended for the post-card-stock prints generally measures about 370 x 275 mm. The signature in the lower margin of the post-card-stock prints or on the vellum mount is for the most part consistent: "A. Kertész" to the lower left and "Paris" to the lower right.

The following three sections (viz., Stamps, Reproductions, and Exhibitions) contain information relevant to the individual catalogue entries, where annotations are frequently given in an abbreviated form.

Stamps

Kertész was systematic in applying wet stamps to the verso of his photographs. He used indelible alcohol-based inks, as was customary for photographers who made part of their living by selling reproduction rights to their photographs. Since his stamps were changed when he changed his address, the stamps are an aid to dating when prints were made. Although early prints sometimes bear later stamps, the reverse is never the case. The hiatus between moving to a new location and obtaining a new stamp is reflected by manuscript alterations of the old address to the new one. This is particularly true of the New York addresses. Occasionally, manuscript alterations are accompanied by a specific day and month.

Paris stamp #1:
ANDRE KERTESZ / 5, rue de Vanves / PARIS 14e
(This stamp was used between 1926 and 1929.)

Paris stamp #2:
Andre KERTESZ / 75 Bould. Montparnasse / PARIS 6e
(This stamp was used between 1929 and 1931.)

Paris stamp #3:
PHOTO / ANDRE KERTESZ / 32 bis, Rue du Cotentin, PARIS XV / COPYRIGHT BY
(This stamp was used between 1931 and 1936.)

Paris stamp #4:
REPRODUCTION RESERVEE / EN CAS DE REPRODUCTION / LA SIGNATURE EST OBLIGATORE
(This stamp was used after 1929.)

Paris stamp #5:
PHOTO PERSONELLE
(This stamp occasionally appears on the verso of the 1933 nude distortion photographs.)

New York stamp #1:
PHOTO COPYRIGHT BY / ANDRE KERTESZ / 307 E. 44th ST. NEW YORK / TEL. MURRAY HILL 4–4800
(This stamp was used in 1936 and 1937.)

New York stamp #2:
ANDRE KERTESZ / 67 W. 44th St. VA 6–2759
(This stamp occasionally occurs without any
telephone number; on others the number was
changed to VA 6–3012. The stamp was used in
1938 and 1939.)

New York stamp #3:
André Kertész
(This stamp, with no address, was used throughout
the 1950s and 1960s.)

New York stamp #4:
ANDRE KERTESZ
(This stamp, again with no address, was used
from 1941 to about 1948.)

New York stamp #5:
ANDRÉ KERTÉSZ / 31 UNION SQ. N.Y.C.3, /
GR 3–2564 / #
(This stamp was used between 1946 and 1952.)

New York stamp #6:
ANDRE KERTESZ / 2 FIFTH AVE. / NEW YORK,
N.Y. 10011 / GR 7–5737
(This stamp was made after the introduction of
Zip Codes in 1962. It has been used from the 1960s
to the present.)

New York stamp #7:
Photo by André Kertész
(This stamp, with no address, was used between
1939 and 1941.)

Levy stamp:
JULIEN LEVY GALLERY, INC. / 15 EAST 57th
STREET / NEW YORK CITY
(This stamp was applied after October 1937 when
the Levy Gallery moved from 602 Madison Avenue.
Levy, however, had purchased all of the photographs by Kertész in his collection by 1930, and this
stamp was most likely applied when the collection
was packed for moving. None of the photographs
in the Levy collection bears Paris stamp #1 or #3.)

Reproductions

In citing the early and important publications that
reproduced photographs by André Kertész, short
titles have been used whenever practical. Works
frequently cited have been identified by the
following short titles.

Abrams *André Kertész: A Lifetime of Perception*, introduction by Ben Lifson (New York:
Harry N. Abrams, 1982).

Aperture *André Kertész*, text by Carole Kismaric
(Millerton, N.Y.: Aperture, 1977).

Day of Paris André Kertész, *Day of Paris*, ed.
George Davis (New York: J. J. Augustin, 1945).

Distortions André Kertész, *Distortions*, introduction by Hilton Kramer (New York: Alfred A.
Knopf, 1976).

Enfants André Kertész, *Enfants*, text by
Jaboune (Jean Nohain) (Paris: Librairie Plon,
1933).

Fárová Anna Fárová, *André Kertész*, adapted by
Robert Sogalyn (New York: Paragraphic Books,
1966).

Film und Foto Film und Foto, *Internationale
Ausstellung des Deutschen Werkbunds* (Stuttgart,
1929). (exh. cat.)

J'aime Paris André Kertész, *J'aime Paris:
Photographs Since the Twenties*, ed. Nicolas

Ducrot (New York: Grossman Publishers,
1974).

Manchester *André Kertész*, text by Harold Riley
and others (The Manchester Collection, 1984).

Of New York André Kertész, *Of New York*, ed.
Nicolas Ducrot (New York: Alfred A. Knopf,
1976).

Paris Vu André Kertész, *Paris vu par André
Kertész*, text by Pierre Mac Orlan (Paris: Librairie
Plon, 1934).

Portraits André Kertész, *Portraits*, ed. Nicolas
Ducrot (New York: Mayflower Books, 1979).

Sixty Years André Kertész, *Sixty Years of
Photography, 1912–1972*, ed. Nicolas Ducrot
(New York: Grossman Publishers, 1972).

Szarkowski The Museum of Modern Art, *André
Kertész, Photographer*, text by John Szarkowski
(New York, 1964). (exh. cat.)

Travis The Art Institute of Chicago, *Photographs
from the Julien Levy Collection, Starting with
Atget*, text by David Travis (Chicago, 1976).
(exh. cat.)

Washington Square André Kertész, *Washington
Square* (New York: Grossman Publishers, 1975).

Wilde *André Kertész*, ed. Thomas Walther
(Cologne: Galerie Wilde, 1982).

Exhibitions

The following list of selected exhibitions includes the most notable ones of the 1920s and 1930s that showed photographs by André Kertész, as well as three important later exhibitions. Whenever extant catalogues and gallery flyers or the photographer's personal archives have made possible the identification of individual images, specific reference to these exhibitions has been made in the respective catalogue entries.

Paris, Au Sacre du Printemps, 1927. (This was an untitled exhibition of photographs by Kertész and paintings by Ida Thal.)

Zaragosa, III Salon Internacional de Fotografie, 1927.

Paris, XXIIIe Salon International d'Art Photographique, 1927.

Paris, Salon de l'Escalier, 1928. (The official title of this exhibition was "1er Salon Indépendent de la Photographie.")

Brussels, Galerie L'Epoque, 1928. (This exhibition was entitled "Exposition de Photographie.")

Rotterdam, Internationale Foto-Salon, 1928.

Prague, Svaz cs. Klubu Fotografu Amateru, 1928.

Essen, Fotographie der Gegenwart, 1929.

Stuttgart, Film und Foto, 1929. (This exhibition, organized by the Deutscher Werkbund, was officially entitled "Der International Ausstellung von Film und Foto.")

Munich, Das Lichtbild, 1930.

Buenos Aires, Primer Salon Anual de Fotografia, 1930.

Paris, 11e Salon de l'Araignée, 1930. (This exhibition was held at the Galerie G. L. Manuel Freres.)

Paris, Galerie d'Art Contemporain, Photographies d'aujourd'hui, 1930.

Paris, Galerie d'Art Contemporain, Deuxieme Groupe de Photographes, 1931.

Brussels, Xe Salon de Photographie, Association Belge de Photographie, 1931.

Paris, Galerie d'Art Contemporain, Photographies d'aujourd'hui, 1931.

Vienna, Graphische Lehr- und Versuchsanstaldt, Neue Sportbauten, 1931.

New York, The Art Center, 1931. (This show was entitled "An Exhibition of Foreign Photography.")

Brussels, Internationale de la Photographie, Palais des Beaux-Arts, 1932.

New York, Julien Levy Gallery, Modern European Photography, 1932.

New York, Brooklyn Museum, International Photographers, 1932.

Buffalo, N.Y., Albright Art Gallery, Modern Photography, 1932.

Essen, Museum Folkwang, 1932.

Brussels, Deuxieme Exposition Internationale de la Photographie et Cinema, 1933.

Paris, Galerie de la Pléiade, Groupe Annuel des Photographes, 1933.

London, The Royal Photographic Society of Great Britain, The Modern Spirit in Photography, 1933.

Paris, Leleu's, 1934.

Paris, Galerie de la Pléiade, Groupe Annuel des Photographes, 1934.

Paris, Studio Saint-Jacques, Exposition de la société des artistes photographes, 1934.

London, The Royal Photographic Society of Great Britain, The Modern Spirit in Photography and Advertising, 1934.

Paris, Galerie de la Pléiade, 1935.

Paris, Musée des Arts Décoratifs, Exposition Internationale de la Photographie Contemporaine, 1936.

New York, The Museum of Modern Art, 1937. (This exhibition, organized by Beaumont Newhall, was entitled "Photography 1839–1937.")

New York, P M Gallery, An Exhibition of 60 Photographs by André Kertész, 1937.

New York, Julien Levy Gallery, Pioneers of Modern French Photography, 1937.

New York, The Museum of Modern Art, Image of Freedom, 1942.

Chicago, The Art Institute of Chicago, 1946. (This was Kertész's first one-man museum exhibition in America.)

New York, The Museum of Modern Art, 1964. (This exhibition, organized by John Szarkowski, was entitled "André Kertész, Photographer.")

Catalogue

1. *The Eiffel Tower*, 1925
Silver gelatin contact print on post-card
   stock, 72 x 40 mm
Repr.: *Vu*, no. 10 (May 23, 1928), p. 254;
   J'aime Paris, frontispiece facing full
   title page; Manchester, #56, p. 54
Lent by the J. Paul Getty Museum, Malibu

This photograph was made from the
window of a building designed by the
Hungarian architect André Szivessy (later,
André Sive), the partner of Ernő
Goldfinger, whom Kertész was visiting.
This photograph appears framed on the
wall in a 1927 self-portrait (see cat. no.
40). Kertész sent this contact print to
Elizabeth in Budapest probably during his
first year in Paris. Most of the Paris contact
prints on post-card stock were printed from
negatives made between 1925 and 1928.
For reproduction, see p. 127.

2. *The Fountain in the Place de la
   Concorde*, 1925
Silver gelatin contact print on post-card
   stock, 52 x 38 mm
Inscribed on verso in pencil "Place de la
   Concorderól"
Repr.: Jean-Louis Vaudoyer, "Les
   Nymphes de Paris," *Art et Médecine*,
   Oct. 1931, p. 33; *Day of Paris*, p. 126;
   "Day of Paris," *Minicam Photography* 8,
   no. 10 (July 1945), p. 29; *J'aime Paris*,
   p. 65
Lent by the J. Paul Getty Museum, Malibu

This print was sent to Elizabeth in
Budapest. For reproduction, see p. 128.

3. *Notre Dame at Night*, 1925
Silver gelatin contact print on post-card
   stock, 70 x 83 mm
Signed on recto in pencil "Notre Dame,
   1925, A. Kertész" in a later hand
Repr.: *Day of Paris*, p. 144–45; *J'aime
   Paris*, p. 154
Exh.: Paris, Au Sacre du Printemps, 1927
Lent by the Susan Harder Gallery, New
   York

This photograph was made while Kertész
was returning to his residence in the
neighborhood of the Hôtel de Ville, after
an evening with friends at the Café du
Dôme. Attracted by the patterns made by
rain, he set up his camera on a tripod for a
half-hour exposure. For reproduction, see
p. 129.

4. *Behind the Hôtel de Ville*, 1925
Silver gelatin contact print on post-card
   stock, 79 x 108 mm
Repr.: *Paris Vu*, n. pag.; *Coronet* 4, no. 4
   (Aug. 1938), p. 116
Lent by Nicholas Pritzker, Chicago

A few weeks after his arrival, Kertész
moved to the 1st arrondissement in an area
near the Hôtel de Ville because a friend
lived nearby. This is one of his first
Parisian night views, a subject he had
experimented with in Hungary. He gave
this print to one of his friends, the sculptor
István (later, Etienne) Beőthy. For reproduction, see p. 129.

5. *Quai d'Orléans, Fishermen Behind
   Notre Dame*, 1925
Silver gelatin contact print on post-card
   stock mounted on vellum, 102 x 61 mm
Repr.: Marcel Prévost, "L'Ame de Paris,"
   Art et Médecine, Oct. 1931, p. 17; *Paris
   Vu*, frontispiece; *J'aime Paris*, p. 14
Exh.: probably New York, Julien Levy
   Gallery, 1932 or 1937
Lent by Brenda and Robert Edelson,
   Baltimore

Within four to five months of his arrival
in Paris, Kertész had found his own quarters at 5, rue de Vanves, where he lived
until 1928. There he was able to set up his
own modest darkroom and print his work
regularly. Before he discovered the post-
card stock he so favored, he used several
available papers: velox, one produced by
Lumière, and another made in Belgium.
This photograph has been cropped very
slightly. For reproduction, see p. 130.

6. *Boulevard Malesherbes at Midday*, 1925
Later semi-glossy, single-weight silver
   gelatin print made by Igor Bakht
130 x 125 mm
Repr.: *J'aime Paris*, p. 56; Abrams, p. 56
Lent by the Susan Harder Gallery, New York

This photograph, made within a month or
two of Kertész's arrival, was taken from
the window of an art gallery then exhibiting the work of the social satirists George
Grosz, Frans Masereel, and Kertész's
friend Gyula Zilzer, who had recently
arrived in Paris from Germany. Zilzer had
been politically active in Hungary with the
Commune. Later he immigrated to the
United States and worked briefly in Holly-
wood, before settling in New York. It was
Zilzer who had shown Kertész's work to
Alfred Stieglitz in New York, before
Kertész arrived from Europe. For reproduction, see p. 131.

7. *The Café du Dôme*, 1925
Semi-glossy, single-weight silver gelatin
   print, 130 x 170 mm
Repr.: *Das Illustrierte Blatt*, no. 44 (1926),
   p. 984; Fernand Vallon, "Montparnasse,"
   Art et Médecine, Oct. 1931, p. 41
   (slightly cropped); *Day of Paris*, p. 61;
   Sixty Years, p. 86; *J'aime Paris*, p. 110;
   Abrams, p. 25; Manchester, #67, p. 60
Lent by Ernő Goldfinger, London

The Hungarian painter Lajos (Louis)
Tihanyi is seated at the café table. Ernő
Goldfinger, a Hungarian architect, is
standing to the left, speaking to Marie
Wassilieff, a Russian painter who exhibited
at the Au Sacre du Printemps gallery.
For reproduction, see p. 25.

8. *Legs*, 1925
Silver gelatin contact print on post-card
   stock, 98 x 61 mm
Signed on recto in pencil "A. Kertész,
   Paris"; inscribed on verso "Erdekes
   véletlen. Ráfogják, hogy szürrealista
   legyen, ha az embereknek úgy jobb."
   (Interesting coincidence. They claim it
   as being surrealistic, if it suits people
   better.)
Repr.: *Variétés* 1 (1928), opposite p. 488;
   Szarkowski, p. 23; *Sixty Years*, p. 155
Lent by the J. Paul Getty Museum, Malibu

The image reproduced in *Sixty Years* includes more of the negative on the left side of the photograph. The Hungarian inscription demonstrates that Kertész was not a confirmed believer in or member of Surrealism as an artistic movement, but did understand its appeal and was able to make photographs immediately after his arrival in Paris that incorporated its delight in the coincidental. This print was sent to Elizabeth in Budapest. See remarks on cat. no. 11. For reproduction, see p. 66.

9. *Pont Louis-Philippe*, 1925/26
Silver gelatin contact print on velox paper, 51 x 38 mm
Inscribed on verso in pencil "Pont Louis-Philippe"
Lent by the J. Paul Getty Museum, Malibu

This print was sent to Elizabeth in Budapest. For reproduction, see p. 128.

10. Self-Portrait with Friends in the Hôtel des Terraces, 1926
Silver gelatin contact print on post-card stock, 80 x 99 mm
Signed on recto in pencil "A. Kertész, Paris"; inscribed on verso in ink "Ocskösnek!/Bandi/Paris, 1926. dec./ Onarckép, egy amerikai ujságírónővel es egy cseh festővel." (To little brother/ Bandi/Paris 1926 dec./Self-portrait with American woman journalist and a Czech painter.)
Lent by Nicholas Pritzker, Chicago

Several of Kertész's friends and acquaintances lived in the Hôtel des Terraces, including Michel Seuphor, Tihanyi, Brassaï, and the young Frank Dobo. Several early photographs Kertész took of Seuphor were made there. The woman depicted here was a German actress visiting Paris, and the painting on the wall was made of her by the man to the right, an artist named Reichental, who later immigrated to the United States. This print was sent to Kertész's brother Jenő in Buenos Aires. For reproduction, see p. 56.

11. *Lajos Tihanyi*, 1926
Silver gelatin contact print on post-card stock, 109 x 79 mm
Titled on verso in pencil "Louis Tihanyi" in a later hand
The Art Institute of Chicago, Ada Turnbull Hertle Fund, 1984.544

Lajos Tihanyi had been a member of the Hungarian avant-garde Group of Eight and a member of the Nyugat circle and had had contact with Endre Ady, its most important poet. He maintained as well a friendship with Ady's biographer, György

Bölöni, in Paris. Tihanyi's work in Hungary was an Expressionist version of Cubism. He left Hungary after the Republic of Councils, stayed briefly in Vienna and Germany, and lived in Paris from 1923 until his death in 1939. In Paris he made portraits of his friends and associates, Mihály Károlyi, Tristan Tzara, Ivan Goll, and others also known to Kertész, and gradually became involved in abstraction. Kertész has said that Tihanyi took him to a studio where he found mannequin legs to photograph (see cat. no. 8), as well as to a flophouse. Tihanyi was also interested in the anthropomorphic shapes of Paris chimneys, and Kertész has in his collection one of Tihanyi's chimney drawings. Kertész himself had photographed chimney shapes in Hungary. For reproduction, see p. 132.

12. *József Csáky*, 1926
Silver gelatin contact print on post-card stock, 109 x 73 mm
Signed on recto in pencil "A. Kertész, Paris"; inscribed on verso in pencil "Csáky, most már nemzetközileg elismert szobrász." (Csáky now has an international reputation.)
Exh.: probably Essen, Fotographie der Gegenwart, 1929
Lent by Nicholas Pritzker, Chicago

József Csáky left Hungary for Paris in 1908 and settled at La Ruche, the famous beehive-shaped studios where many Eastern European artists lived, including Chagall, Zadkine, and Lipchitz. (Léger too resided there for a time.) Marie Wassilieff operated a canteen nearby. Csáky's important contributions to Cubist sculpture— stylistically related to the work of his good friends Léger, Lipchitz, and Archipenko— are now recognized. He was a good friend of Kertész and gave him two of his sculptures. The poster in the background is his design. This print was sent by Kertész to his brother Jenő in Buenos Aires. This photograph also exists in a large format, mounted on laid paper. For reproduction, see p. 132.

13. Anne-Marie Merkel, profile, 1926
Silver gelatin contact print on post-card stock, 91 x 66 mm
The Art Institute of Chicago, Wirt D. Walker Fund, 1984.533

Anne-Marie Merkel was a sculptor and a special friend of Kertész and his wife, Elizabeth. Kertész admired what he called her "face of the Middle Ages." On the verso of other portraits of the same woman, which Kertész sent to Elizabeth in Budapest, he recorded her name as Anne-Marie Reps. For reproduction, see p. 133.

14. *Anne-Marie Merkel*, 1926
Matte, single-weight silver gelatin print mounted on a laid paper, 215 x 130 mm
Signed on mount recto in pencil "A. Kertész, Paris"
Repr.: Au Sacre du Printemps announcement; Wilde, no. 4
Exh.: Paris, Au Sacre du Printemps, 1927; probably Paris, Salon de l'Escalier, 1928; Brussels, Galerie L'Epoque, 1928
Lent by Thomas Walther

Kertész photographed his friend several times, and he considered these portraits important enough to include in several of his early exhibitions. This photograph was reproduced on the announcement for his first show (Au Sacre du Printemps). For reproduction, see p. 133.

15. *Mlle. Jaffe*, 1926
Silver gelatin contact print on post-card stock, 73 x 69 mm
Signed on recto in pencil "A. Kertész, Paris"; inscribed on verso in ink by the photographer "Mlle Jaffe/amerikai ujságírónő, a világ legnagyobb jiddisch lapjának, a Der Tag-nak munkatársnője." (Mlle. Jaffe, American journalist, a correspondent for the world's biggest Yiddish newspaper, *Der Tag*.)
Repr.: Wilde, no. 3
Lent by Nicholas Pritzker, Chicago

Jean Jaffe was another friend from the Dôme. The mirror was in Kertész's studio, and this photograph is one of the earliest to show his interest in mirror imagery (see also cat. nos. 10, 16). Miss Jaffe died in 1958. *Der Tag* became *The Jewish Daily Journal* after 1972. Kertész sent this print to his brother Jenő in Buenos Aires. For reproduction, see p. 133.

16. *Miss Gundvor Berg*, 1926
Silver gelatin contact print on post-card stock, 73 x 95 mm
Signed on recto in pencil "A. Kertész, Paris"
Repr.: *Sixty Years*, p. 89; Fárová, p. 39; Manchester, #232, p. 147
Lent by Nicholas Pritzker, Chicago

Gundvor Berg was a Swede studying painting in Paris. Kertész knew her from the Dôme, and he asked her permission to take some photographs. Another image made at this same time shows her wrapped in a shawl of Norwegian peasant design. This print was sent to his brother Jenő in Buenos Aires. For reproduction, see p. 133.

17. *Chairs, the Medici Fountain*, 1926
Semi-glossy, single-weight silver gelatin print mounted on vellum, 158 x 186 mm

Inscribed on mount verso in ink "No.6" and titled "Jardin du Luxembourg"; stamped on mount verso Paris stamp #2; exhibition label from "Primer Salon Anual de Fotografia, 1930/Buenos Aires."
Repr.: Rolf Henkl, "Neue Fotografie/ Ausstellungen/Kunstbücher/Theatre-aufführungen," *Tageschronik der Kunst* 8, no. 4 (July 1927), p. 27; *Der Querschnitt* 8, no. 9 (Sept. 1928), between pp. 630 and 631 (reproduced reversed right to left); *Paris Vu*, n. pag.; *J'aime Paris*, p. 107; Wilde, no. 12; Abrams, p. 235; Manchester, #138, p. 91
Exh.: Paris, Au Sacre du Printemps, 1927; Paris, Salon de l'Escalier, 1928; Stuttgart, Film und Foto, 1929; Buenos Aires, Primer Salon Anual de Fotografia, 1930
The Art Institute of Chicago, Wirt D. Walker Fund, 1984.536

The first of his many images of chairs in Paris, this photograph was made in the early spring after Kertész's arrival. Michel Seuphor remembers that it was he who pointed out these shadows to Kertész. Certainly their configurations would have interested this friend of Mondrian. Kertész, however, recalls that Tihanyi was with him when he made this photograph. This print was undoubtedly sent to his brother Jenő in Buenos Aires for exhibition. Five other photographs were sent to that exhibition: *Boy Archer* (cat. no. 76), Woman washing clothes, *Quai d'Orléans* (cat. no. 5), *Chez Mondrian* (cat. no. 22), and *Montparnasse, Square Jolivet* (cat. no. 44). It is not known how many were actually exhibited. This photograph is often titled *Chairs, Luxembourg Gardens*. See remarks on cat. no. 63. For reproduction, see p. 134.

18. *The Stairs of Montmartre*, 1926
Semi-glossy, single-weight silver gelatin print mounted on vellum, 155 x 202 mm
Signed and dated on mount recto in pencil; signed and titled on mount verso; inscribed "No 1, (Agr.)" in pencil and "441" in red crayon; stamped on mount verso Paris stamp #1
Repr.: Jean Gallotti, "La Photographie est-elle un art?—Kertész," *L'Art vivant* 5 (Mar. 1, 1929), p. 208; Pierre Mac Orlan, "Photographie," *Das Kunstblatt*, May 1929, p. 137; Jean Cocteau, "Le Montmartre," *Art et Médecine*, Oct. 1931, p. 38; Szarkowski, p. 26; *J'aime Paris*, p. 157; Abrams, p. 109
Exh.: Paris, Salon de l'Escalier, 1928; Brussels, Galerie L'Epoque, 1928
Lent by the Jedermann Collection, N.A.

This is one of the most well loved and often reproduced of Kertész's works. Here he used a Voigtlander f6.3 lens, which he

took apart to achieve a flatness and a more extreme perspective. He also cropped down the original negative to emphasize the composition. There were several photographs made from this same vantage, as Kertész was clearly attracted to the abstract potential of Montmartre's many stairs. One sent to his brother Jenő, showing a man with a cart instead of the woman and *clochard*, was taken a week or so earlier (see Travis, fig. 2). Another variant, showing a group of schoolgirls led by a nun, with several *clochards* on the steps, was made in 1930 (see Phillips, fig. 38). *The Daisy Bar, Montmartre* (cat. no. 91) was taken not far from this location, at night. For reproduction, see p. 135.

19. *Cello Study*, 1926
Matte, single-weight, silver gelatin print mounted on vellum, 206 x 44 mm
Repr.: *Sixty Years*, p. 120
Exh.: Paris, Salon de l'Escalier, 1928; Brussels, Galerie L'Epoque, 1928; probably Essen, Fotographie der Gegenwart, 1929; Stuttgart, Film und Foto, 1929
Lent by the Jedermann Collection, N.A.

This is a much cropped image derived from a close-up study of the Feri Róth Quartet made at the same time as cat. no. 20. Kertész's archives show that he sent a print of this image to the photography exhibition at the Folkwang Museum in Essen (Fotographie der Gegenwart). For reproduction, see p. 138.

20. *Quartet*, 1926
Silver gelatin contact print on post-card stock, 40 x 72 mm
Signed on recto in pencil "A. Kertész, Paris"
Repr.: *Vu* 1, no. 5 (Apr. 18, 1928), p. 125; *Sixty Years*, p. 121; Aperture, p. 59; Abrams, p. 43
Exh.: Paris, Au Sacre du Printemps, 1927; probably Paris, Salon de l'Escalier, 1928
Lent by Nicholas Pritzker, Chicago

From the group of about five photographs he made for Feri Róth, Kertész chose this particular image to crop down severely. The Róth Quartet performed Bartók, as well as the classical repertoire. This photograph is often titled in French as *Quatuor*. For reproduction, see p. 138.

21. *Mondrian's Glasses and Pipe*, 1926
Silver gelatin contact print on post-card stock, 80 x 95 mm
Signed and dated on recto in pencil "A. Kertész, 1926" in a later hand
Repr.: Hans Nachod, "Die Photographie

der Gegenwart," *Neue Leipziger Zeitung*, Aug. 20, 1929; *Sixty Years*, p. 116; Travis, no. 63, back cover; Fárová, no. 47; Wilde, no. 16; Abrams, p. 201; Manchester, #258, p. 162
Exh.: Paris, Au Sacre du Printemps, 1927; probably Paris, Salon de l'Escalier, 1928; Brussels, Galerie L'Epoque, 1928; Essen, Fotographie der Gegenwart, 1929; Stuttgart, Film und Foto, 1929; probably New York, Julien Levy Gallery, 1932 or 1937
Lent by Nicholas Pritzker, Chicago

Kertész was asked to make some photographs of Mondrian's studio and living quarters by the editor and aesthetician Michel Seuphor. Here Kertész slightly rearranged the pipes to modify the "static" quality he found in the studio. See remarks on cat. no. 63. For reproduction, see p. 136.

22. *Chez Mondrian*, 1926
Silver gelatin contact print on post-card stock mounted on vellum, 108 x 79 mm
Stamped on mount verso Paris stamp #2, Paris stamp #4, Levy stamp
Repr.: *The Complete Photographer*, ed. Willard D. Morgan, vol. 5 (New York: National Educational Alliance, 1943), between pp. 1584 and 1585; Brassaï, "My Friend André Kertész," *Camera* 42, no. 4 (Apr. 1963), p. 23; "The World of Kertész," *Show*, Mar. 1964, p. 61; Dan Budnik, "A Point Vue," *Infinity* 14, no. 3 (Mar. 1965), p. 11; Fárová, no. 43; *Sixty Years*, p. 119; Travis, no. 58, p. 6; Aperture, p. 87; Wilde, no. 15; Abrams, p. 206; Manchester, #112, p. 78
Exh.: Paris, Au Sacre du Printemps, 1927; probably Paris, Salon de l'Escalier, 1928; Brussels, Galerie L'Epoque, 1928; probably Buenos Aires, Primer Salon Anual de Fotografia, 1930; probably New York, Julien Levy Gallery, 1932 or 1937
The Art Institute of Chicago, The Julien Levy Collection, 1975.1136

Kertész moved the vase further into the center of the composition to concentrate the focus of attention. The exposure was made with available daylight. The straw hat belonged to Seuphor, everything else was Mondrian's. This is a very slightly cropped version of the original negative. For reproduction, see p. 136.

23. Mondrian's Studio, 1926
Silver gelatin contact print on post-card stock mounted on vellum, 108 x 68 mm
Signed and inscribed on mount recto in pencil "Paris"
Repr.: Fárová, no. 42; Szarkowski, p. 39;

Aperture, p. 77; Wilde, no. 17
Exh.: New York, The Museum of Modern
    Art, 1964
Lent by the Jedermann Collection, N.A.

This image also exists in several cropped
states, one of which is horizontal. For
reproduction, see p. 136.

24. *Mondrian*, 1926
Matte, single-weight, silver gelatin print
    mounted on a laid paper, 208 x 159 mm
Signed on mount recto in pencil "A. Kertész,
    Paris"
Repr.: Brassaï, "My Friend André
    Kertész," *Camera* 42, no. 4 (Apr. 1963),
    p. 23
Lent by Dr. Richard L. Sandor, Chicago

The prints made on matte paper and
mounted on a laid paper are rare. This
presentation seems to be for portraits only.
Other known portraits on this paper are of
Anne-Marie Merkel (cat. no. 14), Tristan
Tzara (cat. no. 42), Tihanyi (Magyar
Nemzeti Galleria, Budapest), and Csáky.
For reproduction, see p. 137.

25. *Satiric Dancer*, 1926
Silver gelatin print, 97 x 79 mm
Signed on mount recto in pencil "A.
    Kertész, Paris"
Repr.: *Die Dame*, Oct. 1927, p. 2;
    Szarkowski, p. 22; Fárová, no. 28;
    Sixty Years, p. 70; Aperture, p. 75;
    Abrams, p. 243; Manchester, #223,
    p. 138
Private Collection, New York

Along with *The Stairs of Montmartre* and
Chez Mondrian (cat. nos. 18, 22), this must
be one of the photographer's most well
known images. In recent years it has
become the most often reproduced photograph of Kertész's entire oeuvre. It was
made in the studio of a friend, the sculptor
István Beőthy, whose work can be seen on
the pedestal and wall. Michel Seuphor was
a supporter of his, and he wrote a monograph on Beőthy's work. Kertész made
several variants two and three years later,
one with the sculptor himself on the couch
and another with his wife and friends surrounding Magda Förstner, posed like a piece
of sculpture on a table. For reproduction,
see p. 139.

26. *Magda Förstner*, 1926
Silver gelatin contact print on post-card
    stock, 91 x 38 mm
Signed on recto in pencil "A. Kertész,
    Paris"
Repr.: *Portraits*, p. 16
Lent by Thomas Walther

Magda Förstner was a popular cabaret dancer
in Europe at this time, admired for her
humor and spontaneity. This photograph
was made at the same time as *Satiric
Dancer* (cat. no. 25). For reproduction, see
p. 139.

27. *Quai d'Orsay*, 1926
Later, semi-glossy, single-weight silver
    gelatin print made by Igor Bakht,
    110 x 79 mm
Repr.: *Paris Vu*, n. pag.; *Day of Paris*,
    p. 93; "Day of Paris," *Minicam Pho-
    tography* 8, no. 10 (July 1945), p. 27;
    Brassaï, "My Friend André Kertész,"
    Camera 42, no. 4 (Apr. 1963), p. 15
    (where it is dated 1927); Szarkowski,
    p. 20; Fárová, no. 33; *Sixty Years*,
    p. 130; *J'aime Paris*, p. 192; Aperture,
    p. 57; Abrams, p. 33
Exh.: Paris, Au Sacre du Printemps, 1927;
    New York, The Museum of Modern Art,
    1964
Lent by the Susan Harder Gallery, New
    York.

Between 1912 and 1926 Kertész favored a
4.5 x 6 cm camera, which was stolen from
him while he napped in the Luxembourg
Gardens. He replaced it with a square
format Ikaret, which he used until he
purchased a Leica in 1928. This negative
has been printed in several different croppings. According to the photographer, the
subject is a snobbish Frenchman, playing
at being a member of the gentry class,
while two proletarians pass by. For
reproduction, see p. 140.

28. Wall of Posters, 1926
Silver gelatin contact print on post-card
    stock, 105 x 80 mm
Signed on verso in pencil "A. Kertész,
    Apr. 23, 1980" and dated "1927" in a
    later hand
Repr.: *Das Illustrierte Blatt*, no. 44 (Nov.
    30, 1926) as "Reklamewand für die
    Tänzerin Spinelli"; Wilde, no. 6
Exh.: Paris, Au Sacre du Printemps, 1927
Lent by Thomas Walther

The office of *Vu* magazine on the Champs
Elysées was opposite this scene. In the late
1920s Kertész made several photographs of
clochards, most with ironic content. For
reproduction, see p. 140.

29. *Fête Foraine*, 1926
Silver gelatin contact print on post-card
    stock, 75 x 72 mm
Signed on recto in pencil "A. Kertész,
    Paris"; inscribed on verso in pencil
    "Typikus párisi búcsú" (typical
    Parisian festival)

Lent by the J. Paul Getty Museum, Malibu

This print was sent to Elizabeth in
Budapest. For reproduction, see p. 142.

30. *Clowns of the Fête Foraine*, 1926
Silver gelatin contact print on post-card
    stock, 102 x 79 mm
Signed on recto in pencil "A. Kertész,
    Paris"
Repr.: *J'aime Paris*, p. 178
Lent by the J. Paul Getty Museum, Malibu

Kertész was especially fascinated by the
folk characters of these street fairs. This
print was sent to Elizabeth in Budapest.
For reproduction, see p. 142.

31. Caretaker's House, 1926
Silver gelatin contact print on post-card
    stock, 108 x 79 mm
Repr.: Wilde, no. 9
Lent by Nicholas Pritzker, Chicago

Kertész sent this photograph of a concierge's
entrance in a modest section of Paris to his
brother Jenő in Buenos Aires. For reproduction, see p. 143.

32. *Boats on the Seine Outside Paris*,
    1926/27
Silver gelatin contact print on post-card
    stock, 57 x 102 mm
Signed on recto in pencil "A. Kertész,
    Paris"
The Art Institute of Chicago, Wirt D.
    Walker Fund, 1984.547

Kertész made two very similar photographs
of this subject, the barges on the Seine just
outside Paris where workmen lived; both
the subject and its location greatly appealed
to him. For reproduction, see p. 143.

33. *Seuphor on the Pont des Arts*, 1926
Silver gelatin contact print on post-card
    stock, 48 x 109 mm
Signed on recto in pencil "A. Kertész,
    Paris"
Repr.: *Paris Vu*, n. pag.
Lent by the New Orleans Museum of Art,
    Museum Purchase through the Women's
    Volunteer Commitee Funds, 73.178

The man in the straw hat is Seuphor, who
sometimes explored the city with Kertész.
For reproduction, see p. 143.

34. *Zadkine in His Studio*, 1926
Silver gelatin contact print on post-card
    stock, 108 x 69 mm
Signed on recto in pencil "A. Kertész,
    Paris"
Repr.: Pierre Mac Orlan, "Le Centenaire
    de l'accordéon," *Les Annales*, no. 2 (Feb.

15, 1929), p. 172; *J'aime Paris*, p. 113
Private Collection, New York

The sculptor Ossip Zadkine is shown in his studio in Montparnasse. He was an admirer of African sculpture, as his mask on the wall reveals. Like Kertész, Zadkine was one of the many Central European artists who immigrated to Paris at this time and endowed the art of the 1920s with a special decorative style that departed from earlier Cubism. He was also a proficient accordian player; his instrument lies next to him on the couch. For reproduction, see p. 144.

35. At Zadkine's, 1926
Silver gelatin contact print on post-card
  stock mounted on heavy paper, 105 x
  67 mm
Signed on mount recto in pencil "A.
  Kertész, Paris"
Repr.: Fárová, no. 44
Exh.: New York, PM Gallery, 1937
Lent by Thomas Walther

Zadkine was also a good friend of Modigliani, whose influence can be inferred from the sculpted head. Kertész was fond of selecting the corner of a room that would signify the personality of the inhabitant. Léger's and Mondrian's studios, to name only two, are described in this manner. Zadkine's penchant for convivial drinking with friends and his attraction to popular art forms like puppetry are represented in this composition. For reproduction, see p. 144.

36. Woman on Stairs, 1926/27
Silver gelatin contact print on post-card
  stock, 105 x 51 mm
Signed on recto in pencil "A. Kertész,
  Paris"
Lent by the J. Paul Getty Museum, Malibu

This woman was a Yugoslav ballerina. Kertész sent this print to Elizabeth in Budapest. For reproduction, see p. 141.

37. Young Woman with a Curl of Hair,
  1926/27
Silver gelatin contact print on post-card
  stock, 87 x 67 mm
The Art Institute of Chicago, Wirt D.
  Walker Fund, 1984.546

This young woman was a relative of József Csáky's wife whom Kertész asked to pose. He thought she was "a lovely French girl with a beautiful, typically French face." For reproduction, see p. 141.

38. Portrait of a Young German Doctor,
  1926/27
Silver gelatin contact print on post-card
  stock, 109 x 68 mm

The Art Institute of Chicago, Wirt D.
  Walker Fund, 1984.538

Kertész was introduced to this woman, visiting Paris from her native Germany, by their mutual friend Gyula Zilzer (see remarks on cat. no. 6). For reproduction, see p. 141.

39. Portrait of a Young Yugoslav
  Bibliophile, 1926/27
Silver gelatin contact print on post-card
  stock, 108 x 79 mm
The Art Institute of Chicago, Wirt D.
  Walker Fund, 1984.545

The sitter, an acquaintance of Kertész from the Dôme, commissioned him to make this portrait. For reproduction, see p. 141.

40. Self-Portrait at Table, 1927
Silver gelatin contact print on post-card
  stock, 79 x 108 mm
Repr.: Szarkowski, p. 6 (detail)
Lent by the J. Paul Getty Museum, Malibu

For remarks on this photograph, see Phillips, p. 30. For reproduction, see p. 16.

41. The Studio Cat, 1927
Silver gelatin contact print on post-card
  stock mounted on vellum, 90 x 79 mm
Signed and dated on mount recto in pencil
Repr.: Sylviac, "Superstitions," *Vu*, no.
  143 (Dec. 10, 1930), p. 1343; William
  Houseman, "André Kertész," *Infinity* 8,
  no. 4 (Apr. 1959), p. 6; Manchester,
  #136, p. 90
Exh.: Paris, Au Sacre du Printemps, 1927;
  Essen, Fotographie der Gegenwart, 1929;
  Munich, Das Lichtbild, 1930
Lent by Harriette and Noel Levine, New
  York

Kertész visited the studio of a Swiss sculptor who was a friend of Vincent Korda. According to Kertész, the cat was an important ingredient of this photograph; in fact, he returned the day after he had first seen it in this position and waited for the cat to resume the same pose. He illuminated the subject with a magnesium flash. For reproduction, see p. 144.

42. *Tristan Tzara*, 1927?
Matte, single-weight, silver gelatin print
  mounted on a laid paper, 216 x 159 mm
Signed on mount recto in pencil "A.
  Kertész, Paris"; titled and dated on verso
  in pencil; stamped on verso New York
  stamp #7
Repr.: "The World of Kertész," *Show*,
  Mar. 1964, p. 59; *Sixty Years*, p. 101;

Abrams, p. 143
Lent by Dr. Richard L. Sandor, Chicago

Kertész was invited to inspect the building progress of Tzara's house with the architect Adolf Loos. A variant was published in the *Documents internationaux de l'esprit nouveau*, as an illustration to a fragment of Tzara's poem "L'Homme approximatif." For reproduction, see p. 145.

43. Avenue Junot, 1927?
Photographische Rundschau und Mitteilungen magazine printed in halftone
  278 x 212 mm
Repr.: Wilhelm-Kästner, "Photographie
  der Gegenwart, Grundsätzliches zur
  Ausstellung im Museum Folkwang,"
  *Photographische Rundschau und
  Mitteilungen* 66, no. 5 (1929), p. 99;
  Film und Foto, no. 20, p. 162
Exh.: Essen, Fotographie der Gegenwart,
  1929; Stuttgart, Film und Foto, 1929
Lent by André Kertész, New York

This photograph was made from the window of Tzara's new house; the street below was being repaired at that time. For reproduction, see p. 32.

44. *Montparnasse, Square Jolivet*, 1927
Semi-glossy, single-weight silver gelatin
  print mounted on vellum 215 x 160 mm
Stamped on mount verso Paris stamp #2
Repr.: A.H. Kober, "Die Unterwelt der
  Grosstädte," *Uhu*, Sept. 1929, pp. 74–75;
  Photographie, 1930, p. 49; Pierre Bost,
  Photographies modernes (Paris, 1930),
  pl. 1; "Images," *L'Illustration*, no.
  4539 (Mar. 1, 1930), p. 291; *Paris Vu*,
  n. pag.; *Coronet* 4, no. 1 (May 1938), p.
  117; *Day of Paris*, p. 131; *Sixty Years*,
  p. 139; *J'aime Paris*, p. 9; Manchester,
  #184, p. 122
Exh.: Stuttgart, Film und Foto, 1929;
  Buenos Aires, Primer Salon Anual de
  Fotografia, 1930; New York, PM Gallery,
  1937
Lent by the Jedermann Collection, N.A.

Kertész made one photograph of this park in daylight from the window of a friend's apartment. He then returned specifically at night to make this other, more characteristic view. The daylight exposure is horizontal in format. This image has been cropped down from an originally horizontal negative. See remarks on cat. no. 63. For reproduction, see p. 147.

45. *Bistro*, 1927
Semi-glossy, single-weight silver gelatin
  print, 200 x 129 mm
Stamped on verso Paris stamp #2, Paris
  stamp #4, Levy stamp

Repr.: "Les Heures de Paris," *L'Image*, no. 27 (1932), p. 7; *Paris Vu*, n. pag.; *Day of Paris*, p. 133; *Sixty Years*, p. 104

Exh.: probably New York, Julien Levy Gallery, 1932 or 1937

The Art Institute of Chicago, The Julien Levy Collection, 1979.72

During an assignment to photograph the mosque in Paris, Kertész noticed this little café, adjacent to an Arab coffee shop. He went back later to photograph the café and using his tripod made this image just before the lights were turned off. The exposure took about one half hour. For reproduction, see p. 149.

46. *Primel*, 1927
Silver gelatin contact print on post-card stock, 68 x 64 mm
Titled and dated on recto in pencil "Primel, 1927"
Lent by the J. Paul Getty Museum, Malibu

Primel is in Brittany, which Kertész visited with Beőthy. This print was sent to Elizabeth in Budapest. For reproduction, see p. 142.

47. *Les Halles in the Early Morning*, 1927
Semi-glossy, single-weight silver gelatin print, 238 x 177 mm
Stamped on verso Paris stamp #2, Paris stamp #4, Levy stamp
Repr.: *Day of Paris*, p. 27; *J'aime Paris*, p. 88
Exh.: probably New York, Julien Levy Gallery, 1932 or 1937
The Art Institute of Chicago, The Julien Levy Collection, 1979.74

This is another of the many photographs Kertész made over the years of one of his favorite subjects. He was naturally drawn to the peasant who enters the city, bringing nature with him. For reproduction, see p. 150.

48. *Siesta*, 1927
Semi-glossy, single-weight silver gelatin print, 239 x 155 mm
Stamped on verso Paris stamp #2, Paris stamp #4, Levy stamp
Repr.: Carlo Rim, "Curiosités photographiques," *L'Art vivant* 6, no. 135 (Aug. 1930), pp. 604-05; Pierre Mac Orlan, "Visages et paysages populaires de Paris," *Art et Médecine*, Oct. 1931, p. 46; *Jeunesse*, no. 3 (Dec. 1935), p. 1; *Paris Vu*, n. pag.; *Coronet* 4, no. 1 (May 1938), p. 167; *Day of Paris*, p. 91; *Sixty Years*, p. 131; *J'aime Paris*, p. 17; Aperture, p. 49; Abrams, p. 67; Manchester, #104, p. 70
Exh.: probably Paris, Au Sacre du Prin-

temps, 1927; probably Munich, Das Lichtbild, 1930; probably New York, Julien Levy Gallery, 1932 or 1937; New York, PM Gallery, 1937

The Art Institute of Chicago, The Julien Levy Collection, 1979.80

This image was made looking down on a quai in the Hôtel de Ville area (not the quai d'Orsay as sometimes identified). The composition was much admired by Florent Fels, who published it in *L'Art vivant*. Kertész recalls that it was also published in 1928 by the Larousse firm to illustrate a guidebook to Paris. The photograph was made on a glass-plate negative. For reproduction, see p. 151.

49. *Chairs, the Tuileries*, 1927
Semi-glossy, single-weight silver gelatin print, 225 x 166 mm
Inscribed on verso in pencil "Les Tuileries, 1927"; inscribed "n.p. 114," "A. Kertész, Nov. 3, 1983" in a later hand; stamped on verso Paris stamp #2, Paris stamp #4, New York stamp #1 with manuscript address change to 67 W.
Repr.: Florent Fels, "Photographie— nouvel organe, "*L'Art vivant* 7, no. 147 (Apr. 1931), p. 146; *Paris Vu*, n. pag.; *Sixty Years*, p. 114; Manchester, #103, p. 70
Exh.: probably New York, Julien Levy Gallery, 1932 or 1937
The Art Institute of Chicago, Wirt D. Walker Fund, 1984.537

In his article on photography as a new aesthetic medium, Florent Fels chose this photograph along with others by Kertész's contempories (including Roger Parry and Man Ray) to illustrate his point that light and shadow can be used mysteriously and evocatively. The treatment is here sharper and more clarified than in the earliest example (see cat. no. 17), still distinctively personal in comparison to the other photographs shown in *L'Art vivant*. Photographs of the same subject were made by Ilse Bing and others. For reproduction, see p. 146.

50. Mrs. Rosskam, 1927
Silver gelatin contact print on post-card stock mounted on vellum at an angle, 53 x 70 mm
Signed on mount recto in pencil
Repr.: *Vu*, no. 5 (Apr. 18, 1928), p. 128 (not reproduced at an angle)
The Art Institute of Chicago, Restricted gift of Mrs. Leigh B. Block, 1980.43

Edwin Rosskam, an American photographer and writer, then living in Paris, knew Kertész from the Café du Dôme and asked him to take photographs of himself and his wife in their Montmartre studio, an apart-

ment designed by Le Corbusier. Kertész was fascinated by the space and made a series of photographs of the Rosskams from various angles and in different parts of the interior. These photographs were cropped in several different ways, and a version with both Mr. and Mrs. Rosskam was shown at the Salon de l'Escalier show, and later in 1937 at the PM Gallery show in New York. This particular version is unique because of the angular way Kertész mounted it. Alfred Stieglitz took two photographs meant to be viewed at a similar angle in the same year. Perhaps both photographers were responding to Mondrian's diamond paintings of the period. For reproduction, see p. 152.

51. *Pierre Mac Orlan*, 1927
Silver gelatin contact print on post-card stock, 107 x 79 mm
Inscribed on verso in pencil by the photographer "Pierre Mac Orlan/1927"
Repr.: Variant published in Pierre Mac Orlan, "Defense et illustration de l'accordéon," *Mon Programme*, Feb. 2, 1934, p. 33; *Sixty Years*, p. 106
The Art Institute of Chicago, Wirt D. Walker Fund, 1984.532

Pierre Mac Orlan, whose real name was Pierre Dumarchey (or variously, Dumarchại or Dumarchais), was a novelist and poet who wrote about the lives of the lower class, mainly in cities. Like Kertész, he also considered himself a journalist. He was interested in crossing the line that separated "popular" culture from high art. Therefore, photography, especially documentary and anonymous photography, was appealing to him, and he wrote eloquently about it. His own work has a folklike primitivism and atmospheric sensitivity—especially to grey days in poorer sections of cities. He was naturally sympathetic to Kertész's photography, as the photographer was to him. A variant of this portrait was published in the Belgian magazine *Variétés*, where Mac Orlan's work frequently appeared (see Phillips, fig. 30). For reproduction, see p. 152.

52. *Paul Dermée*, 1927?
Silver gelatin contact print on post-card stock, 93 x 68 mm
Repr.: *Portraits*, p. 7
Lent by the Edwynn Houk Gallery, Chicago

The poet Paul Dermée had been a Dadaist, a proto-Surrealist, and had helped to found the original magazine *L'Esprit Nouveau*. (For a discussion of this, the *Documents internationaux*, and the events surrounding Kertész's opening, see pp. 34–35.) This photograph, which has been cut down slightly, was made before Kertész knew that Dermée had written a very sensitive poem about his work. On the back of the announcement for the exhibition, Dermée wrote:

Frère voyant

Ne fût-ce que pour la rime, Hamlet, tu devais ajouter: Il y a plus de choses dans la nature que dans les oeuvres d'art et les littératures.

Seuls les découvreurs et les inventeurs créent, enrichissent le domaine public. Il n'existe que par eux, ce dont on leur sait mal gré.

Dans le monde visuel, pour faire de perpétuelles découvertes, il suffit d'y promener des yeux dont la rétine redevient vierge à chaque clin — film qui se dévide san fin.

Mais tous, ne photographiez-vous pas la nature sur une plaque que vous n'avez pas changée depuis le jour de votre naissance!

Kertész,

  des yeux d'enfant dont chaque
   regard est le premier;
   qui voient le grand roi nu, lorsqu'il
   est vêtu de mensonges;
   qui s'effraient des fantômes drapés
   de bâches hantant les quais de Seine;
   qui s'extasient devant les tableaux
   tout neufs que créent, sans malice,
   trois chaise au soleil du Luxembourg,
   la porte de Mondrian s'ouvrant sur
   l'escalier, des lunettes jetées sur une
   table à côté d'une pipe.

Pas d'arrangement, de rangement, de trucage, de contreplacage.

Votre technique est aussi loyale, aussi incorruptible que votre vision.

Dans notre hospice des Quinze-Vingts. Kertész est un frère voyant.

For reproduction, see p. 152.

53. Still Life in Bookshop Window, 1927?
Silver gelatin contact print on post-card
 stock mounted on vellum, 99 x 72 mm
Signed on recto in pencil; inscribed on
 verso in pencil "Evsa Model."
Lent by Ealan J. Wingate, New York

The bookstore L'Esthétique, located near the Café du Dôme, was owned by a cousin of the Russian painter Evsa Model, the future husband of the photographer Lisette Model. Kertész and Evsa Model were good friends, and Model decorated the window in very fanciful ways and asked Kertész to record these arrangements. L'Esthétique was one of the establishments that regularly stocked books and related materials from all over Europe on contemporary trends in art. Kertész's other photographs of

L'Esthétique appeared in *Documents internationaux de l'espirit nouveau* and in Gallotti's 1929 *L'Art vivant* article on Kertész's photography. For reproduction, see p. 153.

54. Hands and Books, 1927
Silver gelatin contact print on post-card
 stock mounted on vellum, 95 x 58 mm
Signed and dated on mount recto in pencil
 "A. Kertész, 1927"
Repr.: "Les Médecins littérateurs," *Art et
 Médecine*, no. 4 (Jan. 1931), p. 39
Exh.: Paris, Salon de l'Escalier, 1928;
 Essen, Fotographie der Gegenwart, 1929;
 Stuttgart, Film und Foto, 1929
Lent by Harriette and Noel Levine, New
 York

Kertész also knew the manager of another bookstore, the Librairie H. Soudier at 174–76, boulevard St. Germain, and made this photograph for his own interest. It was later printed and used by the store for bookcovers. Kertész also photographed in a globe the bookstore of Edouard Loewy, now operated by his brother, Alexandre Loewy. For reproduction, see p. 153.

55. *L'Elégance du Métier*, 1927/28
Vu magazine printed by rotogravure,
 370 x 270 mm, each page
Repr.: *Vu* 6, no. 264 (Apr. 5, 1933),
 pp. 504–05
Lent by Sandra S. Phillips, Annandale-on-
 Hudson, New York

Attracted by the activity around Les Halles, Kertész in 1927 started to photograph its inhabitants, first a butcher, later other workmen in this area. Lucien Vogel, editor of *Vu*, was attracted by Kertész's photographs and asked him to complete this series for publication. For reproduction, see p. 154.

56. Smokestacks at Night, 1927/28
Semi-glossy, single-weight silver gelatin
 print, 157 x 181 mm
Stamped on verso Paris stamp #2, Paris
 stamp #4, Levy stamp
Exh.: probably New York, Julien Levy
 Gallery, 1932 or 1937
The Art Institute of Chicago, The Julien
 Levy Collection, 1978.1079

For reproduction, see p. 148.

57. *Mr. Titus, Editor and Publisher, Rue
 Delambre*, 1928
Silver gelatin contact print on post-card
 stock, 109 x 77 mm
Inscribed on recto in pencil "Mr. Titus
 (editeur) Rue Delambre (Paris 1928)";
 stamped on verso New York stamp #1

Lent by the New Orleans Museum of Art, Museum Purchase through the Women's Volunteer Committee Funds, 73.168

Edward Titus, the husband of Helena Rubenstein, and an important though small-scale expatriate publisher, took over the little magazine *This Quarter* after its founder Ernest Walsh died. He also published a novel by Manuel Komroff (whom Kertész also photographed) and an English translation of Kiki's memoirs. Titus's bookstore was virtually next door to the Café du Dôme. For this photograph Kertész asked Titus to step outside and look in the window at the display. For reproduction, see p. 153.

58. *Meudon*, 1928
Later silver gelatin print,
 230 x 170 mm
Repr.: *Day of Paris*, p. 83; Szarkowski,
 p. 32; Fárová, no. 25; *Sixty Years*,
 p. 141; Aperture, p. 53; Abrams, p. 31;
 Manchester, #44, p. 42
Lent by the Susan Harder Gallery, New
 York

With the Leica camera that he bought in 1928, Kertész was finally able to make images with the ease and spontaneousness that he had long wanted. He had known this area well before 1928, and he happened to be wandering around when he made this photograph and another that immediately preceded it before the train appeared overhead. Since its publication in *Day of Paris* in 1945, this image has become as popular as *Chez Mondrian* (cat. no. 22) and *Satiric Dancer* (cat. no. 25). Kertész recalls making a print in the late 1920s, but no record exists of his submitting it to exhibitions or publications—leaving us to assume that it was not a well-known image at the time it was made. For reproduction, see p. 165.

59. *Paul Arma*, 1928
Silver gelatin contact print on post-card
 stock, 79 x 79 mm
The Art Institute of Chicago, Wirt D.
 Walker Fund, 1984.534

Paul Arma, whose actual name is Imre Weisshaus, was a piano student of Béla Bartók in Budapest. He has led an extremely active and eventful life, which, after Paris, took him to America, where he befriended Edward Weston, and later to the Bauhaus in Dessau. Kertész photographed him on March 15, 1928 (according to Arma), when Arma was actively involved in concertizing in Paris. Presently he is a composer and an arranger of folk music, living in Paris. For reproduction, see p. 156.

60. Paul Arma's Hands, 1928
Silver gelatin contact print on post-card
    stock, 61 x 65 mm
Repr.: Jean Gallotti, "La Photographie
    est-elle un art?—Kertesz," L'Art vivant
    5 (Mar. 1, 1929), p. 208; Raymond
    Edwards, "A Note or Two on Music,"
    The Argus (San Francisco), Mar. 1929,
    p. 12; Photographie, 1930, p. 48;
    "Lectures," Art et Médecine, no. 4
    (Jan. 1931), p. 38
Exh.: Munich, Das Lichtbild, 1930;
    probably New York, The Art Center,
    1931; probably New York, Julien Levy
    Gallery, 1932 or 1937
The Metropolitan Museum of Art, New
    York, 1979.687

After Kertész made the above portrait of
Paul Arma (cat. no. 59), he made several
others (see cat. nos. 61, 62) that were
details and variations. Some of these were
later cropped down, as this example has
been. For reproduction, see p. 156.

61. Paul Arma's Hands and Shadows I,
1928
Silver gelatin contact print mounted later,
    96 x 72 mm
Signed on recto in pencil "A. Kertész";
    inscribed on verso in pencil "Paul Arma's
    hand, Paris 1928" and "A. Kertész,
    July 2, 1982," all in a later hand
Repr.: Salon of Ultra Modern Art, Program
    Notes for a concert by Imre Weisshaus,
    Hollywood, California, Feb. 25, 1929
Lent by John C. Waddell, New York

For reproduction, see p. 157.

62. Paul Arma's Hands and Shadows II,
1928
Silver gelatin contact print on post-card
    stock, 103 x 45 mm
Inscribed on mount "A mon Ami Paul,
    A. Kertész"
Lent by Paul Arma, Paris

This is the least known and most dramatic
version of the Arma series. Its long,
attenuated format is similar to that of
Cello Study (cat. no. 19). For reproduction,
see p. 157.

63. Ropes, 1928
Semi-glossy, single-weight silver gelatin
    print mounted on vellum, 225 x 167 mm
Signed and dated on mount recto in pencil
    "A. Kertész"; inscribed in lower right
    "451"; inscribed on mount verso in
    pencil in another hand "Des cordes,
    1928, Kertész"; "15" and in red "4521"
    with the "2" effaced to read 451
Repr.: [Wilhelm] Lotz, "Film und Foto,"
    Die Form, June 1929, p. 279

Exh.: Essen, Fotografie der Gegenwart,
    1929; Stuttgart, Film und Foto, 1929
The Art Institute of Chicago, Ada Turnbull
    Hertle Fund, 1984.542

While on a trip to Deauville to visit two
friends, the painter and illustrator Marcel
Vertès and the Japanese artist Foujita,
Kertész observed these discarded, tangled
ropes. He included this image in the photographs sent to the "Film und Foto"
exhibition in Stuttgart in 1929. The
Staatliche Museen Kunstbibliothek, Berlin,
bought this photograph along with others
(cat. nos. 17, 44, and one titled Chimneys).
Other museums made purchases of
Kertész's work including the König Albert
Museum in Zwickau, which bought two
photographs (cat. nos. 21 and 44). These
sales marked the first time Kertész's works
entered public collections. For reproduction,
see p. 158.

64. In Les Halles, 1928
Semi-glossy, single-weight silver gelatin
    print, 165 x 215 mm
Stamped on verso Paris stamp #2, Paris
    stamp #4
Repr.: Photographie, 1931, no. 112;
    Fárová, no. 49; Sixty Years, p. 123;
    Abrams, p. 121
Exh.: Munich, Das Lichtbild, 1930; Paris,
    11e Salon de l'Araignée, 1930; probably
    New York, Julien Levy Gallery, 1932
    or 1937
The Art Institute of Chicago, The Julien
    Levy Collection, 1979.71

This photograph was also made with the
new Leica. Unlike the more complicated
procedure he had to follow in the earlier
Stairs of Montmartre (cat. no. 18), this was
a composition Kertész had seen before but
was now able to take easily. Without the
Leica, Kertész recalls that the perspective
would have been wrong. For reproduction,
see p. 159.

65. Fork, 1928
Semi-glossy, single-weight silver gelatin
    print, 75 x 93 mm
Repr.: [Wilhelm] Lotz, "Film und Foto,"
    Die Form, June 1929, p. 279; "Eine
    neue Künstler-Gilde: Der Fotograf
    erobert Neuland," Uhu 6, no. 1 (Oct.
    1929), p. 36; Die Dame 4 (Nov. 1929),
    p. 72 (as an advertisement); Pierre Bost,
    Photographies modernes (Paris, 1930),
    pl. 2; Photographie, 1930, p. 85; Fárová,
    no. 48; Sixty Years, p. 117; Wilde,
    no. 13; Abrams, p. 199
Exh.: Paris, Salon de l'Escalier, 1928;
    Brussels, Galerie L'Epoque, 1928;
    Rotterdam, Internationale Foto-Salon,

1928; Essen, Fotografie der Gegenwart,
    1929; Stuttgart, Film und Foto, 1929;
    New York, PM Gallery, 1937
The Art Institute of Chicago, Ada Turnbull
    Hertle Fund, 1984.539

This photograph was very well known to
Kertész's contemporaries in both Germany
and France. Asked to contribute to an article on the new photography for the popular
German magazine Uhu, Kertész chose to
represent his work with this photograph.
Peter Bruckmann, a member of the organization that sponsored the "Film und Foto"
show, asked that he be permitted to use
this photograph as an advertisement for his
silverware company. Kertész finally permitted its use, since the photograph was by
then recognized as an aesthetic expression.
The fork itself, however, was an ordinary
utensil he had picked up at the Bazaar de
l'Hôtel de Ville. The following year (1930)
Charles Peignot reproduced this image in
his annual, Photographie, opposite a
Steichen photograph of a pear on a plate.

For exhibitions Kertész often preferred
semi-glossy, single-weight silver gelatin
prints mounted on vellum; his exhibition
in 1927 at the gallery Au Sacre du Printemps consisted of such a presentation. This
print and several others like it, however,
were made to the size of the carte postale
photographs, but on a different stock. It is
probable that the post-card stock was no
longer available around 1928 and that for a
short period Kertész continued to print this
small format on other papers. There are at
least three other examples of this photograph in this format on a non-post-card
stock in the Pritzker Collection (the same
print which he sent to his brother Jenő in
Argentina), in the Walther Collection, and
in Kertész's own collection (the same print
which he sent to Elizabeth in Budapest).
The same stock was used to print cat. no. 73.
For reproduction, see p. 160.

66. African Sculptures, 1928
Silver gelatin contact print on post-card
    stock, 81 x 79 mm
Signed on recto in pencil "A. Kertész,
    Paris"; inscribed on verso "Kicsit sötét
    kópia. Néger szobrok." (A print, a bit
    dark. Negro sculptures.)
Repr.: Ida Treat, "La Femme il y a 25,000
    ans," Vu, no. 15 (June 1928), p. 376
Lent by Nicholas Pritzker, Chicago

An artist whose name Kertész has now
forgotten had a collection of African sculptures. Kertész, while visiting him, asked to
photograph them. He set the figures next
to a chair to indicate proportion. Vogel, the
director of Vu, was very interested in this

photograph and included it in an article comparing the prehistoric female figure, primitive sculpture (exemplified by this photograph), and African and modern European body types. Kertész sent this print to his brother Jenő in Buenos Aires. For reproduction, see p. 144.

67. Ady's Poem, c. 1928
Semi-glossy, single-weight silver gelatin
    print, 231 x 172 mm
Stamped on verso Paris stamp #3
Repr.: György Bölöni, *Az Igazi Ady*,
    (Paris, 1934), between pp. 120 and 121
Lent by the Petőfi Irodalmi Museum of
    Hungarian Literature, Budapest

Kertész knew the Hungarian writer György Bölöni as a journalist in Paris, but he had been a good friend of the poet and patriot Endre Ady and wrote a critical biography of Ady that concentrated on the poet's years in Paris. Kertész's sensitive photographs of Ady's milieu visualized those years of the expatriate's life for his countrymen. Ady frequently composed his poems in cafés; this photograph shows a manuscript of one. Bölöni's caption for it was, "The way a poem of Ady's began on a café table in Paris." For reproduction, see p. 162.

68. Still Life in Ady's Room, c. 1928
Semi-glossy, single-weight silver gelatin
    print, 238 x 179 mm
Repr.: György Bölöni, *Az Igazi Ady*,
    (Paris, 1934), following p. 184
Lent by the Petőfi Irodalmi Museum of
    Hungarian Literature, Budapest

This still life arranged in a cheap hotel room includes a French newspaper, a Hungarian Bible, and a glass of wine. The Hungarian Bible—based on John Calvin's translation—was an important source for Ady's verse; he admired the spare rhythms of its special language. Bölöni gave it the caption, "Ady's hotel room looked something like this." For reproduction, see p. 162.

69. In the Chartier Restaurant, c. 1928
Semi-glossy, single-weight silver gelatin
    print, 230 x 177 mm
Stamped on verso Paris stamp #3
Lent by the Petőfi Irodalmi Museum of
    Hungarian Literature, Budapest

Ady visited Paris during the turn of the century—a period reflected in the restaurant's elegant art nouveau decoration, which Kertész also admired. Like Ady, Kertész was an habitué of cafés and parks, a foreigner enjoying the places open to everyone. The man in the restaurant is György Bölöni. This is a close variant of a photograph reproduced in Bölöni's book on Ady (between pp. 120 and 121), where it is captioned, "The student quarter restaurant, Chartier, where Ady used to lunch, unchanged since 1900." For reproduction, see p. 163.

70. *Rue de Lévis, Montmartre*, c. 1928
Semi-glossy, single-weight silver gelatin
    print, 176 x 234 mm
Repr.: György Bölöni, *Az Igazi Ady*,
    (Paris, 1934), following p. 88; *Day of
    Paris*, p. 23; *J'aime Paris*, p. 87
Lent by the Petőfi Irodalmi Museum of
    Hungarian Literature, Budapest

When Kertész went with György Bölöni to visit the street where Ady lived, the rue de Lévis, they found this flock of goats led by a goatherd selling milk and cheese. Bölöni can be seen standing to the right, next to the building. Bölöni gave the photograph this caption, "In Ady's street goats are still seen." For reproduction, see p. 164.

71. *Rue de Médicis*, c. 1928
Semi-glossy, single-weight silver gelatin
    print, 237 x 178 mm
Stamped on verso Paris stamp #3
Repr.: *Paris Vu*, n. pag.
Lent by the Petőfi Irodalmi Museum of
    Hungarian Literature, Budapest

Again, this photograph is a variant of one in Bölöni's book that was in fact taken just before it (the man is farther away). For a caption Bölöni chose the opening line of an Ady poem, "Autumn entered Paris unnoticed. . . ." In this photograph Kertész shares some of Ady's attitudes toward the common man. Ady was one of the early and important Hungarians to take a serious look at the inequalities of the Hungarian social system and to seek to reform it. He was deeply interested in the common man, whether a city dweller or a peasant, as a vehicle both for his own symbolism and for his political idealism. Ady lived to see the dissolution of the Austro-Hungarian Empire, the idealism of Károlyi's short-lived democratic republic, but he died before the establishment of the Commune and, soon thereafter, Horthy's fascist regime. For reproduction, see p. 166.

72. The Luxembourg Gardens, c. 1928
Semi-glossy, single-weight silver gelatin
    print, 178 x 238 mm
Stamped on verso Paris stamp #3
Repr.: *Paris Vu*, n. pag.
Lent by the Petőfi Irodalmi Museum of
    Hungarian Literature, Budapest

Kertész took a series of photographs of chairs in Parisian parks and gardens. This image was not published in the Ady book although Bölöni felt its spirit corresponded to the mood of Ady's poetry; instead, he used a very similar photograph. For reproduction, see p. 167.

73. *St. André des Arts*, 1928?
Semi-glossy, single-weight silver gelatin
    print, 81 x 105 mm
Repr.: *Day of Paris*, pp. 46–47
The Art Institute of Chicago, Ada Turnbull
    Hertle Fund, 1984.540

See remarks on cat. no. 65. For reproduction, see p. 143.

74. Study of People and Shadows, 1928?
Semi-glossy, single-weight silver gelatin
    print, 155 x 216 mm
Stamped on verso Paris stamp #1
Repr.: Jean Gallotti, "La Photographie
    est-elle un art?—Kertesz," *L'Art vivant*
    5 (Mar. 1, 1929), p. 209
Exh.: probably Essen, Fotografie der
    Gegenwart, 1929
Lent by the J. Paul Getty Museum, Malibu

Kertész made many photographs from windows, looking at his subject from above, and this is one of the earliest. Often the subjects are children on their way to school, because there were schools not far from Kertész's first and third residences in Paris. A photograph similar to this one was used by Marcel Natkin to demonstrate the artful components photography can possess. What attracted Kertész were not only the abstract shapes made by the shadows and the abstracted figures seen from this uncustomary angle, but their eery and amusing relationship to the actual people and things. For reproduction, see p. 161.

75. Street Work, 1929
Semi-glossy, single-weight silver gelatin
    print made in New York, 249 x 289 mm
Signed and dated on verso in pencil;
    stamped on verso New York stamp #1
Exh.: New York, The Museum of Modern
    Art, 1937
Lent by Robert Koch, Berkeley

Although this photograph resembles one by Eugène Atget, Kertész asserts today that he was not aware of Atget's work until later. A small selection of Atget's work was seen publicly for the first time in Paris at the Salon de l'Escalier, courtesy of Berenice Abbott. A variant of this was published in *J'aime Paris*, p. 53. Few if any of Kertész prints made in Paris were this large. This photograph was taken with a Leica and has been cropped. For reproduction, see p. 155.

76. Boy Archer, 1929
Semi-glossy, single-weight silver gelatin
    print mounted on vellum, 178 x 216 mm
Signed and dated on mount recto in pencil;
    stamped on mount verso Paris stamp #2,
    Paris stamp #4, Levy stamp
Repr.: S.V., "Les Archers de nos jours,"
    Vu, no. 63 (May 29, 1929), p. 422;
    Enfants, p. 32
Exh.: Buenos Aires, Primer Salon Anual de
    Fotografia, 1930; Paris, 11ᵉ Salon de
    l'Araignée, 1930; probably New York,
    Julien Levy Gallery, 1932 or 1937
The Art Institute of Chicago, The Julien
    Levy Collection, 1979.73

This photograph was originally made for
an essay on archery in *Vu*. The negative
has been printed in several croppings.
For reproduction, see p. 168.

77. *Alexander Calder*, 1929
Semi-glossy, single-weight silver gelatin
    print made in New York, 251 x 224 mm
Inscribed on verso in pencil "Calder" and
    dated
Repr.: Szarkowski, p. 38; Fárová, no. 36;
    Portraits, p. 56
Exh.: New York, PM Gallery, 1937
Lent by André Kertész, New York

This photograph is one of several that were
made when Kertész visited Calder's studio
with friends to watch the artist perform his
Circus. Kertész knew him from the Dôme.
For reproduction, see p. 169.

78. *Storefront* and *Montparnasse, rue de
    Vanves*, c. 1929
Rotogravure reproduction in *Bifur*,
    235 x 190 mm
Repr.: *Bifur* 1 (May 1929), opposite p. 72;
    Day of Paris, p. 132
Lent by Sandra S. Phillips, Annandale-on-
    Hudson, New York

Bifur was one of the many literary publications in Paris that showed some acquaintance with Surrealism. Its editor, Georges
Ribemont-Dessaignes, knew Kertész's work
and asked to choose photographs for
publication. His photographs were reproduced in the first and third issues. For
reproduction, see p. 39.

79. *Vert Galant on a Wintry Day*, c. 1929
Rotogravure reproduction in *Photographie*,
    313 x 242 mm
Repr.: Marcel Natkin, *L'Art de voir et la
    photographie* (Paris: Editions Tiranty,
    1935), p. 23; *Photographie*, 1936, no.
    114; *Art et Décoration*, Jan. 1936, p. 22;
    J'aime Paris, p. 40
Exh.: Paris, Musée des Arts Décoratifs,

1936; New York, The Museum of
    Modern Art, 1937
The Art Institute of Chicago, Ryerson
    Library

Despite the fact that not much snow falls
in Paris, Kertész was moved by its spectacle
and its transformation of the city. This
little park is at the western tip of the Ile de
la Cité, a pleasant, natural area surrounded
by the Seine, a roadway, and official
buildings. This photograph was used by
Marcel Natkin as a demonstration of
compositional design. The same subject by
Marie et Borel from the same vantage
point in the same season was published in
Photographie, 1940, no. 13 (see Travis,
fig. 37). For reproduction, see p. 84.

80. Maeterlinck Still Life, c. 1929
Rotogravure reproduction in *Art et
    Médecine*, 311 x 244 mm
Repr.: Andre Thérive, "Maurice Maeter-
    linck," *Art et Médecine*, Nov. 1932,
    pp. 8–9; Maurice Maeterlinck, "La Vie
    des pigeons, *Les Annales* 52, no. 2
    (July 6, 1934), p. 6
Lent by The New York Academy of Medicine

The Belgian Symbolist writer Maurice
Maeterlinck, although both older and considerably more established, had been interested in photography for many years and
appreciated Kertész's work. Kertész
admired his cultivated simplicity, and
responded to the symbolic presence of the
bird, here integrated in the photograph, by
the author of *The Bluebird*. This was
included in an issue on Maeterlinck by *Art
et Médecine*, an artfully produced magazine founded in 1930. Kertész photographed Maeterlinck's milieu on two
different occasions. Not reproduced.

81. Paris Chimneys, 1929
Semi-glossy, single-weight silver gelatin
    print mounted on vellum, 173 x 224 mm
Signed and dated on mount recto in pencil;
    inscribed on mount verso "Pariser
    Kamine"; stamped on mount verso
    Paris stamp #2, Paris stamp #4
Exh.: Munich, Das Lichtbild, 1930
Lent by Ealan J. Wingate, New York

Kertész often acclimated himself to his
environment by making photographs out
of his window. This one was made just
before he left the rue de Vanves apartment
to move into new quarters on boulevard
Montparnasse. For reproduction, see p. 173.

82. Shadows of the Eiffel Tower, 1929
Semi-glossy, single weight silver gelatin
    print mounted on vellum, 165 x 219 mm

Signed and dated on mount recto in pencil;
    stamped on mount verso Paris stamp
    #2, Paris stamp #4, Levy stamp
Repr.: *Paris Vu*, n. pag.; "40 Jahre Eiffel-
    turm," *Münchner Illustrierte Presse*,
    no. 19 (May 12, 1929), p. 637; Jean
    d'Erleich, "La Tour à quarante ans,"
    Vu, no. 63 (May 29, 1929), p. 433; *Art
    et Médecine*, Oct. 1931, frontispiece;
    Coronet 4, no. 4 (Aug. 1938), p. 117;
    Sixty Years, p. 137; *J'aime Paris*,
    p. 207; Aperture, p. 45; Abrams, p. 71;
    Manchester, #83, p. 64
Exh.: Munich, Das Lichtbild, 1930;
    probably New York, Julien Levy
    Gallery, 1932 or 1937
The Art Institute of Chicago, The Julien
    Levy Collection, 1979.77

On the fortieth anniversary of the Eiffel
Tower, Kertész went with his friend
Brassaï to prepare a piece of reportage.
Brassaï was then supporting himself writing essays for German and French magazines. On this occasion, Brassaï had the
opportunity to observe at close range how
Kertész structured a photoessay. Kertész and
Brassaï also photographed Eiffel's private
apartments in the tower. For reproduction,
see p. 170.

83. *Clock of the Academy*, *Pont des Arts,
    and the Louvre*, 1929
Semi-glossy, single-weight silver gelatin
    print, 252 x 197 mm
Inscribed on verso in pencil "Paris, Academy
    Française"; stamped on verso New York
    stamp #5, with address, etc. crossed out
Repr.: Abel Hermant, "Le Tricentenaire
    de la Académie Française", *Les Annales*,
    Mar. 25, 1935, p. 306; *Coronet* 5, no. 5
    (Mar. 1939), p. 59; *Day of Paris*, p. 75;
    Brassaï, "My Friend André Kertész,"
    Camera 42, no. 4 (Apr. 1963), p. 16;
    J'aime Paris, on half-title page; *Sixty
    Years*, p. 136; Aperture, p. 51; Abrams,
    p. 73 (where it is dated 1932)
Lent by the J. Paul Getty Museum, Malibu

In 1929 Kertész visited the august Académie
Française. In addition to photographing the
more obvious views, he examined the
building's unseen aspects. This image was
made in the attic, looking out from behind
an ancient clockface. For reproduction,
see p. 171.

84. *The Seine from Lady Mendl's
    Apartment*, 1929
Semi-glossy, single-weight silver gelatin
    print mounted on vellum, 222 x 166 mm
Signed on mount recto in pencil "A.
    Kertész, Paris"; stamped on verso Paris
    stamp #2

Repr.: *Paris Vu*, n. pag.; *J'aime Paris*,
p. 10
Lent by George H. Dalsheimer, Baltimore

Lady Mendl was a fashionable interior
decorator. Kertész made her portrait on this
occasion, probably for *Vogue*. He also saw
this view, but was unable to realize it because his lens was not sufficent to capture
what he visualized. He therefore took a
much larger general view and cropped it
down severely to achieve this image.
For reproduction, see p. 172.

85. Child in Mother's Arms, 1929
Semi-glossy, single-weight silver gelatin
    print mounted on vellum, 163 x 155 mm
Signed and dated on mount recto in pencil;
    stamped on mount verso Paris stamp
    #2, Levy stamp
Repr.: Travis, p. 80
Exh.: probably New York, Julien Levy
    Gallery, 1932 or 1937
The Art Institute of Chicago, The Julien
    Levy Collection, 1979.75

The child was the daughter of one of
Kertész's artist-friends. For reproduction,
see p. 175.

86. *Clayton "Peg Leg" Bates*, 1929
Semi-glossy, single-weight silver gelatin
    print mounted on vellum, 226 x 168 mm
Signed and dated on mount recto in pencil;
    stamped on mount verso Paris stamp
    #2, Levy stamp
Exh.: probably Munich, Das Lichtbild,
    1930; probably New York, Julien Levy
    Gallery, 1932 or 1937
The Art Institute of Chicago, The Julien
    Levy Collection, 1979.76

Kertész was commissioned to take photographs for a feature on an American jazz
troupe that included a male dancer with a
wooden leg. His portraits of Clayton "Peg
Leg" Bates, as well as views of him dancing,
were reproduced in the *Münchner Illustrierte Presse* ("Der Tanzer mit dem
Holzbein," 1929, p. 1319; see Phillips,
fig. 31) and also in a Hungarian paper.
None, however, was made from such a
small portion of the negative as this
example, a treatment that aestheticized the
composition. For reproduction, see p. 174.

87. At the Fortune Teller's, 1929
Vu magazine printed in rotogravure,
    370 x 275 mm
Repr.: *Vu* 3, no. 129 (Sept. 30, 1930),
    back cover; "Parijasche Waarzegsters
    Hebben Het Druk," *Het Leven*
    (*Geillustreerd*), no. 52 (Dec. 30, 1933),
    n.pag.

Lent by Sandra S. Phillips, Annandale-on-
Hudson, New York

In response to a general fascination for
mystery, superstition, and religious mysticism during this period in France, *Vu*
commissioned Kertész to supply images of
fortune tellers. His initial experiments
with distortions in a crystal ball were later
extensively pursued in the Distortion series
of 1933. Other photographs from this series
were reproduced in *Berliner Illustrirte
Zeitung*, no. 38 (1929), p. 1709.
For reproduction, see p. 183.

88. Distortion Portrait of André Kertész
    and Carlo Rim, 1930
Semi-glossy, single-weight silver gelatin
    print
Lent by Carlo Rim

Carlo Rim was appointed editor of *Vu*
magazine in August 1930. Previously he
had worked as editor for a lively arts
journal *Jazz*. He was a caricaturist and a
highly cultured, very witty man, who
submitted to these distorted portraits with
relish. Not reproduced.

89. Distortion Portrait of Carlo Rim, 1930
Vu magazine printed in rotogravure,
    370 x 275 mm
Repr.: *Vu* 3, no. 125 (Aug. 6, 1930), back
    cover
Lent by Sandra S. Phillips, Annandale-on-
Hudson, New York

Lucien Vogel asked Kertész to make some
amusing photographs that would express
Rim's many-sidedness. Kertész accompanied Rim to Luna Park, the amusement
park of Paris, and there found distorting
mirrors with which to experiment. An
article inside this issue of *Vu* shows Rim
in other forms. For reproduction, see p. 182.

90. *Tuileries Gardens*, 1930
Glossy, single-weight silver gelatin print
    made in New York, 194 x 241 mm
Inscribed on verso in ink "1928"
Repr.: *Day of Paris*, pp. 114–15; *J'aime
    Paris*, p. 45
Lent by André Kertész, New York

In the afternoon university students among
others came out to refresh themselves in
the park. Kertész, who was nearby, noticed
this and photographed them. For reproduction, see p. 177.

91. *The Daisy Bar*, Montmartre, 1930
Semi-glossy, single-weight, silver gelatin
    print made in New York, 241 x 199 mm
Inscribed on verso in pencil "Montmartre

(Paris), 'Daisy Bar,' 1930"; stamped on
verso New York stamp #2, New York
stamp #5; signed "A. Kertész, Dec. 5,
1983" in a later hand
Repr.: *Day of Paris*, p. 128; *J'aime Paris*,
    p. 163
Lent by the Edwynn Houk Gallery,
    Chicago

This photograph was made in approximately the same location as the 1926 *Stairs of
Montmartre* (cat. no. 18). For reproduction,
see p. 176.

92. From the Louvre, c. 1931
Art et Médecine magazine printed in
    rotogravure, 311 x 244 mm
Repr.: Marcel Prévost, "L'Ame de Paris,"
    Art et Médecine, Oct. 1931, p. 21
Lent by André Kertész, New York

Among the Kertész photographs used to
illustrate the article were: cat. no. 4 and
three other views of the Seine. On the
opposite page was reproduced a photograph
by Man Ray of Notre Dame, seen from the
rue Saint-Séverin. For reproduction, see
p. 44.

93. Quartier Saint-Jean, Lyon, and The
    Saint-Barthélemy Steps, Lyon, 1932
Art et Médecine magazine printed in
    rotogravure, 311 x 244 mm, each page
Repr.: Pierre Scize, "Simplicité de Lyon,"
    Art et Médecine, Apr. 1932, pp. 20–21
Lent by André Kertész, New York

In 1933, *Aspects de Lyon*, a selection of
views of Lyon by Blanc et Demilly, many
of which were similar to Kertész's photographs of a year earlier, was published in
gravure in a set of ten portfolios. For
reproduction, see p. 45.

94. *Elizabeth*, 1931
Silver gelatin print made in New York,
    240 x 189 mm
Stamped on verso New York stamp #7;
    dated in pencil
Repr.: Szarkowski, p. 7; Fárová, p. 17;
    Sixty Years, half-title frontispiece;
    Abrams, p. 138; Manchester, #226, p. 141
Exh.: New York, The Museum of Modern
    Art, 1964
Lent by André Kertész, New York

In 1931 Kertész wrote to Elizabeth, still
living in Hungary, to come and join him
in Paris. She arrived shortly afterwards,
and this photograph, a refined and cropped
version of the following one, celebrates
their intended marriage. The exposure was
made in Kertész's rue du Cotentin
apartment. For reproduction, see p. 179.

95. Elizabeth and André, 1931
Silver gelatin print made in New York,
  175 x 230 mm
Lent by André Kertész, New York

This represents another version of the same
negative used for the above photograph.
For reproduction, see p. 178.

96. Mrs. Hubbell, 1931
Rotogravure reproduction in *Photographie*,
  308 x 242 mm
Repr.: *Photographie*, 1931, no. 4; *Die
  Dame* 59, no. 3 (Nov. 1931), pp. 8–10
The Art Institute of Chicago, Ryerson
  Library

The photographic annual *Photographie*
invited ten prominent photographers to
pose and take portraits of the same model.
Man Ray, Lee Miller, Maurice Tabard,
and others all photographed this attractive
young Irishwoman in very different ways.
Another Kertész portrait of the same
woman owned by the J. Paul Getty
Museum is titled "Miss X." For reproduction, see p. 82.

97. Father Christmas, c. 1931
Vu magazine printed in rotogravure,
  370 x 275 mm
Repr.: *Vu* 4, no. 197 (Dec. 23, 1931),
  front cover; part of the negative is
  reproduced in *Enfants*, n. pag.
Lent by David Travis, Chicago

This photograph was made close to its
publication date. The little boy at the
center of the window is Lucien Vogel's son.
A cropped version of the children's faces in
the window was used in *Enfants*.
For reproduction, see p. 181.

98. Infant on a Scale, and Two Mothers
  and Infants Waiting for the Doctor,
  1931
Rotogravure reproduction in *Art et
  Médecine*, 311 x 244 mm
Repr.: Paul Strauss, "Puériculture nation-
  ale," *Art et Médecine*, May 1931, p. 12
Lent by André Kertész, New York

The second image represents only a portion
of the full negative. For reproduction, see
p. 51.

99. On the Teeter-Totter, 1931
Semi-glossy, single-weight silver gelatin
  print made in New York, 171 x 229 mm
Inscribed on verso in pencil in the hand of
  Anne Fried "aus dem Buch L'Enfant."
Repr.: *Enfants*, n. pag.; Manchester,
  #86, p. 65
Lent by the Trustees of the Theodore
  Fried Trust

A similar view, with the title *Rue du
Cotentin*, was reproduced in *J'aime Paris*,
p. 171. Both were made out the window of
his third Paris residence. For reproduction,
see p. 180.

100. *Chez Kisling*, 1933
Semi-glossy, single-weight silver gelatin
  print, 178 x 249 mm
Inscribed on verso in pencil "Chez Kisling,
  1933"
Repr.: *Day of Paris*, pp. 100–101
The Art Institute of Chicago, Ada Turnbull
  Hertle Fund and Wirt D. Walker Fund,
  1984.549

This photograph carries on the theme of
representing famous artistic personalities
through studio still lifes (see cat. nos. 21–
23, 25, 35, 41, and 80; Phillips, fig. 21), a
theme that was perpetuated by Brassaï and
other photographers after Kertész.
For reproduction, see p. 192.

101. Eiffel Tower and Iron Bridge, 1933
Semi-glossy, single-weight silver gelatin
  print, 244 x 183 mm
Repr.: Brassaï, "My Friend André
  Kertész," *Camera* 42, no. 4 (Apr. 1963),
  p. 14; *J'aime Paris*, p. 204
The Art Institute of Chicago, Ada Turnbull
  Hertle Fund, 1984.541

Kertész recalls that this photograph was
published in a German magazine, but no
record of it has been found. This composition was a new departure for him, as it
tended to deny the sense of solid space,
which up to this point had been the hallmark of most of his photographs, by the
bold juxtaposition of part of an iron bridge
in front of the subject. This compositional
motif was used in several of his photographs
illustrating a privately published book,
Les Cathédrales du vin in 1936 and later in
New York in such photographs as *Manhattan Span of the Queensborough Bridge* in
1947 (cat. no. 180). For reproduction,
see p. 193.

102. *Distortion#17*, 1933
Semi-glossy, single-weight silver gelatin
  print, 238 x 178 mm
Inscribed on verso in pencil "No 17," and
  "AK" in a later hand
Lent by André Kertész, New York

On the first day of shooting this series the
publisher hired two models. The older one
was a dance-hall girl and the younger one
was from a wealthy family. The mirror was
obtained from the flea market (*marché aux
puces*). Often such mirrors were used as
funhouse mirrors, although distorting

mirrors were also made expressly for that
purpose. For reproduction, see p. 186.

103. *Distortion #31*, 1933
Semi-glossy, single-weight silver gelatin
  print, 237 x 170 mm
Inscribed on verso in pencil "#31," and
  "AK" in a later hand
Repr.: *Distortions*, n. pag.
Lent by André Kertész, New York

For reproduction, see p. 187.

104. *Distortion #20*, 1933
Semi-glossy, single-weight silver gelatin
  print, 232 x 117 mm
Inscribed on verso in pencil "#20," and
  "AK" in a later hand; stamped on verso
  New York stamp #7
Repr.: *Distortions*, n. pag.
Lent by André Kertész, New York

For reproduction, see p. 188.

105. *Distortion #68*, 1933
Semi-glossy, single-weight silver gelatin
  print, 110 x 57 mm
Inscribed in pencil on verso "#68," and
  "AK" in a later hand
Repr.: *Distortions*, n. pag.
Lent by André Kertész, New York

For reproduction, see p. 185.

106. *Distortion #72*, 1933
Semi-glossy, single-weight silver gelatin
  print, 73 x 53 mm
Inscribed on verso in pencil "#72," and
  "AK" in a later hand
Repr.: *Distortions*, n. pag.
Lent by André Kertész, New York

For reproduction, see p. 184.

107. *Distortion #91*, 1933
Semi-glossy, single-weight silver gelatin
  print, 178 x 230 mm
Inscribed on verso in pencil "91a, 886/32,"
  and "AK" in a later hand; stamped on
  verso Paris stamp #3
Repr.: *Distortions*, n. pag.
Lent by André Kertész, New York

For reproduction, see p. 189.

108. *Distortion #164*, 1933
Semi-glossy, single-weight silver gelatin
  print, 238 x 178 mm
Inscribed on verso in pencil "164," and
  "AK" in a later hand; stamped on verso
  Paris stamp #3, Paris stamp #5
Repr.: *Distortions*, n. pag.
Lent by André Kertész, New York

For reproduction, see p. 190.

109. *Distortion #167*, 1933
Semi-glossy, single-weight silver gelatin
   print, 238 x 166 mm
Inscribed on verso in pencil "167," and
   "AK" in a later hand; stamped on verso
   Paris stamp #3
Repr.: *Distortions*, n. pag.
Lent by André Kertész, New York

For reproduction, see p. 191.

110. *Place Saint Sulpice*, 1934
Semi-glossy, single-weight silver gelatin
   print mounted on illustration board,
   236 x 178 mm
Signed and dated on mount recto in pencil;
   stamped on verso Paris stamp #3
Repr.: *Day of Paris*, p. 143; "Day of
   Paris," *Minicam Photography* 8, no. 10
   (July 1945), p. 28
The Art Institute of Chicago, Ada Turnbull
   Hertle Fund, 1984.543

This was made with a primitive zoom lens.
It exists in a much less severely cropped
state (see Phillips, fig. 39 and *Day of
Paris*, p. 143). For reproduction, see p. 195.

111. *On the Boulevards*, 1934
Semi-glossy, single-weight silver gelatin
   print, 238 x 181 mm
Stamped on verso "For reproduction only";
   signed in pencil "A. Kertész, April 22,
   1983" in a later hand; label of European
   agency
Repr.: *Paris Vu*, n. pag.; *Photo-Illustrations*
   2 (1935); Dan Budnik, "A Point Vue,"
   Infinity 14, no. 3 (Mar. 1965), p. 4;
   Fárová, p. 10; *Sixty Years*, p. 129;
   Aperture, p. 43; Abrams, p. 61
Lent by John C. Waddell, New York

The posters in this photograph were
created by the well-known and important
Art Deco designer Cassandre, who had also
designed the logo for *Vu*. Here the decorative motif of Paris is combined with a
sense of the coincidental, as well as a feeling
of melancholy. Here too is a playful denial
of space in the positioning of the charactered
head, as compared to his earlier work (see
cat. no. 28). For reproduction, see p. 194.

112. *Self-Portrait in the Hotel Beaux-Arts*,
   1936
Semi-glossy, double-weight silver gelatin
   print, 247 x 168 mm
Titled and dated on verso in pencil
The Metropolitan Museum of Art, Pur-
   chase, Rogers Fund, The Elisha Whittelsey
   Collection, The Elisha Whittelsey Fund,
   Mary Livingston Griggs and Mary Griggs
   Burke Foundation, and Mrs. Vincent Astor
   Gifts, 1984.1083.10
(*Note*: In subsequent credit lines to the

Metropolitan Museum, an asterisk (*)
indicates that a photograph was acquired
with the above funds.)

This photograph was made looking southwest from Kertész's room in the Hotel
Beaux-Arts, 310 East 44th Street. In the
background is the Crystal Building, 801
Second Avenue (corner of 43rd Street),
designed in 1930 by Blum & Blum. Here
Kertész is holding a monorail view camera
designed for 4 x 5 inch sheets of film. In
Europe he had always preferred the smallest and lightest camera, but in New York
he found himself, unhappily, working on
assignment, mostly with a view camera,
until 1962. He did, however, take his Leica
on all assignments and used it in offhand
moments to create a body of personal work
simultaneous with the assigned subjects.
For reproduction, see p. 197.

113. At The Metropolitan Museum of Art, 1936
Semi-glossy, double-weight silver gelatin
   print, 333 x 270 mm
Signed on verso in pencil "Kertész" with a
   bold stroke; stamped on verso New York
   stamp #1; designer's notation in pencil
   "same size"
The Metropolitan Museum of Art*,
   1984.1083.72

Kertész was a bystander while his friend
Richard Statile photographed on assignment. Today this picture would be impossible because the stairs leading to the
Metropolitan Museum have been enlarged
and the driveway has been replaced by two
fountains. For reproduction, see p. 198.

114. Crippled Woman, 1936
Glossy, single-weight silver gelatin print,
   200 x 246 mm
Stamped on verso New York stamp #3
Repr.: *Of New York*, p. 166
The Metropolitan Museum of Art*,
   1984.1083.9

Itinerant persons always attracted Kertész,
whether they were beggars and Gypsies in
Hungary or *clochards* in Paris. Here, the
figure and its context seem more European
than American. Kertész lived near the
corner of 43rd Street and Third Avenue;
the stanchions of the Third Avenue elevated
railroad may be seen in the background.
For reproduction, see p. 199.

115. Distortion with Vase, 1936
Semi-glossy, single-weight silver gelatin
   print mounted on board, 344 x 185 mm
Signed on mount recto in pencil; stamped
   on verso New York stamp #1; paper
   label with number "45" affixed on verso
   (PM Gallery number)

Exh.: New York, PM Gallery, 1937
The Metropolitan Museum of Art*,
   1984.1083.104

For reproduction, see p. 208.

116. Clothes Lines, 1937
Semi-glossy, double-weight silver gelatin
   print, 246 x 197 mm
Dated on verso in ballpoint pen; stamped
   on verso New York stamp #1 (altered
   with addition in fountain pen "67 W.");
   telephone number added in fountain pen
   "Va6–2759"; designer's scaling marks
Repr.: *Of New York*, p. 87 (reproduced
   from this print)
The Metropolitan Museum of Art*,
   1984.1083.60

This is the earliest surviving print of a
subject distinctly different from the reper-
tory of subjects Kertész had formed in
Hungary and Paris. Clothes lines hung
between tenements were for this period in
New York as picturesque as the wire chairs
of the Tuileries. For reproduction, see
p. 202.

117. *Sutton Place*, 1937
Glossy, single-weight silver gelatin print,
   242 x 193 mm
Titled on verso; stamped on verso New
   York stamp #6, applied about 1976
Repr.: *Of New York*, p. 136 (reproduced
   from this print)
The Metropolitan Museum of Art*,
   1984.1083.37

This photograph was taken from a vantage
looking north across River House dock into
Sutton Place toward the Queensborough
Bridge. For reproduction, see p. 203.

118. *Lost Cloud*, 1937
Later silver gelatin print, 216 x 137 mm
Repr.: Szarkowski, p. 44; *Sixty Years*, p. 166;
   Of New York, p. 14 (where it is incor-
   rectly dated 1932); Abrams, p. 131
Exh.: New York, The Museum of Modern
   Art, 1964
Lent by The Museum of Modern Art, New
   York, gift of the photographer, 312.65

Later this picture of the Empire State
Building became Kertész's most often
reproduced photograph of the early New
York period. Like cat. no. 117, this image
is dependent upon a chance encounter
between a roving eye and a short-lived
event. For reproduction, see p. 200.

119. *Third Avenue*, 1937
Semi-glossy, double-weight silver gelatin
   print, 245 x 196 mm
Inscribed on verso in pencil "New York

3rd Ave., 1937" in a later hand
Repr.: *Of New York*, p. 37; Manchester, #141, p. 97
Lent by the Edwynn Houk Gallery, Chicago

For reproduction, see p. 201.

120. Arm and Ventilator, 1937
Later silver gelatin print made by Igor Bakht, 200 x 183 mm
Repr.: Szarkowski, p. 46; Abrams, p. 253
Exh.: New York, The Museum of Modern Art, 1964
Lent by the Susan Harder Gallery, New York

Kertész has characterized himself as a "naturalist Surrealist." In Paris his photographs were admired by the Surrealists because he frequently used the camera to remove his subjects from their expected context. The mundane process of a workman repairing a drugstore ventilator has resulted in a disembodied figure rearranged by the eye of the photographer into an improbable actuality. For reproduction, see p. 209.

121. *Bronx, New York*, 1937
Glossy, single-weight silver gelatin print 259 x 202 mm
Titled on verso; stamped on verso New York stamp #2 (effaced in ballpoint pen); partial Rapho Guillumette blue paper label
Repr.: *Of New York*, p. 150 (reproduced from this print)
The Metropolitan Museum of Art*, 1984.1083.102

For reproduction, see p. 204.

122. Nicholas Luddington, Jr., 1937
Glossy, single-weight silver gelatin print mounted on illustration board, 233 x 190 mm
Signed on recto "A. Kertész"; stamped on verso New York stamp #1, New York stamp #2 (former effaced in pencil)
Repr.: *Harper's Bazaar* 70, no. 2698 (Aug. 1937)
Exh.: New York, PM Gallery, 1937
The Metropolitan Museum of Art*, 1984.1083.3

This photograph was made during Kertész's first out-of-town assignment after termination of the Keystone Studios contract. The trip to Haverford, Pennsylvania, was his first trip out of New York since his arrival from Europe. The presence of both New York stamp #1 and New York stamp #2 suggests that #2 was in existence by the spring of 1938. Prints in the possession of Merloyd Lawrence are marked with

Harper's Bazaar notations that indicate the prints were received by the editors on July 1, 1937, for publication in the August issue. The trip was made in all likelihood in mid-June. The Lawrence prints also have the New York stamp #1, indicating its use was not abandoned until after July 1. For reproduction, see p. 210.

123. Merloyd Luddington, 1937
Matte, double-weight silver gelatin print, 195 x 237 mm
Stamped on verso New York stamp #1
Repr.: *Harper's Bazaar* 70, no. 2698 (Aug. 1937)
Lent by Merloyd Lawrence, Boston

For reproduction, see p. 210.

124. *Poughkeepsie, New York*, 1937
Semi-glossy, single-weight silver gelatin print, 236 x 184 mm
Signed and dated on verso in pencil; stamped on verso New York stamp #2
Repr.: Szarkowski, p. 45; Aperture, p. 71; Abrams, p. 111
Exh.: New York, The Museum of Modern Art, 1964
Lent by John C. Waddell, New York

For reproduction, see p. 205.

125. Men Seated on Bench, 1937
Glossy, single-weight silver gelatin print, 200 x 256 mm
Dated on verso in pencil and ink; stamped on verso New York stamp #6; designer's scaling marks
The Metropolitan Museum of Art*, 1984.1083.25

For reproduction, see p. 212.

126. The Lake, Central Park, Near Bow Bridge, c. 1937
Semi-glossy, double-weight silver gelatin print, 115 x 92 mm
Inscribed on verso in pencil "E.5"
The Metropolitan Museum of Art*, 1984.1083.76

During his Hungarian and early Paris period, Kertész made contact prints from glass-plate and sheet-film negatives. After 1928 these small format contact prints are rare, since the prints were needed for exhibitions and publications. With the exception of this photograph and the following group of nine prints (cat. nos. 127–35), all bearing on verso the letter "E" followed by a numeral, Kertész in his American work generally made enlargements on eight-by-ten or eleven-by-fourteen inch paper. The prints were made for distribution to editors and publishers

and were passed from hand to hand unmounted. He did make, however, at least sixty exhibition enlargements for display at the PM Gallery in 1937, all mounted on rag-content board and signed on recto in pencil. For reproduction, see p. 214.

Cat. nos. 126–35 are finely made contact prints that, with the exception of cat. no. 127, which may be a small 35mm enlargement, are from four-by-five inch negatives. Cat. nos. 126 and 133 are especially perfect in their range of tone and fine finish. Although larger and of a colder tone, they resemble the post-card prints of the Paris period more so than any other prints of the New York period.

127. Elevated Train Platform, Bowery (?), 1937
Glossy, single-weight silver gelatin print, 74 x 114 mm
Dated on verso in pencil
The Metropolitan Museum of Art*, 1984.1083.26

This photograph was taken from a vantage looking toward the financial district. At the left center is the Cities Service Building at 60 Wall Street, designed in 1931 by the firm of Clinton & Russell, Wells, Holton & George; at the right is the Bank of Manhattan Building, 40 Wall Street, designed by the firm of Severance & Matsui in 1930. For reproduction, see p. 216.

128. From 85 Fifth Avenue, c. 1937
Glossy, single-weight silver gelatin print, with cracks in emulsion in sky area, 115 x 95 mm
Inscribed on verso in pencil "E.12"
The Metropolitan Museum of Art*, 1984.1083.79

One of Kertész's favorite motifs is to include a small genre detail, like the figure on the scaffold, as counterpoint to a broader composition. The massive building is located at 853 Broadway (at the southwest corner of 14th Street), designed in 1928 by Emery Roth. For reproduction, see p. 216.

129. Third Avenue Elevated at 43rd Street, c. 1937
Semi-glossy, double-weight silver gelatin print, 122 x 85 mm
Inscribed on verso in pencil "E.13"; stamped on verso New York stamp #2
The Metropolitan Museum of Art*, 1984.1083.75

The marquee of the Grand Central Hotel is evident to the left on the far side of the elevated train platform. This composition may be compared to that of cat. no. 119, which is also a tightly structured composition based upon the improbable intersection of architectural elements. For reproduction, see p. 217.

130. East River Pier Around 23rd Street, c. 1937
Semi-glossy, double-weight silver gelatin print, 93 x 113 mm
Inscribed on verso in pencil "E.15"
The Metropolitan Museum of Art*, 1984.1083.80

Like many of Kertész's compositions, this one is about two chance intersections. A figure, hand to face in a pensive gesture, is bisected diagonally by the curved edge of the enormous cleat forming a miraculous intersection of lines and shapes; in the right background, perfectly occupying its space, is a tugboat with its bow delicately brushing the edge of the composition. For reproduction, see p. 214.

131. New York Public Library Plaza, c. 1937
Semi-glossy, double-weight silver gelatin print, 113 x 94 mm
Inscribed on verso in pencil "E.20"
The Metropolitan Museum of Art*, 1984.1083.77

For reproduction, see p. 215.

132. Steps of the New York Public Library, c. 1937
Semi-glossy, double-weight silver gelatin print, 122 x 99 mm
Stamped on verso New York stamp #1, overprinted with New York stamp #2; designer's scaling marks in pencil
The Metropolitan Museum of Art*, 1984.1083.78

The idea of this image is very similar to that of cat. no. 130: a picturesque figure interrupted by an improbable shape. The diagonal thrust of the steps, a recurrent compositional element, creates a strong sense of space. For reproduction, see p. 215.

133. The East River from 42nd Street, c. 1937
Semi-glossy, double-weight silver gelatin print, 94 x 118 mm
Inscribed on verso in pencil "E.21"
The Metropolitan Museum of Art*, 1984.1083.30

The preceding three works (cat. nos. 130–32) demonstrate the photographer's arresting a chance event through a flash of the eye. Here a different principle is operative. The photographer has built a composition from stationary objects through the force of his own powers of observation. The stacks at right are those of the 34th Street power station; in the distance are the stacks of the 14th Street power station.
For reproduction, see p. 217.

134. Apartment Houses in the Bronx (?), c. 1937
Semi-glossy, double-weight silver gelatin print, 79 x 120 mm
Inscribed on verso in pencil "E.21"
The Metropolitan Museum of Art*, 1984.1083.74

For reproduction, see p. 216.

135. Ornamental Sphere on the North Tower of the Hippodrome, c. 1937
Glossy, single-weight silver gelatin print, 87 x 115 mm
Inscribed on verso in pencil "E.28"
The Metropolitan Museum of Art*, 1984.1083.44

The sphere atop the Hippodrome was illuminated at night to act as an enormous sign, while by day it was a latticework sculpture. The Hippodrome was designed by J. H. Morgan and constructed in 1905; it is no longer standing. For reproduction, see p. 217.

136. Man with Spaniel on Leash, 1938
Glossy, single-weight silver gelatin print, 253 x 198 mm
Stamped on verso New York stamp #6; dated on verso in ballpoint pen "7-3-38"; inscribed in pencil "67 W. 44th St." (effaced in ballpoint pen)
Repr.: Of New York, p. 174
The Metropolitan Museum of Art*, 1984.1083.57

Kertész has continually attempted to endow anecdotal subjects with a rigorous sense of form. Here the physical energy of the straining dog and the line formed by the taut leash work in opposition to the carpet of diagonal shadows. Kertész quite reliably inscribed his dates in the American style of month/day/year, but here he seems to have reverted to the European style of day/month/year, since the figures are in winter clothes. The fact that this print was made before the stamp for 67 West 44th Street was used suggests that the photographer's relocation took place early in 1938. For reproduction, see p. 206.

137. Rockefeller Center, 1938?
Semi-glossy, double-weight silver gelatin print, 190 x 243 mm
Stamped on verso New York stamp #1 (altered in pencil by addition of "67 W")
The Metropolitan Museum of Art*, 1984.1083.59

During the 1960s and 1970s, when opportunities to make monographic anthologies of his work arose, Kertész went to his files and looked at prints he had not seen for years. This one was pulled in 1975/76 as a candidate (later rejected) for Of New York (1976), at which time it was erroneously dated 1937. The stamp for 67 West 44th Street existed by the spring of 1938, and the stamp would not have required pencil alteration. The exposure was made from approximately 49th Street and Rockefeller Plaza, showing in the background buildings at 28–56 West 48th Street on the south side of the street. For reproduction, see p. 207.

138. Washington Square, New York, 1938
Glossy, single-weight silver gelatin print, 240 x 191 mm
Inscribed on verso in ballpoint pen "Washington Square (N.Y.)"; stamped on verso New York stamp #2 (effaced in pencil), New York stamp #5
Repr.: Washington Square, n. pag.
The Metropolitan Museum of Art*, 1984.1083.35

During the summer of 1938, Kertész discovered Greenwich Village. The flagpole in front of the Washington Square arch is approximately 100 yards from the location at 2 Fifth Avenue, where he moved in 1952 and has lived ever since. The building in the right background is 1 Fifth Avenue, which at this time faced upon a row of brownstone houses. An unpublished variant shows the boys mounting the base of the pole. For reproduction, see p. 213.

139. Cecil Beaton, 1938
Semi-glossy, double-weight silver gelatin print, 236 x 144 mm
Titled and dated on verso in pencil "5-I-1938"
The Metropolitan Museum of Art*, 1984.1083.70

A version showing Beaton's full face also exists. For reproduction, see p. 220.

140. The Set Designer, c. 1938
Matte, double-weight silver gelatin print, 306 x 257 mm
The Metropolitan Museum of Art*, 1984.1083.88

The subject was illuminated by the light of a slide projector showing a transparency of a drawing. For reproduction, see p. 221.

141. Midtown Manhattan, 1938
Matte, double-weight silver gelatin print,
    251 x 201
Dated on verso in ballpoint pen about
    1976; stamped on verso New York stamp
    #1 (altered in pencil by addition of
    "67 W"); designer's scaling marks
Repr.: *Of New York*, p. 178 (reproduced
    from this print)
The Metropolitan Museum of Art*,
    1984.1083.100

The palmette in the foreground is super-
imposed upon the finials and gabled roof of
the now-demolished Savoy-Plaza Hotel
and the spire of the Sherry-Netherland
Hotel, both at opposite corners of Fifth
Avenue and 59th Street. Both buildings
date from 1927, the former a late work by
the firm of McKim, Mead and White, and
the latter by Schultze and Weaver.
For reproduction, see p. 232.

142. Children in an Art Gallery, 1938
Semi-glossy, double-weight silver gelatin
    print, 249 x 185 mm
Dated on verso in pencil "3-18-38";
    stamped on verso New York stamp #1;
    Atlas Photos, 45 West 45th Street;
    "Kertész from Atlas Photos"
The Metropolitan Museum of Art*,
    1984.1083.89

Kertész avoided the use of artificial illumination whenever possible, but it was
unavoidable here. The conception remains
natural by virtue of the sunbonnets that
shielded the eyes from the burst of light
issued from the flashbulb. For reproduction,
see p. 211.

143. *44th Street and the East River*, 1938
Glossy, double-weight silver gelatin print,
    203 x 241 mm
Titled on verso in ballpoint pen and dated
    (about 1976) in pencil; stamped on verso
    New York stamp #2 (telephone number
    effaced)
Repr.: *Of New York*, p. 173 (reproduced
    from this print)
The Metropolitan Museum of Art*,
    1984.1083.36

The essential difference between this
photograph and cat. no. 120 is that the arm
remained in position for an instant, was
caught by a flash of the eye, and required
cropping to realize the final composition,
while the stationary subject permitted the
photographer to choose the exactly desired
point of view. For reproduction, see p. 223.

144. *Beekman Terrace*, 1938
Semi-glossy, single-weight silver gelatin
    print, 250 x 200 mm

Signed and dated on verso
Repr.: *Of New York*, p. 129
Lent by Harriette and Noel Levine, New
    York

After his arrival in New York, Kertész
could not erase from his mind the idea of
European cities. This view calls to mind his
vision of Paris and may be compared to cat.
no. 44. The lighted lamppost in the little
Paris square occupies the same compositional function as the wagon here, subjects that
in both cases are flanked by different
degrees of tracery from tree branches.
For reproduction, see p. 218.

145. Model Inspecting Tea, 1938
Semi-glossy, double-weight silver gelatin
    print, 251 x 200 mm
The Metropolitan Museum of Art*,
    1984.1083.69

When this photograph was made, the
highest paid photographers in the world
were those who did fashion assignments for
the Condé Nast and Hearst publications.
This photograph and cat. nos. 146 and 147
are the product of Kertész's attempt at
this line of work. Judging by the results,
he could have made quite a success of this
direction. Kertész attempted to realize
natural poses and gestures, while
accommodating the necessities of illustration.
For reproduction, see p. 224.

146. Model and Delivery Man, c. 1938
Glossy, single-weight silver gelatin print,
    242 x 193 mm
Stamped on verso New York stamp #3
The Metropolitan Museum of Art*,
    1984.1083.71

Kertész took his model to the brownstone
district near The Metropolitan Museum of
Art. The delivery man's wagon bears the
name and address of the Madison Avenue
Market, then located on the west side of
the street between 83rd and 84th. The
delivery man forms a naturalistic counterpoint to the stylishly dressed model caught
in mid-stride exiting from a fashionable
residence. At this time only sportswear was
photographed on location. More formal
costume was generally photographed in the
studio to delineate the nuances of cut and
tailoring. The fact that no reproduction of
this photograph has been located suggests
that it was found by the editors of *Vogue*
to be unacceptable, though perhaps they
merely found no room for it in their final
layouts. For reproduction, see p. 224.

147. Model Jumping Stones, c. 1938
Glossy, single-weight silver gelatin print,
    237 x 190 mm

Stamped on verso New York stamp #3
The Metropolitan Museum of Art*,
    1984.1083.90

Shoes are difficult to photograph as anything other than still-life objects. Here
Kertész attempted to bring a resistant subject to life. Typical of his attention to
compositional details is the elegant perspective of the foreground and its finely
visualized relationship to the one behind.
For reproduction, see p. 223.

148. Hand Holding Mushrooms, c. 1938
Glossy, single-weight silver gelatin print
    mounted on illustration board,
    196 x 243 mm
The Metropolitan Museum of Art*,
    1984.1083.61

Kertész turned in all directions in the
attempt to forge a livelihood from the art
of photography. The subject here is a
worker at a mushroom farm, and the
photograph bears comparison to the study
of modern winery facilities Kertész did in
France in 1936, under the title *Les Cathédrales du vin*, privately published a year
after his departure (see Naef, fig. 18).
There is an important difference between
the two projects: in the former, an entire
suite of pictures was realized, but here an
equally complex activity has been distilled
to a single image. The hand and its contents
appear to be carved in stone, an impression
that is enhanced by the block of wood upon
which the hand rests. For reproduction,
see p. 209.

149. Great Danes, c. 1938
Matte, double-weight silver gelatin print,
    199 x 246 mm
The Metropolitan Museum of Art*,
    1984.1083.62

This exposure was made on an excursion
with Ylla, the noted photographer of
animals, who could not resist sentimental-
izing her subjects. Kertész here overlaid his
Constructivist sensibilities upon a subject
that he, too, was known to sentimentalize.
For reproduction, see p. 219.

150. Workmen on Waterfront, c. 1938
Glossy, single-weight silver gelatin print,
    237 x 190 mm
Stamped on verso New York stamp #2,
    New York stamp #6
The Metropolitan Museum of Art*,
    1984.1083.21

Four men energetically engaged in their
work presented an irresistible subject to
Kertész, although the available points of
view were extremely limited. The chal-

lenge was to observe the scene from a vantage such that each figure retained a strong pose and gesture, and to make the best of very confusing foreground and background elements. Lacking the possibility of complete clarity, Kertész's chose to create a latticework of lines and shapes. For reproduction, see p. 226.

151. New York Harbor, c. 1938
Glossy, double-weight silver gelatin print with faint yellowing at edges, 335 x 262 mm
Stamped on verso New York stamp #2, New York stamp #4
Repr.: *Of New York*, p. 104
The Metropolitan Museum of Art*, 1984.1083.19

Kertész observed the New York Harbor at the peak of its activity in the twentieth century. His challenge here was to depict the character of this lively intercourse in a single image. This photograph was taken in lower Manhattan near the Battery, with Pier A partially visible at the upper left and Pier 1 occupied by the Hudson River Night Line Company. Kertész stood on the roof of the Whitehall Building (17 Battery Place) to make this exposure. For reproduction, see p. 231.

152. The Tugboat Eugene F. Moran, New York Harbor, c. 1938
Glossy, double-weight silver gelatin print, 331 x 263 mm
Stamped on verso New York stamp #2, New York stamp #4
The Metropolitan Museum of Art*, 1984.1083.20

This and the preceding work have tugboats as a central subject. They are thought to be a part of the *Life* magazine waterfront series that was never published. Several related pictures were published in *The Compass* 8, no. 8 (1942), pp. 6–7, and the question is whether they were commissioned by Socony-Vacuum Oil Company, the publisher of the magazine, or were left over in Kertész's files. The latter is more probably the case, since he and all enemy aliens were not allowed to photograph sensitive subjects during the war. The vantage is from lower Manhattan on the East River looking south toward the power station located on Hudson Avenue in Brooklyn. For reproduction, see p. 227.

153. Bridge and Ship's Stack, 1938
Glossy, single-weight silver gelatin print, 201 x 258 mm
Stamped on verso New York stamp #2
The Metropolitan Museum of Art*,

1984.1083.49

Kertész very often reacts like a sculptor by fixing his subjects in a gracefully drawn spatial context. He rarely sacrifices a strong spatial context in favor of surface design, as he did here. This location is believed to be looking northeast along Kill Van Kull toward New York Harbor under the Bayonne Bridge; Staten Island is at the right. For reproduction, see p. 229.

154. *Sixth Avenue, New York*, 1939
Glossy, single-weight silver gelatin print, 251 x 200 mm
Titled and dated on verso in fountain pen; stamped on verso New York stamp #2, overprinted with New York stamp #7
Repr.: *Of New York*, p. 136
The Metropolitan Museum of Art*, 1984.1083.24

This photograph and the next one (cat. no. 155) are excellent examples of how Kertész prospects for his pictures. The question indirectly raised here is whether he was addressing the curiously juxtaposed shops in the background, or tracking the figures who gravitated that way along the block. For reproduction, see p. 225.

155. *Sixth Avenue*, 1939
Glossy, single-weight silver gelatin print, 250 x 195 mm
Titled on verso in pencil and dated in ballpoint pen in a later hand; stamped on verso New York stamp #2 (telephone number effaced with pencil, address effaced with ballpoint pen)
The Metropolitan Museum of Art*, 1984.1083.58

See remarks on cat. no. 154. For reproduction, see p. 225.

156. Children in Playground with Sprinkler, 1939
Glossy, single-weight silver gelatin print, 245 x 191 mm
Dated on verso in pencil; stamped on verso New York stamp #3; designer's scaling marks
Repr.: *The Complete Photographer*, ed. Willard D. Morgan, vol. 1 (New York: National Educational Alliance, 1942), between pp. 16 and 17; *Of New York*, p. 43 (reproduced from this print)
The Metropolitan Museum of Art*, 1984.1083.6

This picture must be seen in light of Kertész's biography: in Europe the war was deepening, and Kertész was at the point of having to decide whether his two-year sabbatical from Paris should come to an

end as planned, or whether America would be his home for the duration. By choosing to cast his eye on this instant of pure childhood ecstacy, Kertész suggested a message of personal optimism. For reproduction, see p. 211.

157. Ballet Dancer, Roof Garden of Rockefeller Center, 1939
Glossy, single-weight silver gelatin print mounted on pulp illustration board, 240 x 194 mm
Inscribed on verso in pencil "New York/ 1939"; stamped on verso New York stamp #3
Repr.: Maria Giovanna Eisner, "Citizen Kertész," *Minicam Photography* 7, no. 10 (June 1944), p. 27; *Sixty Years*, p. 155
The Metropolitan Museum of Art*, 1984.1083.31

A favorite Kertész strategy is to compass his subject in a context other than the one in which we expect to find it. A dancer dressed to perform classical ballet may be expected to be found in a theater. The imperfections of stone and grass give the dancer a porcelainlike perfection. This photograph also exists in an uncropped state. For reproduction, see p. 223.

158. Female Torso with Plaster Relief, 1939
Glossy, single-weight silver gelatin print, 250 x 204 mm
Repr.: *Sixty Years*, p. 77; Abrams, p. 242
The Metropolitan Museum of Art*, 1984.1083.86

This subject is a manifestation of how fond Kertész is of opposites. He had already treated the female nude in Hungary and in the Paris Distortions, with which this seems to have the most in common. Kertész himself had already made this connection, when, in the sequencing of *Sixty Years*, this subject was placed out of chronological order as the last picture in the Distortions suite. For reproduction, see p. 222.

159. *Melancholic Tulip*, 1939
Semi-glossy, single-weight silver gelatin print, 340 x 216 mm
Dated on verso in pencil; signed in a later hand with the date "5/6/81"; stamped on verso New York stamp #2, New York stamp #4
Repr.: *Sixty Years*, p. 78; Aperture, p. 79; Abrams, p. 173; Manchester, #259, p. 163
Lent by The Detroit Institute of Arts, Founders Society Acquisition Fund, F1983.69

In the layout for *Sixty Years* Kertész placed this image after cat. no. 158, following his nude Distortions. For reproduction, see p. 208.

160. Carousel Horses, Shelburne, Vermont, c. 1939
Semi-glossy, double-weight silver gelatin print, 342 x 270 mm
Stamped on verso New York stamp #6; designer's scaling marks
The Metropolitan Museum of Art*, 1984.1083.34

For reproduction, see p. 219.

161. The Empire State Building, 1939
Matte, double-weight silver gelatin print, 333 x 265 mm
Signed on verso in pencil "A. Kertész Sept. 20, 1982" (in a later hand by way of authentication); stamped on verso New York stamp #4; dated in pencil contemporaneous with the print
Repr.: "The Blimp," *The Lamp* 22, no. 3 (Dec. 1939), p. 23
Lent by Michael G. Wilson, London

The circumstances surrounding an invitation by the editors of *Life* magazine to attempt an essay on waterfront life around New York Harbor have been related elsewhere (see Naef, pp. 102–04). Placed at Kertész's disposal were the formidable resources of a large corporation, including access to a dirigible to enable an overview of the subject. This image and the following two photographs (cat. nos. 162 and 163) represent a selection from the approximately two dozen exposures that Kertész chose to present for publication. By the standards of yesterday or today, what he chose to present represents a very sparing number of pictures and exemplifies his conviction that less is more. The photographs have been sequenced here on the principal that the overview preceded the return on foot to a specific locations. Cat. no. 163 is sequenced as it is to coincide with other Weehawken views, even though it was made in a separate venture.

Kertész had no control over the height of the airship as it passed by his subject, and he was left with two essential compositional decisions: where would the base of the structure fall in relation to the frame of the picture, and how would the grid of the intersecting streets fall in relation to the rectangle of the picture? He timed his exposure so that the corner of the building's base (representing the southwest corner) would fall in the precise center of the bottom edge of the photograph, a

decision he coordinated instinctively with the spatial orientation of the camera that was aimed to insure that the most prominent diagonal formed by 34th Street would commence precisely at the upper right corner. For reproduction, see p. 233.

162. *Weehawken, New Jersey,* 1939?
Glossy, single-weight silver gelatin print mounted on rag-content illustration board trimmed flush with the image, 338 x 258 mm
Stamped on verso New York stamp #2, effaced and overprinted with New York stamp #6
The Metropolitan Museum of Art*, 1984.1083.13

Once this particular array of piers, tracks, waterway, and highway had been decided upon as the subject, the central artistic decision was how to treat the light-reflecting roadway as an element of design rather than as an interruption. Kertész chose to maximize the degree of reflection by facing into the light; from any other viewpoint, the roadway would have become as gray as the other surfaces, and he would have lost the highlights that delineate the ribbons of track. For reproduction, see p. 229.

163. *Weehawken, New Jersey,* 1939?
Matte, double-weight silver gelatin print, 253 x 197 mm
Titled and dated on verso in pencil, c. 1982; stamped on verso New York stamp #2 (effaced in ballpoint pen)
The Metropolitan Museum of Art, Purchase, Harriette and Noel Levine Gift and Matching Funds from the National Endowment for the Arts, 1981.1022

It is not absolutely certain that this photograph was made on the *Life* assignment discussed in remarks on cat. no. 161. For reproduction, see p. 230.

164. Near Coxsackie, New York, 1939?
Glossy, single-weight silver gelatin print, 240 x 198 mm
The Metropolitan Museum of Art*, 1984.1083.5

The otherwise nondescript factory represented here is rendered from a point of view such that every building appears placed by some rule of divine proportion. This act of creative judgment reflects more the skill of the photographer than it demonstrates particular truths about the subject itself, or the skills of the architect. For reproduction, see p. 228.

165. Waterfront Buildings, c. 1939
Glossy, single-weight silver gelatin print probably printed in the 1950s, 193 x 241 mm
Stamped on verso New York stamp #6
The Metropolitan Museum of Art*, 1984.1083.23

Kertész reverted here to thoughts of Paris. Like cat. no. 164, this is an arrangement of various building shapes, but far more improbable ones than those of the former. The figure observing the photographer at work from the window recalls a similar figure in *J'aime Paris,* p. 129. For reproduction, see p. 228.

166. Pilings, Weehawken, New Jersey, 1941
Glossy, double-weight silver gelatin print, 249 x 197 mm
Dated on verso in pencil; stamped on verso New York stamp #2, overprinted with New York stamp #4; telephone number "Va6–3012" effaced in fountain pen and replaced with "Mu2–9366"
The Metropolitan Museum of Art*, 1984.1083.32

Water has always been endowed with symbolic content, but it is rarely photographed in ways that go beyond the obvious literary associations. Here the network of decayed wooden shapes is contrasted with the life-sustaining quality that water usually connotes. This photograph is a kind of answer to the formalist Constructivism that America welcomed from Bauhaus-trained immigrants who arrived here about the same time as Kertész, and whose presence resulted in the establishment of the New Bauhaus in Chicago in late 1937. For reproduction, see p. 230.

167. *Armonk, New York,* 1941
Semi-glossy, single-weight silver gelatin print, 243 x 198 mm
Titled on mount recto, not in the photographer's hand; inscribed on verso "April 6, 1941," not in the photographer's hand
Repr.: *The Bulletin of the Museum of Modern Art* 9, no. 2 (Nov. 1941), p. 15; *The Complete Photographer,* ed. Willard D. Morgan, vol. 4 (New York: National Educational Alliance, 1943), p. 1529; Maria Giovanna Eisner, "Citizen Kertész," *Minicam Photography* 7, no. 10 (June 1944), p. 31; Brassaï, "My Friend André Kertész," *Camera* 42, no. 4 (Apr. 1963), p. 27; *Sixty Years,* p. 209
Exh.: New York, The Museum of Modern Art, "Image of Freedom," 1942
Lent by The Museum of Modern Art, New York

In 1941 Beaumont Newhall, Curator of Photography at The Museum of Modern Art, issued a call for submissions to a photographic competition entitled "Image of Freedom." More than seven hundred photographs from sixteen states were submitted, from which sixty-five were selected for purchase at twenty-five dollars each. The jury was composed of some of the most respected experts on art and photography in the United States, namely, members of the museum's Committee on Photography, including the Chairman, David Hunter McAlpin, and the Vice Chairman, Ansel Adams; A. Hyatt Mayor, then Associate Curator of Prints at the Metropolitan Museum; Nancy Newhall; and James Thrall Soby. The museum staff was represented by Beaumont Newhall himself; Director Alfred H. Barr, Jr.; and Monroe Wheeler, Director of Exhibitions. Five photographs by Kertész were selected for display, including this one that was reproduced in the museum's *Bulletin*. For reproduction, see p. 234.

168. *Richfield, New Jersey*, 1941
Glossy, single-weight silver gelatin print, 254 x 202 mm
Titled on verso in fountain pen; stamped on verso New York stamp #2
The Metropolitan Museum of Art*, 1984.1083.2

When Kertész began to focus his attention on typically American subjects such as the dilapidated front porch of a house in Richfield, New Jersey, he was moving close to ground covered by Alfred Stieglitz, Paul Strand, Walker Evans, Berenice Abbott, and Ansel Adams. What distinguishes Kertész is the humor and irony embodied in the design of the benches, which seem to be the center of his interest. For reproduction, see p. 235.

169. *Rye, New York*, 1941?
Semi-glossy, single-weight silver gelatin print, 231 x 189 mm
Stamped on verso New York stamp #5 (effaced in ink)
The Metropolitan Museum of Art*, 1984.1083.97

This undated photograph seems to be part of the work inspired by the "Image of Freedom" competition. (See remarks on cat. no. 167.) The subject has strong human associations as well as being a tightly composed geometric network. For reproduction, see p. 236.

170. Shadow of a Tree, 1944
Semi-glossy, single-weight silver gelatin print, 165 x 182 mm
Dated on verso in pencil "Aug. 6, 1944"; stamped on verso New York stamp #4
The Metropolitan Museum of Art*, 1984.1083.33

Kertész would have passed many walled gardens during the course of his walks through Greenwich Village, among them Thompson Street and West Third Avenue; Sixth Avenue and Bleeker Street; the walled playground at Downing Street and Sixth Avenue; or the walled cemetery of Old St. Patrick's Church at Prince and Mott streets. For reproduction, see p. 236.

171. Riverside Park Near 153rd Street, 1944
Glossy, single-weight silver gelatin print, 244 x 198 mm
Dated on verso in pencil "10-8-44"; stamped on verso New York stamp #4
The Metropolitan Museum of Art*, 1984.1083.40

In September 1944, when this photograph was made, Kertész had been in America nearly five years. Its date nearly coincides with his becoming a naturalized citizen, the date of which is believed to be about October 15, 1944. The new status freed him from the restrictions governing enemy aliens. Kertész was celebrated in Paris for his nocturnes, but he made very few here. By 1944 he had explored the island of Manhattan from the Battery to its northern tip, represented here. For reproduction, see p. 240.

172. Hudson River, Henry Hudson Parkway, and Riverside Park, 1944
Glossy, single-weight silver gelatin print, 195 x 244 mm
Inscribed on verso in pencil "Riverside Drive, New York"
Repr.: *Of New York*, p. 188
The Metropolitan Museum of Art*, 1984.1083.8

Throughout his creative career Kertész has operated, alternately, from a deeply Constructivist sensibility or from a romantic one that in its most extreme moments some would call sentimentality. This and the following work are relatively isolated examples of romanticism in a body of work Kertész created between 1939 and 1944 that is largely Constructivist. For reproduction, see p. 241.

173. East Walk of Conservatory Pond, Central Park, 1944
Glossy, single-weight silver gelatin print, 247 x 198 mm

Inscribed on verso in ink "10-13-44"; and later in pencil "New York/ 1944 / page 182"
Repr.: *Sixty Years*, p. 182; *Of New York*, p. 182; Aperture, p. 61; Abrams, p. 251; Manchester, #152, p. 108
Lent by Raymond Slater, Altrincham, England

The figure here is carrying a model schooner from Conservatory Pond to the boathouse in Central Park, where citizens may store their models for the payment of a modest annual fee to the city. The image has a curiously European feeling even though its actual subject is typical of one pocket of New York life. This image is referred to by Kertész as *Homing Ship*. For reproduction, see p. 238.

174. *Washington Square, New York—After the Rain*, 1945
Glossy, single-weight silver gelatin print, 249 x 201 mm
Titled on verso in fountain pen and dated in ballpoint pen "April 28/May 2, 1945," with "April 28" effaced; stamped on verso New York stamp #5, overprinted with New York stamp #7
The Metropolitan Museum of Art*, 1984.1083.43

For reproduction, see p. 239.

175. *Ashfield, Massachusetts, Church Spire*, 1945
Glossy, single-weight silver gelatin print, 215 x 157 mm
Titled and dated on verso; stamped on verso New York stamp #5; photofinisher's order number "V9445" effaced in pencil
Repr.: Manchester, #176, p. 120 (where it is titled *St. John's Church Spire* and dated Aug. 8, 1945)
The Metropolitan Museum of Art*, 1984.1083.1

This image is a return to the Constructivism that characterized Kertész's work of 1939–1941. It is also among the earliest photographs not printed personally by Kertész. From the 1950s to the present Kertész has relied upon skillful technicians to make his prints. For reproduction, see p. 235.

176. Game Room, The Joseph B. Platt Residence, 1946
Semi-glossy, double-weight silver gelatin print, 343 x 276 mm
Stamped on verso "André Kertész"
Repr.: "A New House That Looks Old," *House and Garden* 90 (Nov. 1946), p. 159

Lent by Condé Nast Publications, Inc., New York

The Platt house, Little Compton, Rhode Island, was photographed in its entirety by Kertész for *House and Garden*. Joseph Platt was a furniture designer and his wife, June, was an author of cookbooks and a designer of wallpaper. For reproduction, see p. 247.

177. Chair, Lamp, and Sculpture, 1947?
Semi-glossy, double-weight silver gelatin print, 351 x 288 mm
Stamped on verso "André Kertész," "Condé Nast Publications"
Lent by Condé Nast Publications, Inc., New York

No reproduction of this image has been located. The absence of any identification or designer's scaling marks on the verso suggests that the image was not selected for reproduction, perhaps because the image was deemed too personal to Kertész. For reproduction, see p. 247.

178. Crucifix and Light Bulb, 1947
Glossy, single-weight silver gelatin print, 246 x 197 mm
Signed on verso in fountain pen "A. Kertész" and inscribed in pencil "p. 195"
Repr.: William Houseman, "André Kertész," *Infinity* 8, no. 4 (Apr. 1959), p. 12; *Sixty Years*, p. 195 (reproduced from this print?)
The Metropolitan Museum of Art*, 1984.1083.38

This photograph was taken at the entrance of the studio of Theodore Fried, a Hungarian painter who immigrated to America in 1942. Kertész had known Fried from the Café du Dôme and they remained friends until Fried's death in 1980. For reproduction, see p. 245.

179. Overhead Crosswalk with Clock, 1947
Semi-glossy, double-weight silver gelatin print, 251 x 180 mm
Stamped on verso New york stamp #4
Repr.: *Of New York*, p. 107 (where it is erroneously dated 1937); Manchester, #140, p. 96 (where it is dated Apr. 12, 1947)
Lent by Raymond Slater, Altrincham, England

This image may be compared to one of the most notable pictures of the Paris period, *Meudon* (cat. no. 58). Both depend upon the powerful, but static, architectural forms that interact with mobile figures. The arrested motion of the passing train

and of the second hand of the clock refer in different ways to the notion that the passage of time is a fundamental, underlying ingredient in photography. As with *Meudon*, no print contemporaneous with the negative is known to survive. This image appears to have been printed for the first time in the mid-1960s. For reproduction, see p. 249.

180. Manhattan Span of the Queensborough Bridge, 1947
Glossy, double-weight silver gelatin print, 345 x 270 mm
Dated on verso in pencil; stamped on verso New York stamp #4
The Metropolitan Museum of Art*, 1984.1083.17

The Consolidated Gas Company storage tanks were located on York Avenue between 60th and 62nd streets until they they were demolished shortly after this photograph was made. Kertész made this picture while on a *House and Garden* assignment from the roof of a house on the Vanderbilt-Morgan row looking toward the southwest corner of 59th Street and Sutton Place and the Queensborough Bridge. The tall structure whose masonry forms the upper right edge of the picture is located at 25 Sutton Place North. For reproduction, see p. 248.

181. Queensborough Bridge at Night, 1948
Semi-glossy, single-weight silver gelatin print, 258 x 194 mm
Repr.: *Of New York*, p. 50
Lent by the Susan Harder Gallery, New York

For reproduction, see p. 243.

182. River Walk of Carl Schurz Park, 1948
Glossy, single-weight silver gelatin print, 248 x 185 mm
Dated on verso in pencil "Jan. 15, 1948"; stamped on verso New York stamp #3
Repr.: *Of New York*, p. 47
The Metropolitan Museum of Art*, 1984.1083.41

During the first two years in which Kertész was devoting all of his time to projects for *House and Garden*, he made certain works that are classic manifestations of alienation, loneliness, and self-doubt. For reproduction, see p. 242.

183. Book-lined Hallway, Mainbocher Apartment, New York, 1948
Semi-glossy, double-weight silver gelatin print, 342 x 276 mm
Stamped on verso New York stamp #4 and "Condé Nast Publications"; caption

typed on verso; designer's scaling marks
Repr.: "Self-Portrait in Two Rooms," *House and Garden* 93 (Mar. 1948), p. 99
Lent by Condé Nast Publications, Inc., New York

Nine photographs by Kertész were the exclusive illustrations to an article on Mainbocher, a Chicago-born artist who "was the editor of French *Vogue* before making his name in the *haute couture*" [*House and Garden* 93 (Mar. 1948), p.4]. For reproduction, see p. 246.

184. *My Little Indians*, 1948
Semi-glossy, double-weight silver gelatin print, 355 x 284 mm
Stamped on verso New York stamp #4 and "Condé Nast Publications"
Repr.: Charles G. Shaw, "My Little Indians," *House and Garden* 93 (May 1948), p. 135
Lent by Condé Nast Publications, Inc., New York
For reproduction, see p. 250.

185. Watchmaker's Shop, Christopher Street, 1950
Glossy, single-weight silver gelatin print, 227 x 143 mm
Dated on verso in pencil; stamped on verso New York stamp #5
Repr.: *Sixty Years*, p. 219
The Metropolitan Museum of Art*, 1984.1083.27

Berenice Abbott photographed the same storefront in 1949/50. The stylistic differences are notable. Abbott stood back to include the entire store, and printed from her full negative. Kertész cropped his negative to emphasize the scale of the clock, and to include only a sliver of the figure intruding from the left. The scale of the clock may be compared to Kertész's concern for out-of-scale objects between 1948 and 1950. For reproduction, see p. 251.

186. Rooftop Water Tanks, New York, 1951
Glossy, single-weight silver gelatin print, 221 x 170 mm
Stamped on verso New York stamp #4
The Metropolitan Museum of Art*, 1984.1083.50

The exposure was made from the third-floor apartment at 31 East 12th Street that the Kertészes occupied from 1944 until 1952. This is a precursor of the rooftop studies that form an important part of his work beginning in 1952, after the move to the twelfth floor of 2 Fifth Avenue. For reproduction, see p. 237.

187. Stairs, Railing, Shadows, and Woman,
     1951
Glossy, single-weight silver gelatin print,
     180 x 237 mm
Dated on verso in pencil "Feb. 23, 1951"
Repr.: *Of New York*, p. 179
The Metropolitan Museum of Art*,
     1984.1083.52

In Paris one of Kertész's favorite motifs
was the view down an outdoor stair with
the railing forming an out-of-focus foreground element (see cat. no. 18, Phillips,
fig. 38, and Travis, fig. 2). The idea has
been pushed to its radical extreme in this
New York picture. The soft-focus romanticism of the earlier pictures has become
aggressive and Constructivist. For reproduction, see p. 237.

188. *Williamsburg, Virginia*, 1951
Glossy, single-weight silver gelatin print,
     112 x 87 mm
Titled and dated on verso in pencil "Oct. 16,
     1951"
Repr.: *Sixty Years*, p. 165
The Metropolitan Museum of Art*,
     1984.1083.96

Kertész was sent to photograph colonial
Williamsburg by *House and Garden*. This
picture was never used, nor were its particular beauties recognized by Kertész until
much later. Only this tiny damaged print
survives from 1951. Nothing could look less
American than this image. Had it not been
identified on the verso by the photographer
at the time the print was made, this would
seem to be some European location.
Indeed, Kertész has told us nothing about
Williamsburg (its curators have even denied
that this place exists there) and less about
colonial American style than about his own
eccentric view of what he has observed.
For reproduction, see p. 244.

189. Greenwich Village Rooftops, Day,
     c. 1952
Glossy, double-weight silver gelatin print,
     350 x 272 mm
The Metropolitan Museum of Art*,
     1984.1083.18

In 1952 Elizabeth and André Kertész
moved to their first real home in New
York, a twelfth–floor apartment at 2 Fifth
Avenue, which he still calls home today.
The balcony faces south (overlooking
Washington Square Park) and west
toward the heart of Greenwich Village.
The west bedroom permits a slightly
northward vantage and is the location
from which this exposure was made soon
after their relocation. This composition
repeats the Constructivist concerns that
are evident in cat. nos. 149, 169, and 170.
The largest structure at the upper left is
the apartment building located at 1
Christopher Street; the institutional mass
to the right of it is the Woman's House of
Detention (now demolished); and the
gabled building with cruciform finial is the
Jefferson Market branch of the New York
Public Library. The negative was made
with a four-by-five inch camera, which
indicates that not all of Kertész's personal
work was made with the miniature Leica.
For reproduction, see p. 252.

190. Greenwich Village Rooftops, Evening,
     1954
Glossy, single-weight silver gelatin print,
     246 x 200 mm
Inscribed on verso in pencil "January 9,
     1954"
Repr.: *Of New York*, p. 116
The Metropolitan Museum of Art*,
     1984.1083.28

This is from the same vantage point as the
preceding work, but with a view more

toward the north. The finial of the
Jefferson Market Library is at the far left
here. For reproduction, see p. 253.

191. Homage to Robert Capa, 1954
Glossy, double-weight silver gelatin print,
     247 x 350 mm
Stamped on verso New York stamp #6
The Metropolitan Museum of Art*,
     1984.1083.101

The negative was exposed on the day
Kertész learned of the death of Robert
Capa (June 8, 1954). Kertész and Capa
were friends in Paris, and Capa had asked
Kertész to do the sequencing of the photo-
graphs in his book *Death in the Making*
(New York: Covier Friede, 1938). Kertész
was deeply affected by the loss of his friend.
Several of the same buildings visible in the
preceding two works (cat. nos. 189 and
190) are evident in shadowy detail.
For reproduction, see p. 254.

192. Washington Square, Winter, 1954
Later silver gelatin print made by Igor
     Bakht, 350 x 262 mm
Repr.: *Of New York*, p. 81; Aperture, p. 55;
     Abrams, p. 89
Lent by the Susan Harder Gallery, New
     York

Kertész's favorite pastime was to observe
the passersby from his vantage high above
Washington Square Park. He used a telephoto lens to bring his subjects closer. This
image may be compared in its attitude to
his view of the East River in winter (cat.
no. 182), where loneliness is evoked; here
there is a beautiful snowfall and a sense of
joyful ambling. For reproduction, see
p. 255.

Selected Bibliography

1927

"Art and Artist." *Chicago Tribune* (Paris), Mar. 13, 1927.

Henkl, Rolf. "Neue Fotografie Ausstellungen/Kunstbücher/Theatreaufführungen." *Tageschronik der Kunst* 8, no. 4 (July 1927), pp. 26–30.

Montpar. "Kertész." *Chanticler*, Mar. 19, 1927.

S., M. [Michel Seuphor?] "Frère Voyant." *Comoedia*, no. 5184 (Mar. 12, 1927), p. 2.

1928

Bost, Pierre. "Le Salon des indépendants de la photographie" in "Spectacles et Promenades." *Revue hebdomadaire* 37, no. 24 (1928), pp. 356–59.

"Bruxelles, Exposition de photographie. Galerie de L'Epoque." *Cahiers d'Art* 3, no. 8 (1928).

Charensol, [Georges]. "Les Expositions." *L'Art vivant* 4 (June 15, 1928), pp. 486–87.

Fels, F[lorent]. "Le Premier Salon indépendant de la photographie." *L'Art vivant* 4 (June 1, 1928), pp. 444–45.

George, Waldemar. "L'Art photographique, Le XXIIIe Salon internationale." *La Presse*, Oct. 16, 1928.

H., R. "La Photographie est-elle un art? Le Salon indépendant va nous apprendre." *Paris-Midi*, May 14, 1928.

L., F. "L'Exposition de la photographie à la Galerie 'L'Epoque.'" *Variétés*, Nov. 15, 1928, pp. 400–401.

Mac Orlan, Pierre. "La Vie moderne, l'art littéraire d'imagination et la photographie." *Les Nouvelles Littéraires*, Sept. 22, 1928, p.1.

———. "La Photographie et la fantastique sociale." *Les Annales politiques et littéraires*, no. 2321 (Nov. 1, 1928), pp. 413–14.

"Oldest and Newest in Photography Contrasted in Unique Exhibition." *Chicago Tribune* (Paris), May 26, 1928.

"Salon to be Held by Photographers." *New York Herald Tribune* (Paris), May 12, 1928.

1929

"Eine neue Künstler-Gilde: Der Fotograf erobert Neuland." *Uhu* 6, no.1 (Oct. 1929), pp. 34–41.

F., E. "Photographie der Gegenwart: Die neueste Ausstellung in Magdeburg." *Magdeburgische Zeitung*, Nov. 1929, p. 5.

Film und Foto, Internationale Ausstellung des Deutschen Werkbunds. Stuttgart, 1929. (exh.cat.)

Gallotti, Jean. "La Photographie est-elle un art?—Kertész." *L'Art vivant* 5 (Mar. 1, 1929), pp. 208–09, 211.

Lotz, [Wilhelm]. "Film und Foto." *Die Form*, June 1929, pp. 277–79.

Mac Orlan, Pierre. "Photographie." *Das Kunstblatt*, May 1929, pp.136–40.

———. "Photographie: éléments de fantastique sociale." *Le Crapouillot*, Jan. 1929, pp. 3–5.

Nachod, Hans. "Die Photographie der Gegenwart." *Neue Leipziger Zeitung*, Aug. 20, 1929.

Sommer, K. "Film und Foto Ausstellung." *Essener Allgemeine Zeitung*, May 26, 1929.

Wilhelm-Kästner, [K.] "Photographie der Gegenwart, Grundsätzliches zur Ausstellung im Museum Folkwang." *Photographische Rundschau und Mitteilungen* 66, no. 5 (1929), pp. 96–99.

1930

"L'Art de la photographie." *La Revue hebdomadaire*, no. 12 (Mar. 22, 1930), pp. 32, 39–40.

Bost, Pierre. *Photographies modernes.* Paris: Librairie des Arts Décoratifs, n.d.

"Galerie d'Art Contemporain." *Art et Décoration* 57 (Apr. 1930), p. iii.

George, Waldemar. "Photographie, vision du monde." *Arts et métiers graphiques* 3 (Mar. 1930), pp. 5–20, 131–61.

"Images." *L'Illustration*, no. 4539 (March 1, 1930), p. 291.

Kerdyk, René. "Le Salon de l'Araignée." *Le Crapouillot*, June 1930.

Rim, Carlo. "Curiosités photographiques." *L'Art vivant* 6, no. 135 (Aug. 1930), pp. 604–05.

"Le Salon de l'Araignée." *Art et Décoration* 57 (June 1930), pp. iv–v.

Vidal, Jean. "En photographiant les photographes." *L'Intransigeant*, Apr. 1, 1930.

1931

F., F. [Florent Fels?] "Exposition de photographie." *Vu*, no. 161 (Apr. 15, 1931), p. 539.

Fels, Florent. "Actualités photographiques." *L'Art vivant* 7, no. 148 (May 1931), pp. 197–99.

———. "Photographie—nouvel organe." *L'Art vivant* 7, no. 147 (Apr. 1931), pp. 145–47.

"Un Groupe de photographes." *Art et Décoration* 59 (May 1931), p. ii.

Wilhelm-Kästner, K. "Die Fotografie von Heute, zur Ausstellung 'Das Lichtbild' in Essen." *Die Wochenschau*, no. 20 (July 19, 1931), pp. 4–5.

1932

The Brooklyn Museum. *International Photographers*. Brooklyn, N.Y., 1932. (exh. cat.)

Rim, Carlo. "Défense et illustration de la photographie." *Vu*, no. 214 (Aug. 20, 1932), p. 587.

1933

Guégan, Bertrand. "Kertész et son miroir." *Arts et métiers graphiques*, no. 37 (Sept. 15, 1933), pp. 24–25.

P., J. E. "Exposition photographique à la Galerie de la Pléiade." *Arts et métiers graphiques*, no. 36 (July 15, 1933), pp. 52–53.

1934

Alloend Bessand, H. "La Photographie est-elle un art?" *Photocinégraphie*, May 1934, pp. 3–4.

C., P. "L'Album *Enfants* de M. André Kertész." *Photo-Illustration* 7 (1934), p. 15.

de Chambertrand. "L'Avenir de la photo." *Photocinégraphie*, no. 12 (Feb. 1934), pp. 6–7.

Gilson, Paul. Review of *Paris vu par André Kertész. L'Intransigeant*, Dec. 14, 1934.

Malo, Pierre. "A la Galerie de la Pléiade, Groupe annuel des photographes." *L'Homme libre*, Nov 20, 1934.

Rim, Carlo. "Grandeur et servitude de reporter photographe." *Marianne*, Feb. 21, 1934.

1935

Dabit, Eugène. "Paris, par André Kertész." *La Nouvelle Revue française* 45, (Mar. 1, 1935), pp. 474–75.

Natkin, Marcel. *L'Art de voir et la photographie*. Paris: Editions Tiranty, 1935.

S., C. [Charles de Santeuil] "Paris vu par André Kertész." *Photo-Illustrations*, no. 9 (1935), p. 7.

de Santeuil, Charles. "Les Artistes photographes d'aujourd'hui." *Photo-Illustrations* 2 (Jan. 1935), pp. 1–4.

1936

Audiat, Pierre. Review of *Nos Amies les bêtes. Paris-Midi*, Dec. 25, 1936.

Besson, Georges. *La Photographie française*. Paris: Les Editions Braun, 1936.

Guenne, Jacques. "La Photographie vivante, les dix." *L'Art vivant*, Mar. 1936, pp. 44–45.

Musée des Arts Décoratifs. *Exposition Internationale de la Photographie Contemporaine*. Paris, 1936. (exh. cat.)

"Photographer Sails to New York." *New York Herald Tribune* (Paris), Oct. 8, 1936.

Review of *Nos Amies les bêtes. Le Matin*, Dec. 27, 1936.

Review of *Nos Amies les bêtes. Marianne*, Dec. 30, 1936.

Sougez, Emmanuel. "La Photographie." *Le Point* 1, no. 6 (Dec. 1936), pp. 6–26.

1937

The Museum of Modern Art. *Photography 1839–1937*. Text by Beaumont Newhall. New York, 1937. (exh. cat.)

"P M Shorts." *P M* 4, no. 4 (Dec. 1937–Jan. 1938), p. 82.

1938

Strider, Gary. "Kertész—Camera Surrealist." *Popular Photography*, Mar. 1938, p. 42.

1939

Browning, Arthur. "Paradox of a Distortionist." *Minicam Photography* 2, no. 12 (Aug. 1939), pp. 36–41.

King, Alexander. "Are Editors Vandals?" *Minicam Photography* 2, no. 8 (Apr. 1939), pp. 26–33, 80–81.

1941

N., B. [Beaumont Newhall] "Image of Freedom." *The Bulletin of the Museum of Modern Art* 9, no. 2 (Nov. 1941), p. 14–16.

Newhall, Nancy. "What is Pictorialism?" *Camera Craft*, Nov. 1941, pp. 653–63.

1942

Knight, John Adam. "Photography." *New York Post*, Dec. 31, 1942.

1944

Eisner, Maria Giovanna. "Citizen Kertész." *Minicam Photography* 7, no. 10 (June 1944), pp. 26–33.

Rukeyser, Muriel. "The Strong Angel." *Mademoiselle*, Dec. 1944, pp. 106–07.

1945

"Day of Paris." *Minicam Photography* 8, no. 10 (July 1945), pp. 22–29.

Devree, Howard. "Paris, the Well-Remembered." *New York Times Book Review*, June 3, 1945.

Downes, Bruce. "André Kertész' *Day of Paris*." *Popular Photography* 6 (June 1945), pp. 48–49, 101–03.

Paul, Elliott. "A Mood from the Dim Past." *Saturday Review of Literature* 28 (May 19, 1945), p. 10.

1946

Holme, Bryan, and Thomas Forman. *Poet's Camera*. New York: American Studio Books, 1946.

1947

Zucker, Paul. "André Kertész, *Day of Paris*." *Journal of Aesthetics and Art Criticism* 5, no. 3 (March 1947), pp. 235–36.

1948

Dembling, Merwin. "Art in the Kitchen." *Minicam Photography* 12 (Nov. 1948), pp. 26–29.

1951

The Art and Technique of Color Photography. New York: Simon and Schuster, 1951.

1959

Houseman, William. "André Kertész." *Infinity* 8, no. 4 (Apr. 1959), pp. 4–12, 22.

1962

Deschin, Jacob. "Careers in Review." *New York Times*, Oct. 28, 1962.

Poli, Kenneth. "One-Man Show, André Kertész, Photojournalist." *Leica Photography* 5 (1962), pp. 4–8.

Resnick, Nathan. *Kertész at Long Island University*. New York, 1962. (exh. cat.)

1963

Bibliothèque Nationale. *André Kertész, Photographies*. Text by Alix Gambier. Paris, 1963. (exh. cat.)

Brassaï. "My Friend André Kertész." *Camera* 42, no. 4 (Apr. 1963), pp. 7–32.

Gautier, Maximilian. "Quand L'Oeil a du génie." *Les Nouvelles Littéraires*, Nov. 28, 1963, p. 8.

Kertész, André. "Caricatures and Distortions." In *The Complete Photographer: A Complete Guide to Amateur and Professional Photography*, known as *The Encyclopedia of Photography*, ed. Willard D. Morgan, vol. 2, pp. 651–58. New York: National Educational Alliance, Inc., 1942.

"Kertész Exhibit Recalls his Earlier Activity." *New York Times*, June 16, 1963.

Pluchart, François. "Un Grand Photographe: André Kertész." *Combat Paris*, Nov. 16, 1963.

Schwalberg, Carol. "André Kertész: Unsung Pioneer." *U.S. Camera* 26 (Jan. 1963), pp. 54–57, 64–65, 76.

1964

Gruber, L. Fritz. "André Kertész, ein keinesfalls verschollener Altmeister." *Foto Magazin*, July 1964.

———. "Die Gabel." *Die Welt*, July 3, 1964.

Jakowsky, Anatole. "Le Royaume enchanté des naifs." *Beaux Arts*, Oct. 7, 1964.

The Museum of Modern Art. *André Kertész, Photographer*. Text by John Szarkowski. New York, 1964. (exh. cat.)

Plecy, Albert. "André Kertész." *Images du Monde*, no. 815 (Jan. 24, 1964), pp. 18–19.

Weiss, Margaret R. "André Kertész, Photographer." *Saturday Review of Literature* 47 (Dec. 26, 1964), pp. 28–30.

"The World of Kertész." *Show*, Mar. 1964, pp. 56–61.

1965

Budnik, Dan. "A Point Vue." *Infinity* 14, no. 3 (Mar. 1965), pp. 4–11.

"Kertész." *Harper's Bazaar*, June 1965, pp. 66–69.

Vestal, David. "André Kertész, Photographer." *Contemporary Photographer* 5 (Spring 1964–65), pp. 65–66.

1966

Fárová, Anna. *André Kertész*. Adapted by Robert Sogalyn. New York: Paragraphic Books, n.d.

1967

Hood, Robert F. "André Kertész, Soldier and Candid Cameraman in World War I." *12 at War*. New York, 1967.

1968

Capa, Cornell, ed. *The Concerned Photographer*. New York: Grossman Publishers, 1968.

Pollack, Peter. *Picture History of Photography*. New York: Abrams, 1968.

1969

James, Geoffrey. "André Kertész." *Vie des Arts*, Winter 1969–70, pp. 52–55.

Jay, Bill. "André Kertész: A Meeting of Friends." *Creative Camera*, no. 62 (Aug. 1969).

———. "André Kertész: Nude Distortion, An Incredible Experiment." *Creative Camera*, no. 55 (Jan. 1969).

———. "André Kertész: Portfolio." *Creative Camera*, no. 63 (Sept. 1969), pp. 312–21.

1971

Magyar Nemzeti Galleria. *André Kertész Fotomuvesz*. Text by Endre Bajomi Lazar. Budapest, 1971. (exh. cat.)

Moderna Museet. *André Kertész*. Stockholm, 1971. (exh. cat.)

Weiss, Margaret R. "Everyman's Reader." *Saturday Review of Literature*, Aug. 7, 1971, pp. 36–37.

1973

Gidal, Tim N. *Modern Photojournalism: Origin and Evolution, 1910–1933*. From the series *Photography: Men and Movements*, ed. Roméo E. Martinez, trans. Maureen Oberli-Turner. New York: Collier Books, 1973.

Kramer, Hilton. "Kertész Conveys the Poetic Significance of Details." *New York Times*, Jan. 17, 1973.

Weiss, Margaret R. "Anniversary Salute to André Kertész." *Saturday Review of Literature*, Jan. 1973, pp. 26–28.

1974

Gelatt, Dorothy S. "André Kertész at 80." *Popular Photography* 75 (Nov. 1974), pp. 136–43, 154–56, 171.

Kramer, Hilton. "Three Who Photographed the 20s and 30s." *New York Times*, Mar. 3, 1974.

1975

Beaton, Cecil and Gail Buckland. *The Magic Image: The Genius of Photography from 1839 to the Present Day*. Boston: Little, Brown and Company, 1975.

Brassaï. "La Deuxième Vie de Kertész." *Photo*, no. 90 (Mar. 1975), pp. 65, 71.

Bruns, Renée. Review of *J'Aime Paris*. *Popular Photography* 76 (Apr. 1975), pp. 101–02.

Spencer, Ruth. "André Kertész." *British Journal of Photography*, Apr. 4, 1975, pp. 290–93.

1976

The Art Institute of Chicago. *Photographs from the Julien Levy Collection, Starting with Atget*. Text by David Travis. Chicago, 1976. (exh. cat.)

Edwards, Owen. "Zen and the Art of Photography." *Village Voice*, Apr. 5, 1976, pp. 99–100.

Grundberg, Andy. "André Kertész at the French Cultural Services." *Art in America* 64 (July–Aug. 1976), pp. 103–04.

Kramer, Hilton. "Two Masters of Photography Show Work." *New York Times*, Mar. 27, 1976.

Thornton, Gene. "André Kertész' Romance with Paris." *New York Times*, Apr. 4, 1976.

Wesleyan University. *André Kertész, Photographs*. Middletown, Conn., 1976. (exh. cat.)

1977

André Kertész. Text by Carole Kismaric. Millerton, N.Y.: Aperture, 1977.

Centre Nationale d'Art et de Culture Georges Pompidou. *André Kertész*. Paris, 1977. (exh. cat.)

Plains Art Museum. *Sympathetic Explorations, Kertész / Harbutt*. Moorhead, Minn., 1977. (exh. cat.)

Roskill, Mark, and Roger Baldwin. "André Kertész' *Chez Mondrian*." *Arts Magazine* 51 (Jan. 1977), pp. 106–07.

1978

Arts Council of Great Britain. *Neue Sachlichkeit and German Realism of the Twenties*. Text by Ute Eskildsen. London, 1978. (exh. cat.)

Devenyi, Denes. "Kertész: Denes Devenyi Interviews the Father of 35mm Vision." *PhotoLife*, Jan. 1978, pp. 10–13, 30.

Lifson, Ben. "Old Story, Forever New." *Village Voice*, Sept. 25, 1978, p. 114.

1979

Arts Council of Great Britain. *André Kertész*. Text by Colin Ford. London, 1979. (exh. cat.)

Coleman, A. D. "André Kertész Continues." *Camera 35* 24 (Oct. 1979), pp. 12–13.

Hill, Paul, and Thomas Cooper. *Dialogue with Photography*. New York: Farrar, Straus and Giroux, 1979.

Lifson, Ben. "Kertész at Eighty-Five." *Portfolio* 1, no. 2 (June–July 1979), pp. 58–64.

New Orleans Museum of Art. *Diverse Images: Photographs from the New Orleans Museum of Art*. Garden City, N.Y.: Amphoto, 1979.

1980

Borhan, Pierre. *Voyons Voir*. Paris: Créatis, 1980.

Ford, Colin. "André Kertész." *Creative Camera*, no. 193–94 (July–Aug. 1980), pp. 242–45.

Gaillard, Agathe. *André Kertész*. Paris: Pierre Belford, 1980.

1981

Lifson, Ben. "A Great Photographer's Love Story." *Saturday Review of Literature*, Dec. 1981, pp. 21–24.

1982

Davis, Douglas. "I looked, I saw, I did." *Newsweek*, Dec. 6, 1982, pp. 142, 144.

1983

Goldberg, Vicki. "Staking a Claim in the Heart's Territory." *American Photographer*, Feb. 1983, pp. 22–23.

Ugrin, Bela. "Kertész's Photography in Full Bloom." *Houston Post*, Jan. 2, 1983, sec. G, pp. 12–13.

1984

Berman, Avis. "The 'Little Happenings' of André Kertész." *Art News*, Mar. 1984, pp. 67–73.

Thornton, Gene. "Kertész: The Great Democrat of Modern Photography." *New York Times*, July 22, 1984.

Index